Fodo

Virginia

FODOR'S TRAVEL PUBLICATIONS, INC.
New York & London

ISBN 0-679-01713-5

Parts of this book also appear in *Fodor's Chesapeake*.

Fodor's Virginia 1989

Editor: Andrew E. Beresky
Area Coordinator: Editorial Ink, Ltd.
Contributing Editors: Patricia and Edgar Cheatham, Steve Doherty, Eleanor and James Louttit, Rodney N. Smith
Research: Jacqueline Russell
Maps: Burmar Technical Corp.
Drawings: Amy Harold
Cover Photograph: Henley & Savage/Uniphoto
Jodi Cobb/West Light

Cover Design: Vignelli Associates

MANUFACTURED IN THE UNITED STATES OF AMERICA
10 9 8 7 6 5 4 3 2 1

CONTENTS

FOREWORD

Virginia is the place where America began, where it suffered, and where it thrives today. Because of this, millions of people each year visit Virginia to touch the past and to enrich the present.

While every care has been taken to assure the accuracy of the information in this guide, the passage of time will always bring change, and consequently the publisher cannot accept responsibility for errors that may occur.

All prices and opening times quoted here are based on information available to us at press time. Hours and admission fees may change, however, and the prudent traveler will avoid inconvenience by calling ahead.

Fodor's wants to hear about your travel experiences, both pleasant and unpleasant. When a hotel or restaurant fails to live up to its billing, let us know and we will investigate the complaint and revise our entries where the facts warrant it.

Send your letters to the editors of Fodor's Travel Publications, 201 E. 50th Street, New York, NY 10022, or 30–32 Bedford Square, London WC1B 3SG, England.

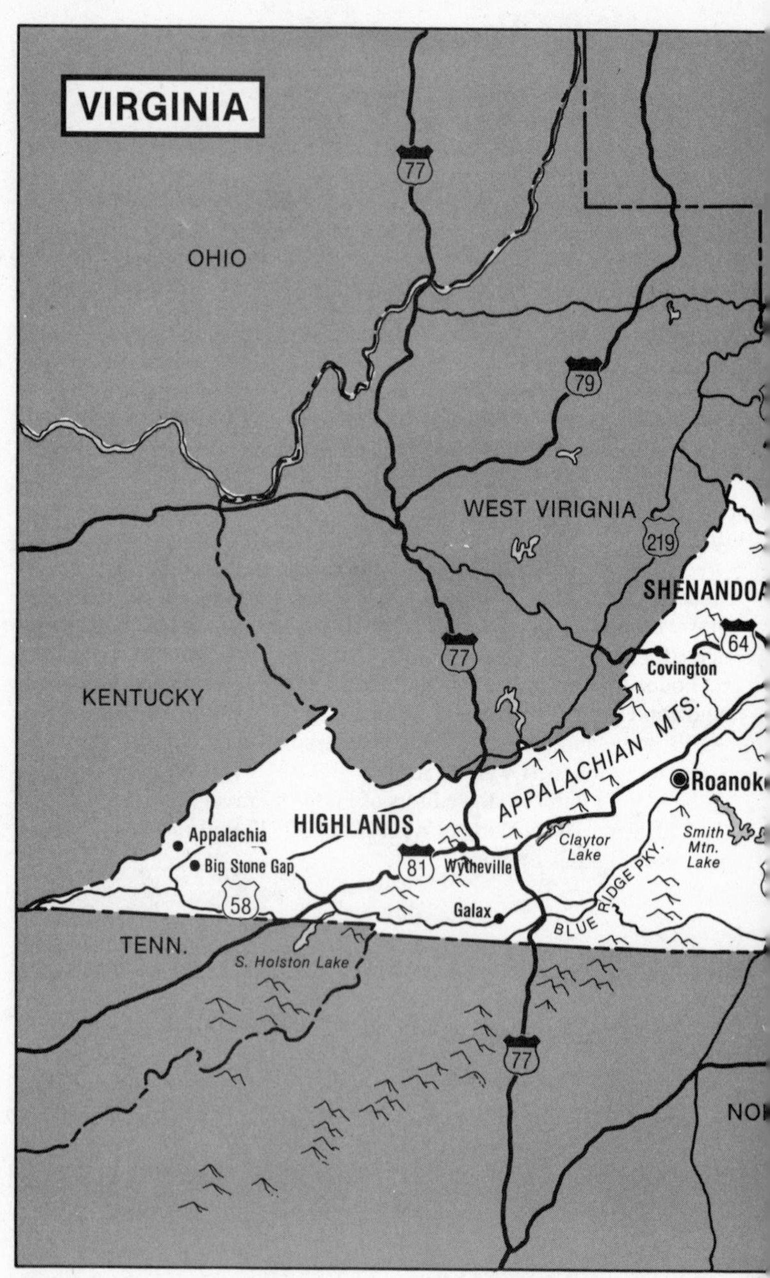

VIRGINIA
OHIO
WEST VIRIGNIA
KENTUCKY
SHENANDOA
Covington
APPALACHIAN MTS.
Roanok
HIGHLANDS
Appalachia
Big Stone Gap
Wytheville
Claytor Lake
Smith Mtn. Lake
BLUE RIDGE PKY.
Galax
TENN.
S. Holston Lake
NO
77
79
219
64
81
58

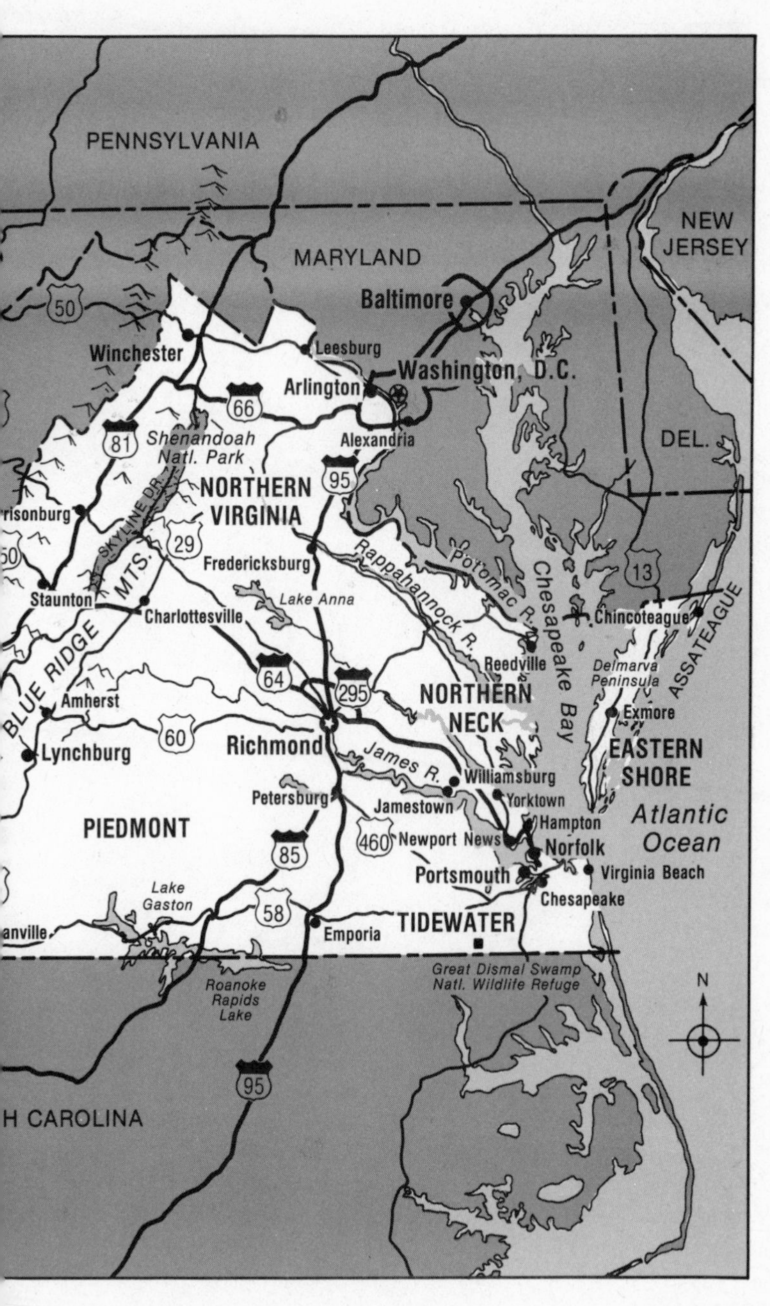

PENNSYLVANIA
MARYLAND
NEW JERSEY
Baltimore
Washington, D.C.
Leesburg
Arlington
Alexandria
Winchester
50
66
81
95
Shenandoah Natl. Park
NORTHERN VIRGINIA
DEL.
risonburg
SKYLINE DR.
29
Fredericksburg
Rappahannock R.
Potomac R.
Chesapeake Bay
13
Staunton
MTS.
Lake Anna
Charlottesville
Chincoteague
ASSATEAGUE
BLUE RIDGE
64
295
Reedville
Delmarva Peninsula
NORTHERN NECK
Amherst
60
Exmore
Lynchburg
Richmond
EASTERN SHORE
James R.
Williamsburg
Petersburg
Jamestown
Yorktown
PIEDMONT
Hampton
Atlantic Ocean
460
Newport News
Norfolk
85
Portsmouth
Virginia Beach
Lake Gaston
Chesapeake
58
anville
Emporia
TIDEWATER
Great Dismal Swamp Natl. Wildlife Refuge
Roanoke Rapids Lake
N
95
H CAROLINA

PLANNING YOUR TRIP

FACTS AND FIGURES. A visit to Virginia is a trip down memory lane to some of the most dramatic—and certainly climactic—events in American history. One need only recall that some of the most stirring figures in America's fight for independence were Virginians—Patrick Henry, Thomas Jefferson, James Madison, and George Washington—and that 60 percent of the battles of the country's deadliest conflict, the Civil War, were fought on Virginia soil, to realize that the "Old Dominion" lies at the very center of the American pageant. Many year-round recreational activities revolve around Virginia's colorful history, all in a climate milder than the U.S. Northeast or Deep South.

As this opening section is devoted to *facts* and *figures,* one point should be set straight: Despite the emphasis in some histories on the landing at Plymouth Rock in Massachusetts in 1620, the keen student of history knows that the "first permanent English settlement in North America" had been established 13 years earlier, in Jamestown, Virginia, in 1607. Without meaning to detract from New England's gallant traditions or glorious contributions to this nation's history, a *fact* is, nevertheless, a *fact.*

Virginia, named for Elizabeth I, the "Virgin Queen" of England, was the tenth state to enter the Union (June 25, 1788). It covers a land area of 39,700 square miles. (The original colony, extending all the way to the Mississippi River, eventually became eight of our present states.) Its range of elevation goes from sea level (the Atlantic Ocean) to 5,729 feet (Mt. Rogers, not far north of the Tennessee–North Carolina border), its capital is Richmond, and its population is 5,346,797. The state is in the Eastern Time Zone.

For Trivial Pursuit buffs, here is some Virginia lore: Nickname—Old Dominion; state flower—American dogwood; state bird—cardinal; state dog—foxhound; state motto—*Sic semper tyrannis* ("Thus always to tyrants"); and state song—"Carry Me Back to Old Virginia."

Tidewater Virginia, that part of the state that forms the southern part of the eastern and western shores of Chesapeake Bay and fronts on the Atlantic Ocean, is a rolling plain that is drained (into Chesapeake Bay) by four rivers: the Potomac, the Rappahannock, the York, and the James—two names coming from the Indians and two from early English settlers. Richmond, the capital, is just over 100 miles from, and due south of, Washington, D.C., on I-95. Richmond lies on the dividing line between Virginia's coastal plain and the Piedmont Plateau, which rises as it edges westward into the Blue Ridge Mountains. These mountains, running in a northeast-to-southwest direction, are cut by several valleys, the best known of which is the Shenandoah. These valleys are bordered on the west by the Allegheny Mountains and the states of West Virginia and Kentucky.

Conscious and proud of its rich heritage, the state has placed more than 1,500 historical markers along its 35,000 miles of paved roads, and more than 100 historically important buildings open to the public all year.

Without the contributions of Virginia's most famous sons, the United States form of government and its guarantees of liberty could hardly exist as we know them today. Consider just four examples: Patrick Henry's stirring, "Give me liberty or give me death," Thomas Jefferson's Declaration of Independence, James Madison's U.S. Constitution, and George Washington, commander in the Revolutionary War and our first president.

Virginia will reward visitors, especially those traveling with children, with a rich tapestry of history, while satisfying any taste for recreational and cultural activities. One visit to Virginia is rarely enough.

TOURIST INFORMATION. The state of Virginia is more than helpful in informing visitors about its many year-round attractions. Nearly 600 travel brochures are available at the many highway information offices operated by the state. For pre-trip planning, write: The Virginia Division of Tourism, 202 North Ninth Street, Suite 500, Richmond, Virginia 23219, or call (804) 786–4484. In either case, give them an idea of your primary interests so they can send you the most appropriate material. A detailed road map, "Virginia, Seasons of Adventure," is also available free from the Virginia Division of Tourism.

Group Meetings or Conferences. If your professional, fraternal, or social organization is planning a get-together in Virginia, special planning help is available. Send for the booklet, "Meet You in Virginia," from the Virginia Travel Council, 7619 Brook Road, Box 15067, Richmond, VA 23227; (804) 266–0444. The booklet contains all the information you'll need—including addresses and phone numbers—to plan a group meeting in any city within the five major regions of the state.

WHEN TO GO. Virginia has year-round allure because of its mid-Atlantic location. As its annual "Calendar of Events" (*free from Virginia Tourist Division; see Tourist Information*) reveals, the schedule of attractions barely drops off in December and January from the other 10 months of the year. If your tour planning is not dictated by school vacation times, you can go any time you want and be assured of plenty to do and to see. For those who can arrange "off-season" travel, there's the special dividend of fewer crowds at major attractions.

CLIMATE. While not as hot in summer as many parts of the Deep South, the traditional vacation months of July and August do see the mercury rise, and you will be aware of humidity; however, the overall climate is mild. Spring and fall are especially appealing. Spring arrives early and it's common to find swimmers taking a plunge in Chesapeake Bay or at Atlantic Ocean beaches well into October. On the shores of Chesapeake Bay, it's not unusual to find roses still in bloom in early December. In the western part of the state, at higher elevations, it's cool and pleasant in autumn, resulting in vivid foliage as the leaves change color, and temperatures are in the 50° to 60° range.

Temperature Statistics

	Winter	Spring	Summer	Fall
Statewide	40°F (4°C)	58°F (14°C)	76°F (24°C)	62°F (24°C)
Mountain areas	35°F (2°C)	56°F (13°C)	70°F (21°C)	57°F (14°C)

HOW TO GET THERE. By Air. The six major airports that have flights into and out of Virginia include: Dulles International in Loudoun County (west of Washington, D.C.); Washington National; Roanoke Municipal; Tri-City Regional (midway between Bristol and the Tennessee state line); Richard E. Byrd International in Richmond; and Norfolk International. These airports provide major air service to the following cities: Bristol, Charlottesville, Danville, Lynchburg, Newport News (also serving Williamsburg), Norfolk, Richmond, Roanoke, and, of course, Washington, D.C.

In addition to these major air terminals, there are several smaller airports from which the smaller air carriers operate, adding these Virginia cities to the above list: Hot Springs, Staunton–Harrisonburg–Waynesboro, and Bluefield (West Virginia) for the southwestern region of the state.

For visitors with a special interest in the southern end of the Shenandoah Valley—especially those approaching the state from the south and west—Roanoke Municipal Airport (Woodrum Field) is the logical choice. It is located in Roanoke Valley, 5.5 miles from downtown Roanoke, and offers scheduled service by Air Virginia, Best Airlines, Henson Airlines, and Piedmont Aviation. There are five charter flight operations there, plus all major car rental companies and limo service. For additional information, write: Airport Manager, Roanoke Municipal Airport, Roanoke, Virginia 24102, or call (703) 981–2531. This airport serves Roanoke and Salem, Lynchburg, Lexington, and Charlottesville as well as Bedford, Botetourt, and Roanoke Counties, and southwest (Highlands) Virginia in general.

By Train. Amtrak serves Washington, D.C., Alexandria, Fredericksburg, Richmond, Petersburg, Culpeper, Danville, Manassas, Staunton, Lynchburg, and Charlottesville. It also provides direct rail service to Williamsburg and Newport News. A word to the wise: As Amtrak service is always under heavy scrutiny by Washington, with cut-backs in service already in the works or under discussion, rail travelers to Virginia should check with their local Amtrak office to make certain of train availability and schedules.

By Bus. Greyhound/Trailways offers service throughout the state. In addition, there's a wide selection of motor coach tours to and through the state from most major cities of the Northeast, and from some large cities of the South. Consult your local travel agent for information on these tours.

By Car. If you're approaching from the northeast, you have two main choices: I-95 through Baltimore and Washington, D.C., into Virginia, then south to Fredericksburg and Richmond, and continuing south on 95—if it suits your itinerary—right to the North Carolina border; or, south on U.S. Rte. 13 along the Delmarva (Delaware-Maryland-Virginia) Peninsula to Cape Charles, and then over and through the Chesapeake Bay (toll) Bridge-Tunnel to Norfolk. With the second choice, you arrive in the southeast corner of the state and have, besides all the attractions of Norfolk and environs, which include ocean swimming in the Virginia Beach area and a good measure of the state's colonial, historical, and cultural attractions, enticements lying just to the west and northwest. Those who enjoy touring by car but like a change of scenery may find it interesting to go south one route and return north by the other.

From the west, there are six principal entry roads from the adjoining states of Kentucky, Tennessee, and West Virginia. From south to north, they are: (1) U.S. 58 (through the Cumberland Mountains); (2) U.S. 23 from Kentucky to Norton; (3) from Kentucky via U.S. 460 to Richlands; (4) from West Virginia via I-77 (West Virginia Turnpike) through Bluefield, West Virginia, to Wytheville; (5) from West Virginia via U.S. 64 through White Sulphur Springs, West Virginia, to Covington, Virginia; and (6) from West Virginia via Route 50 to Winchester, in the northwest corner of Virginia.

Two points worth remembering: The accessibility of your starting point to these "crossings," which are through beautiful, mountainous country, may decide which is best. If you have a choice, the two central roads, I-77 (West Virginia Turnpike) and I-64, may be preferable. Each of the above-mentioned entry routes intersects with I-81, a superhighway that parallels the Blue Ridge Mountains and provides a fast way to cover the state from top to bottom along its western edge. I-64 and I-66 lead eastward from I-81 to the eastern parts of Virginia. I-81 and parallel U.S. 11 also carry south-bound northern tourists from Pennsylvania and Maryland.

From the south, you can drive into Virginia from Tennessee in the far western corner on I-81 or, in the eastern part of the state—about 100 miles from the Atlantic—cross over from North Carolina on I-85 or I-95 (which meet at Petersburg) and, then, continue north on I-95 to Richmond, Fredericksburg, and Washington, D.C.

HINTS TO THE MOTORIST. The speed limit, as elsewhere in the United States, is 55 miles per hour, except where posted at 65 on some Interstates. State law permits a right turn on a red signal, *after a full stop,* unless otherwise directed. Virginia police authorities enforce strictly the state's drunk-driving law. A 0.10 reading of alcohol in the blood is considered drunk. If you're driving a long distance to reach Virginia, and belong to the AAA or another auto club, they will be glad to provide information about the best routes, and help plan accommodations during layovers. If you're not an auto club member—now that gas stations no longer pass out free road maps—a bound map volume of the U.S. highway system, such as those published by Rand McNally, Hammond, and Hagstrom, is a good investment.

Highways in Virginia: The state is criss-crossed by fine roads, a good portion of them part of the federal interstate highway system. The following Virginia cities and towns are close to, and easily reached from, one or another of the Interstates:

I-64 (in the center of the state, generally east/west): Ashland, Charlottesville, Clifton Forge, Covington, Hampton, Jamestown, Lexington, Newport News, Norfolk, Portsmouth, Richmond, Staunton, Virginia Beach, Waynesboro, West Point, Williamsburg, and Yorktown.

I-66 (east/west in the north): Alexandria, Fairfax, Falls Church, Front Royal, Manassas, McLean, and Middletown.

I-77 (north/south in the Highlands): Wytheville.

I-81 (northeast/southwest through Shenandoah and Highlands): Abingdon, Blacksburg, Bristol, Front Royal, Harrisonburg, Lexington, Marion, Middletown, Natural Bridge, New Market, Roanoke, Salem, Staunton, Winchester, Woodstock, and Wytheville.

I-85 (North Carolina to Petersburg): Petersburg and South Hill.

I-95 (north/south, paralleling the coast): Alexandria, Ashland, Emporia, Fairfax, Falls Church, Fredericksburg, Hopewell, McLean, Mount Vernon, Petersburg, Richmond, and Springfield.

Consult your road map or atlas for the exit nearest to each of these places.

HIGHWAY INFORMATION CENTERS. There are 10 of these in Virginia, where the above-mentioned brochures and other help and advice are available. They are located as follows: *Northern Region*—on I-81 in Clear Brook and on I-66 in Manassas; *Northeastern Region*—on I-95 in Fredericksburg; *Tidewater Region*—on Route 13 in New Church; *South-Central Region*—on I-95 in Skippers and on I-85 in Bracey; *Southwest Region*—on I-81 in Bristol and on I-77 in Lambsburg; *Western Region*—on I-64 in Covington. There is a Welcome Center just inside the state line on every interstate highway that enters Virginia.

TIPS FOR BRITISH VISITORS. Passports. You will need a valid passport and a U.S. visa (which can only be put in a passport of the 10-year kind). You can obtain the visa either through your travel agent or directly from the United States Embassy, Visa and Immigration Department, 5 Upper Grosvenor Street, London W1A 2JB (01–499–3443). The embassy no longer accepts visa applications made in person.

Vaccinations. No vaccinations are required for entry into the United States.

Customs. If you are 21 or over, you can take into the United States: 200 cigarettes or 50 cigars or three pounds of tobacco (combination of proportionate parts permitted); and one U.S. quart of alcohol. In addition, every visitor, including minors, is allowed duty-free gifts to a value of $100. No alcohol or cigarettes may be included in this gift exemption, but up to 100 cigars may be. Be careful not to take in meat or meat products, seeds, plants, fruits, etc. Avoid narcotics like the plague.

Returning to the U.K., you may bring home: (1) 200 cigarettes or 100 cigarillos or 50 cigars or 250 grams of tobacco; (2) two liters of table wine and, in addition, (a) one liter of alcohol over 22% by volume (most spirits); (b) two liters of alcohol under 22% by volume (fortified and sparkling wine); or (c) two more liters of table wine; (3) 50 grams of perfume and ¼ liter of toilet water; and (4) other goods up to a value of £32.

Insurance. We heartily recommend that you insure yourself to cover health and motoring mishaps, with Europe Assistance, 252 High Street, Croydon CRO 1NF (01–680 1234). Their excellent service is all the more valuable when you consider the possible costs of health care in the United States. It is also wise to insure yourself against trip cancellation and loss of luggage.

Air Fares. We suggest that you explore the current scene for budget flight possibilities—APEX and other fares offer considerable savings over the full price. Quite frankly, only business travelers who don't have to watch the price of their tickets fly full price these days—and they often find themselves sitting right beside APEX passengers! At presstime (mid-'88) APEX round-trip fares from London to Richmond were from £448, and to Roanoke from £472. You may want to look into available fly-drive programs offered by firms such as Thomas Cook and Trans World Airlines.

Electricity. 100 volts. You should take along an adaptor since American razor and hair-dryer sockets require flat two-prong plugs.

ADDITIONAL READING. For those who like to do a bit of "homework" before they visit a place, a deeper and broader understanding of what Virginia was, is, and has to offer can be obtained from the following books: *Virginia: A Guide to the Old Dominion* (Oxford University Press, New York, 1940) is part of the American Guide Series and is recommended for historical and general background information; next is *Virginia* by Hans Hannau (Doubleday, Garden City, NY, 1966); *Virginia Beautiful* by Wallace Nutting (EPM Publications, McLean, VA, 1974), and for that very special flavor of dining in Virginia, *Virginia's Historic Restaurants* by Dawn O'Brien (John F. Blair, Publisher, Winston-Salem, NC, 1984), and *Fodor's Williamsburg, Jamestown, and Yorktown* (Fodor's Travel Publications, New York, 1988).

INFORMATION FOR THE DISABLED TRAVELER. Virginia is one of the leading states in the United States to make a concerted effort to help the disabled visiting tourist enjoy the state's historical sites and recreational activities with the least possible inconvenience. Well over a hundred state attractions are accessible for the disabled. These include such things as air shows, national battlefields, vineyards, national parks, churches, plantations, Indian reservations, wildlife refuges, museums, zoological parks, botanical gardens, theaters, boat cruises, pony farms, and seashore areas. A helpful guide for planning a trip to Virginia is "Tips for the Physically Disabled Traveler," available from Virginia Division of Tourism, 202 N. Ninth Street, Suite 500, Richmond, VA 23219; (804) 786–2051.

SENIOR-CITIZEN DISCOUNTS. Senior citizens may in some cases receive special discounts on lodgings. The Days Inn chain offers various discounts to those 55 and older. Holiday Inns extend a discount to NRTA members (write to National Retired Teachers Association, Membership Division, 215 Long Beach Boulevard, Long Beach, CA 90802, if you qualify), and to the AARP (American Association of Retired Persons, Membership Division, 215 Long Beach Boulevard, Long Beach, CA 90802). The amounts and availability of such discounts change, so it's wise to check in advance with these organizations or the hotel chain. The National Council of Senior Citizens, 925 15th Street, N.W., Washington, D.C. 20005, is always working to develop low-cost travel opportunities for its members, as well.

PLACES TO STAY. While there are bargains to be had, and an occasional rip-off, you generally get pretty much what you pay for. This is especially true in highly competitive touring areas.

The key to selecting the *right* place for you to stay is "balance"—that is, balancing your needs, desires, and preferences against your ability or willingness to pay. If you insist on a central location, be prepared to pay extra for the convenience. On the other hand, if location is not important to you, you'll probably enjoy substantial savings. Keep in mind that major attractions are not all that far apart, and you'll probably have your own ground transportation anyway.

If you prefer full-service accommodations (restaurants, lounges, room service), again be prepared to pay extra. Here you should be aware that many hotels and motels are near or adjacent to restaurants, ranging from gourmet establishments to pancake houses.

If an accommodation's ambience and amenities are important to you, recognize in advance that you'll pay for those. But if "a view of the garden" and extra-large and fluffy bath towels rank low on your list of priorities, your travel dollars will almost certainly stretch a bit farther. Whatever your preference, reserve your accommodations well in advance, especially during peak seasons. Weighing what you want against what you'll pay is good travel insurance against future disappointment.

In the *Practical Information* sections, you will find a fairly comprehensive selection of Places to Stay. These selections are arranged alphabetically under separate general location headings.

Each of the listings has one or more of the following general price designations: *Deluxe,* \$100 or more; *Expensive,* \$75–\$100; *Moderate,* \$40–\$75; and *Inexpensive,* under \$40. This *very general* pricing structure is based on double occupancy for one night.

Most major hotels and motels accept major credit cards; others may accept a few or none at all. Many of our listings include those cards that are acceptable at a particular hotel, motel, or chain. These are indicated by the following abbreviations at the end of each selection: AE—American Express; CB—Carte Blanche; DC—Diners Club; MC—MasterCard; V—Visa.

A few additional words of caution are appropriate here:

• Our selection of listings, while fairly comprehensive, is not complete; new facilities are added each year, while others go out of business or change their names. If you discover an exceptional place that we've overlooked, we would be delighted to hear about it. By the same token, if you disagree with any of our selections, we would appreciate hearing that, too. Our aim throughout is to give you the widest possible choice of locations, facilities, services, and prices—but we are realistic enough to know that it's impossible to please every traveler every time; the best we can do is try.

• Our pricing structure—*Inexpensive* through *Deluxe*—is a general one. Rates may change seasonally or at the discretion of management, and a facility listed in one price category may slip into another while we're on press or before you read or use this guide. Even service may slip, or improve, sometimes in less than a year.

• Although our four general price ranges are based on current lodging trends, plus our years of personal experience, each of us differs as to what we need, what we will pay, and whether we truly believe that where we sleep and change our clothes is really all *that* important. Only you can make those decisions. We can, as we have done, provide broad guidelines, recognizing that a moderate price to one traveler may seem wildly extravagant to another or "a real bargain" to yet a third.

• Each of our hotel-motel-campground listings includes addresses and telephone numbers (often toll-free 800 numbers). Because these numbers are possibly the most valuable part of the total listing, we recommend you make use of them by calling for more details than our abbreviated descriptions can provide. Above all call well in advance to make a firm reservation. The time and money spent before your trip can save you hours—even days—of aggravation later. In fact, it just might make your trip.

PLACES TO EAT. Virginia is a land of plenty, famous for its ham (especially the smoked Smithfield variety), and for its spoon bread, fried chicken, crabs, and beef. Many surviving favorite dishes from Colonial cookery are still offered in some restaurants. It's claimed that a good Tidewater cook can prepare a crab at least 20 different ways; and crab Norfolk, seasoned with vinegar, salt, red and black pepper, and baked *en casserole,* is just one of them. Hampton (across the harbor from Norfolk) calls itself the "Seafood Capital of Virginia." And at Smithfield, as noted above, hogs are allowed to roam free in the fields until autumn, when they are let into the peanut fields to fatten. It's the peanuts and the special curing method that give the dark red Smithfield hams their distinctive flavor. Virginia is also renowned for the beef from its Black Angus cattle.

Over on the Eastern Shore—from Chincoteague at the northern end with its world-famous oysters, through Wachapreague in the middle, down to Oyster near Cape Charles—the word is seafood *extraordinaire*—especially shellfish in any form. The Delmarva Peninsula produces melons, tomatoes, and potatoes; these, skillfully blended with milk, butter, eggs, sugar, lemon, cinnamon, and nutmeg, produce that regional delight—white potatoe pie.

Immediately following Places to Stay, in the Practical Information section of this guidebook, is a selection of Places to Eat in and around the Historic Triangle, and nearby on the Peninsula. We don't claim that our lists of selections are all-inclusive; instead, we have attempted to provide a broad and well-rounded selection of places to eat that hopefully will satisfy every taste and pocketbook.

Our restaurant listings, although abbreviated, include addresses and telephone numbers, as well as the following general price designations: *Deluxe,* $25 or more; *Expensive,* $15–$25; *Moderate,* $7–$15; and *Inexpensive,* under $7. Most of the selections also include one or more credit card designations. But be aware that all establishments reserve the right to change their minds, and a credit card that was acceptable when we compiled our lists may not be acceptable later. When in doubt, ask when you reserve a table or before you sit down to dine.

Restaurants are in business primarily to serve the touring public, and there is neither joy nor profit in turning away potential customers. Yet, as anywhere else, this is occasionally necessary, much to the regret of the restaurant's staff and the chagrin of the disappointed customer. Rejection, if it amounts to that, may result from two sources: lack of a reservation or improper attire. Some restaurants accept credit cards, others do not; some restaurants insist on advance bookings, while others won't accept them; and some restaurants are fussy about their customers' dress, while others couldn't care less. Wherever possible, we have tried to give you the guidance you need, but keep in mind that rules sometimes change, and a phone call in advance is a wise move.

TIPPING. Whom to tip, how much, and when, are some of the more confusing aspects of travel. There are no written laws or hard-and-fast rules to govern the practice—merely custom and our own inclination. Unlike much of Europe, where a service charge is added automatically to most restaurant (and some hotel) bills, few restaurants in the United States have adopted this practice. In the rare instance where one has, that fact should be noted on the menu and again on your final bill. When in doubt, *ask;* you may add to the tip, but you are not expected to pay double. Fifteen percent of your total food and beverage bill (excluding any tax) is still universally acceptable throughout the United States. In general, tip as you would at home. Since the virtual disappearance of the half-dollar coin, a dollar bill per suitcase is appropriate for bellhops, or for the doorman who makes an extra effort to hail and help you into a cab. However, if there is a long line of waiting cabs, 25 or 50 cents is sufficient for the simple task of helping you into a taxi. For a local cab ride, 15 to 20 percent of the fare is a reasonably generous tip, and it may even earn you a smile. Many establishments add a fixed room-service charge, usually 10 to 15 percent. It is not out of line to add a bit extra, especially for prompt and courteous service. And finally, there are those unsung and often neglected heroines (and an occasional hero)—the housekeepers and chambermaids who make up your bed, collect your trash, and straighten your room. A tip for a special service performed on request is not inappropriate, and if your stay was especially pleasant, leaving a modest monetary gift when you check out is a nice way to show your appreciation.

DRINKING LAWS. In 1968, the state legislature passed a law permitting by-the-drink liquor service, the most radical change in the state's Alcoholic Beverage Control (ABC) laws since 1934. The law permits "qualified establishments"—meaning bona-fide restaurants, not saloons—to serve mixed alcoholic beverages, subject to local option. Licensed restaurants may serve such drinks until 2 A.M.

SEASONAL EVENTS. With its long history (well over three and a half centuries since the first English settlement), rich heritage from major events (the Colonial era, Revolutionary War, Civil War), varied geography (from mountains to ocean shores), and a mild-to-warm climate for nine months of the year, Virginia has developed a wide range of attractions to entice and entertain visitors. Virtually all of them have grown out of the natural, everyday activities of the people, and that's what makes them so varied and interesting. The following is a summary only of Virginia's Calendar of Events. The state's official Calendar may be obtained by contacting the Virginia Division of Tourism, 202 N. Ninth Street, Suite 500, Richmond, VA 23219; (804) 786–4484.

January: This month is marked by birthday celebrations for three native sons. In Alexandria, the American Revolution's "Light Horse Harry" Lee and his even more famous son, Civil War Confederate Commander Robert E. Lee, are honored with mid-month tours of their homes and headquarters. In Lexington, they celebrate the birthday of the Civil War General "Stonewall" Jackson, also mid-month. Late in January, Williamsburg holds its Colonial Weekend, with tours and entertainment (for a fee). Write or phone for the dates of many other Colonial Williamsburg events: Colonial Williamsburg, Box C, Williamsburg, VA 23187; (804) 229–1000, extension 2372.

February: Early in the month, Williamsburg has its regular Antiques Forum (fee). Late in the month, Alexandria and Fredericksburg honor George Washington with birthday celebrations that include tours, parades, music, and refreshments. Fee. Special Washington's Birthday celebrations are also held at his Mount Vernon home (an open house), his birthplace in Wakefield, and at Williamsburg. Richmond holds its annual antiques show. Admission. Phone 285–2977.

March: Virginia Beach opens the month with its now-established Mid-Atlantic Wildfowl Festival, featuring decoys, photos, art, artifacts, carving, and duck-calling contests. For the first three weeks of March, Mt. Vernon holds its Annual Woodlawn Plantation Needlework Exhibit, with entries by amateurs, celebrities, and pros. In the second week, Fredericksburg holds its Fine Art Exhibit, featuring the work of amateurs and professionals. On the last two weekends, Highland County (west of Staunton on the West Virginia border) holds its Maple Sugar Festival, offering craft exhibits, dances, country music, and down-home cooking. Norfolk's big St. Patrick's Day Parade is now an annual affair, and Williamsburg opens its Militia Season with music and demonstrations.

April: With spring arriving early in Virginia, activities swing noticeably to the outdoors. At Natural Bridge there's the Easter Sunrise Service at this unusual rock formation, while in the second week, the town of Grundy stages its yearly Big K Raft Race, with canoes and kayaks and a 10-mile raft race (fee). At mid-month, Beaverdam holds its eighteenth-century Craft Day at Beaverdam, with Colonial crafts exhibits, a modern crafts sale, and eighteenth-century-style food (fee). In the last half of April, Charlottesville holds a two-week Dogwood Festival, which includes a track meet, barbeque, concert, and sporting events (some fees). About the same time, Norfolk holds its weekend International Azalea Festival, which features a parade, ball, and military air show. The month closes out with a statewide celebration of the Historic Garden Week with more than 200 private homes and gardens open to visitors in 32 areas of Virginia. And, in Blacksburg, during April's final days, there's the annual Mountain Arts & Crafts Fair, with 100 artists and artisans, live music, jugglers, and home-cooked food.

May: Chincoteague (on the Delmarva Peninsula) opens the month with its annual Seafood Festival—all you can eat, but advance tickets required; call (804) 787–2460. Equally early are two weekend events: an Arts & Crafts Festival in Winchester, with parades, dances, and family amusements (fee); and, far to the southwest (near Kentucky and Tennessee), Big Stone Gap's annual Lonesome Pine Arts & Crafts Festival, offering the flavor of mountain life with crafts, music, country cooking, antiques, and needlework. In the second week, Charlottesville (with many historical attractions) holds its annual Kite Day at Ash Lawn, with a kite-flying competition (fee for spectators). Up in Arlington (next to Washington, D.C.) there's a Memorial Day Ceremony at the end of the month, held at the National Cemetery, which features a presidential wreath laying.The landing at Jamestown is celebrated on the Virginia Peninsula this month, and on the Sunday preceding May 15. New Market stages its annual battle (1864) reenactment at Battlefield Park, one of a number of similar reenactments around the state.

June: During June through August Middletown's Wayside Summer Theater runs its six-play season, offering musicals, comedies, and drama. During the first week, Middletown (near Winchester) also holds its annual Needlework Exhibition at Belle Grove Plantation (fee). Throughout June, July, and August, Arlington presents the Sunset Parade at the Iwo Jima Memorial, featuring the U.S. Marine Corps Drum & Bugle Corps. A two-day event, the annual Fredericksburg Arts Festival usually occupies a weekend at the end of the first week, exhibiting the work of both amateurs and professionals. Another art event falls about the same time, the annual Seawall Art Show at Portsmouth, which includes entertainment and fireworks; it's sponsored by the Hampton Roads Chamber of Commerce. About the middle of June, Colonial Beach holds its Potomac River Festival, with parades, fireworks, and dances. Finally, in June's third week, Norfolk has its annual Tidewater Scottish Clan Festival & Clan Gathering, which features highland dancing, piping, drumming, and athletic contests.

July: Independence Day celebrations dominate the opening of July, offering every imaginable event and attraction at the following locations during the first four days of the month: Yorktown, Staunton, Chesterfield, Norfolk, Brookneal, Scottsburg, Fairfax, and Chincoteague. In Scottsville, there's an annual Antique Show & Flea Market over a weekend, with more than 200 dealers in attendance. About the same time—the end of the first week—Wachapregue holds its Art Show. During the second weekend of the month Alexandria holds its popular Civil War Reenactment, a two-day event recreating the 1864 battle of St. Stephens. Over in the western part of the state, Orkney Springs holds a 10-day Shenandoah Valley Music Festival in the final days of July, featuring weekend concerts of symphonic, chamber, choral, and big-band music (fee). A reminder: Virginia had 43 separate events in July last year, so there are lots more!

August: Onancock on Virginia's Eastern Shore opens August with its Harbor Festival, offering street dancing, Hobie Cat races, arts, crafts, and music. Galax (southwest Virginia) holds its now time-honored Annual Old Fiddler's Convention (the fifty-first in 1986) over a weekend early in the month. Up in Alexandria, another weekend event is the annual Tavern Days, which celebrates eighteenth-century tavern life with food, drink, and music of the era. At Mt. Solon, they hold Virginia's oldest sporting contest; in 1986 it was the 165th Annual Jousting Tournament, a one-day event held about mid-month. Toward the end of August there's the annual (one-day) Fish Fry in Wachapreague, offering fresh fish, cake, and home-made ice cream (fee). And closing out August, Hillsville (a county seat in southwest Virginia) holds its enduring Gun Show & Flea Circus over a late weekend, with more than 700 dealers exhibiting guns, knives, coins, and antiques. Another Civil War reenactment and living-history encampment is held at Haymarket in Prince William County.

September: In Lorton (on I-95, south of Alexandria), they'll be holding their Annual Gunston Hall Car Show at the end of the first week. The second weekend of the month sees Richmond celebrating its Annual International Festival, with ethnic foods, cultural exhibits, and entertainment (fee). Charlottesville presents an annual Charity Fair on the third weekend, with homemade food and crafts. Late in the month, Emporia (the county seat near the North Carolina border) holds its annual Virginia Peanut Festival, offering entertainment, an arts and crafts show, and parade (some fees). About the same time, Virginia Beach is holding its Neptune Festival, which features a sand-castle contest and live entertainment. The month closes out with arts-and-crafts festivals in Blackstone, Occoquan, and New Market.

October: The weather is still mild in October when Waterford (a National Historic Landmark village on the Maryland border, west of Baltimore) celebrates its eighteenth-century heritage with music, craft demonstrations, art, and a tour of historical homes. Close to mid-month, Chincoteague (on the Eastern Shore) entices shellfish fanciers to its Oyster Festival, and about mid-month Appomattox holds its Historic Railroad Festival. In Richmond, about the third week, it's time for the Annual National Tobacco Festival, highlighted by a Grand Illuminated Parade, Queen's Ball, sports celebrity breakfast, and bluegrass and country music. Late in the month, Vienna (just outside Arlington) will hold its Annual Halloween Parade.

November: Although the schedule slims down in this month, the most recent calendar listed 12 state-wide events. Once again, there will be such events as the Annual Antique Show & Sale in Belle Haven (on the Dalmarva Peninsula), with 100 exhibitors from 10 states; in Fredericksburg the Annual Craft Show is a weekend event around the tenth, and later the Artistry in Wood Show held in Arlington. This is a showcase for mid-Atlantic woodcarvers who exhibit, sell, demonstrate, and compete in their craft (fee).

December: Don't think this first month of winter means lean pickings in Virginia. December is devoted to special Christmas celebrations in Fredericksburg, Williamsburg, Richmond, Lynchburg, and Lexington. Big Stone Gap follows with a weekend celebration called Christmas in the Mountains, a Blue Ridge Mountain version of Yuletide, while Danville holds a Christmas Walking Tour (Victorian homes on Millionaire's Row), and Stratford has candlelight tours and caroling as part of its Christmas Celebration. Note that these are in the first 10 or so days of the month. In the second half of December, it's a string of further Christmas activities all across the state—tree lightings, candlelight tours, carol singing, and dancing, often in eighteenth-century costume. Especially noteworthy are Alexandria, Lorton, Middletown, Arlington, Williamsburg, Jamestown, and Charlottesville. Norfolk closes the month and the year with its annual Waterfront New Year's Eve Festival.

CIVIL WAR BATTLEFIELDS. For the Civil War buff or historian there simply is no other state in the United States where one can see so much preserved of what poet Walt Whitman called "a strange, sad war." It is difficult to realize, but it is nevertheless true, that more Americans lost their lives in the War Between the States than in World Wars I and II, *combined.* Sixty percent of its battles were fought in Virginia, and the most important battle sites of that awesome conflict have been preserved for the present. It should be noted that these preserved areas are not meant to glorify the war, but to honor the men who died in that terrible conflict. Most visitors come away from battlefield visits both awed and deeply moved. At most major sites there are walking or bus tours with narration by guides and descriptive pamphlets available to visitors.

In addition to the battlefields, there are Civil War attractions such as the Museum of the Confederacy at Richmond, Fort Monroe at Hampton, Old Blanford Church and the Siege Museum at Petersburg, and the tombs of both Robert E. Lee and Stonewall Jackson in Lexington. All told there are 250 other marked Civil War sites along Virginia highways. The state of Virginia publishes a comprehensive free guide to Civil War battlefields, monuments, and sites. For further information, contact: Virginia Division of Tourism, 202 N. Ninth St., Suite 500, Richmond, VA 23219, or phone 804–786–4484.

Here are brief descriptions of the battlefields that are considered to be the most famous of the war, all of them administered by the National Park Service, except those at New Market and Sayler's Creek, which are part of Virginia's park system:

Manassas National Battlefield Park. Site of two great battles (called Bull Run by the Union the first time) in 1861 and 1862, this is a 4,500-acre park 26 miles southwest of Washington, D.C. Here the Confederacy lost 11,456 men and the Union, 17,170. Two driving tours trace the ebb and flow of the battles, and a walking tour to Henry Hill affords a panoramic view of the fields where so many died. Located at the junction of I-66 and State Rte. 234.

Fredericksburg and Spotsylvania National Military Park. Here, in a 6,500-acre area, four major battles were fought—Fredericksburg, Chancellorsville, the Wilderness, and Spotsylvania—and 100,000 Americans from both sides lost their lives. Visitors may tour by car or walk the many trails to see the preserved trenches and gunpits, then visit the museums and visitors' centers. Park historians are on hand to answer questions and give directions. The park museums are at Fredericksburg on U.S. 1, and at Chancellorsville, 10 miles west on Rte. 3.

New Market Battlefield Park. This state park is on I-81 in the heart of the Shenandoah Valley. Here, in 1864, 6,000 Union troops met 4,500 Confederates, including young cadets from Virginia Military Institute (at least one movie has touched on this famous episode in the war). New Market was a climactic battle that earned the South's "Stonewall" Jackson his nickname, given to him at the height of the battle by Gen. Robert E. Lee. Each year on the Sunday preceding May 15 (the date of the battle) there is a reenactment of that awful clash. This presentation attracts visitors from far and near.

Richmond National Battlefield Park. Seven times the Union armies hurled assaults at Richmond, the Confederacy's capital and vital center of manufacturing and medical services. Only on Gen. U. S. Grant's final attempt in 1864 did Union troops reach within sight of the capitol building. Ten battlefield sites lie in a loop around Richmond, giving the visitor a sobering insight into this tragic war. During June, July, and August "living history" programs are presented that depict camp life of soldiers on both sides. There are historical trails for those who wish to extend their exploration of this battle area.

Petersburg National Battlefield. The Union's Gen. Grant and the Confederacy's Gen. Lee faced each other's armies for 10 months at this rail center south of Richmond. Petersburg was vital to the South's survival. It was the Civil War's longest siege and biggest battlefield, and when Petersburg finally fell in 1864, the war ended. During the siege the North suffered 42,000 casualties, the South 28,000. Centered in Petersburg, a Living History program (Mid-June to late August) realistically portrays the Civil War soldier's life.

Sayler's Creek Battlefield (Historical State Park). When Petersburg and Richmond fell in 1864, Lee's armies fled south in four columns, a starving army of tattered Confederates seeking to link up in North Carolina with an approaching southern army. But lack of supplies, spring floods that slowed them down, and harassing Union cavalry thwarted their escape. They were forced to stand and fight on ground not of their own choosing. In this final battle of the war, 6,000 Confederate soldiers—including eight generals—were captured. The high ground overlooking the site, with an audio station and visuals, lies on State Rte. 617, two miles north of Virginia Rte. 307, near Rice.

Appomattox Court House (National Historic Park). If Sayler's Creek saw the climax, the village of Appomattox Court House was the place where Lee decided he could no longer accept further bloodshed by his troops and where he surrendered to Grant. Park guides greet visitors with a folder and map, directing them to exhibits, illustrated talks, two 17-minute audio-visual programs, and a walking tour of the village. In addition, there are hourly talks given every day from mid-June to Labor Day. The park, open all year except on holidays in November through February, is located on State Rte. 24, three miles northeast of the town of Appomattox. Phone 804–352–8782.

HISTORIC HOMES. A visitor to Virginia who doesn't know American history may be overwhelmed that so much of the republic's past is housed, cherished, and displayed in just one of the 50 states. That visitor should keep in mind that if it all began here, it could also have *ended* here. Much about the new nation's growing pains is revealed in the homes and houses our forefathers built, from a rustic log cabin at Jamestown to an antebellum planter's mansion a bit further up the James. Virginia, one could say, is a state-wide museum of America's past. As the first, largest, and wealthiest of the British colonies in America, Virginia contains nine homes that belonged to eight U.S. presidents, plus seven homes of eight Virginia signers of the Declaration of Independence. In all, nearly 100 of the state's historic homes are open to visitors, the great majority of them 12 months of the year.

The presidential homes include the following:

Popes Creek Plantation, George Washington's birthplace, and **Mount Vernon,** near Alexandria, built in 1743, where he spent part of his youth and all his later years following two terms as president. Both open all year round. Washington's birthplace is located in Wakefield, Virginia's Northern Neck. Call 804–224–1732. For more information about Mount Vernon, see the Northern Virginia section.

Monticello, in Charlottesville, home of the third president, Thomas Jefferson, framer of the Declaration of Independence. It was designed by him, and built in 1768. Open year round. Call 804–295–8181.

Montpelier, near Orange, home of the fourth president, James Madison. It was built in 1760. This home is *not open* to the public, but there is a James Madison Museum at 129 Caroline Street in Orange, VA 22960 (703–672–1776).

Ash Lawn, in Charlottesville, near Jefferson's home. Ash Lawn was built in 1799 by James Monroe, fifth president; Jefferson helped in its design. In Fredericksburg, there is a Monroe Law Office-Museum exhibiting a large collection from his early career. Open year round. Call 804–293–9539.

Oak Hill, near Leesburg, was built by Monroe in 1819, midway through his term as president. Not open to the public.

Berkeley, in Charles City, belonged to the ninth president, William Henry Harrison. It was *also* the ancestral home of the twenty-third president, Benjamin Harrison, although he was born in Ohio. In 1619, America's first Thanksgiving Day was celebrated here, *one year before* the Pilgrims landed in Massachusetts. Open year round. Daily, 8 A.M. to 5 P.M. Call 804–795–2453.

Sherwood Forest, in Charles City, was owned by *two* presidents, William Henry Harrison (above) and John Tyler, the tenth chief executive. It is the longest frame house in America—300 feet—and is still owned by the Tyler family, with 1,200 of the original acres remaining. The grounds are open daily, but house tours are by appointment only. Daily, 9 A.M. to 5 P.M. Call 804–829–5377.

Montebello, near Gordonsville, was the home of Zachary Taylor, the twelfth president. Taylor was born in a log house (now a guest house on the property) during a stopover while his family was en route to Kentucky. Montebello is not open to the public.

President Woodrow Wilson's Birthplace. In Staunton, this large Greek Revival house, built in 1846, was a Presbyterian manse when Wilson, the twenty-eighth president, was born here in 1856. The reception center exhibits items from Wilson's life as an educator, statesman, and president. Open year round. Call 703–885–0897.

Although the residences listed above are really an impressive collection, they are only a small part of the gracious homes still standing—and often still inhabited—in Virginia. In fact, there are 68 others of historical importance and architectural distinction. The reason for this wealth of surviviing homes—some of them over 300 years old—is that for its first three centuries, Virginia was an agricultural state, with estates founded on land grants received from English kings. The homes tended to remain in each family for generations, on land holdings that were safe from the encroachment of spreading cities. Here are brief descriptions of some other outstanding homes:

Belmont, in Fredericksburg, is a 1761 Rappahannock River manor that became the home and studio of the famous portrait painter, Gari Melchers (1860–1932). Open all year. *Also in Fredericksburg:* **Chatham,** which was built during the 1760s on a plantation overlooking the Rappahannock River. This home belonged to William Fitzhugh, a prominent figure in the Revolutionary period. Open all year. **Kenmore,** home of George Washington's sister, Betty, and Col. Fielding Lewis. This brick mansion was built by Lewis for his bride in 1752 on an 863-acre plantation. Open year round. **St. James House** is a cottage that was built in 1760 by James Mercer on land bought from George Washington. It is furnished with seventeenth- and eighteenth-century English and American antiques, including rare silverware and porcelain. Open by appointment. **Mary Washington House,** which dates back to 1772. Believing war with the British Crown was inevitable, George Washington purchased this house for his widowed mother, Mary, and persuaded her to move here. Open year round. For information, write Fredericksburg Visitor Center, 706 Caroline St., VA 22401, or call 703–373–1776.

Carter's Grove, in Williamsburg, was built in 1750. Robert "King" Carter made this mansion the headquarters of his 300,000-acre plantation with 1,000 slaves. It has been called "the most beautiful house in America." *Also in Williamsburg:* **Brush–Everard House,** built in 1717 by gunsmith and armorer John Brush, was later owned by Thomas Everard, the mayor of the town, who added two wings. Open year round. **James Geddy House.** This L-shaped house, built circa 1750, was the home of the Geddy family—gunsmiths, blacksmiths, silversmiths, and jewelers. George Washington was one of their customers. Furnishings are principally Colonial. Open year round. **Governor's Palace.** No visit to Williamsburg would be complete without a tour of this building, the pre-Revolutionary symbol of the power and prestige of the British Crown and home of seven royal governors. Burned just before the English surrender at Yorktown, it has been faithfully reproduced on the original foundation. **Peyton Randolph House.** Home of a leading statesman in Colonial America, the house was begun in 1716 and served as French General Rochambeau's headquarters during the Revolution. Open year round. **George Wythe House.** The visitor with a "one-stop" limit on his house-appreciation schedule may possibly satisfy his interest here in Williamsburg, finishing with this house, the home of America's first law professor (he taught Thomas Jefferson, John Marshall, and Henry Clay). George Wythe House served as Washington's headquarters before the siege of Yorktown. Open year round. For advance information about the Historic Triangle area, contact Colonial Williamsburg Foundation, Box C, Williamsburg, VA 23185, or phone 804–229–1000.

Stonewall Jackson's Headquarters in Winchester. Commanding Confederate troops in the Shenandoah Valley, Jackson spent the winter of 1861 and spring of 1862 here, planning his valley campaign. The house contains a fine collection of Jackson memorabilia. Open all year. *Also in Winchester:* **Abram's Delight.** In sharp contrast to Civil War architecture is Abraham Hollingsworth's 1729 frontier cabin beside a spring, where his family and later generations lived for 200 years. In 1754 the present stone house was erected and its "conspicuously grand" setting was the site for entertaining Washington, Lafayette, and other notables of the Colonial period. Contact Winchester-Frederick County Chamber of Commerce, 2 North Cameron St., Winchester, VA 22601; 703–662–4118.

John Marshall House. Located in Richmond, America's most famous chief justice, wrote some of his most important Supreme Court decisions here. He built it in 1790 and lived here until his death in 1835. Open year round. *Also in Richmond:* **Agecroft Hall.** This half-timbered manor house, with its original sixteenth-century oak paneling, was purchased in England in 1926, dismantled, shipped here, and reassembled on this James River site. Open all year. **Old Stone House.** Built about 1737, this is Richmond's oldest house. It is constructed of rough field stone and furnished with eighteenth-century pieces. The house is now part of the Edgar Allan Poe Museum. Open all year. **Tuckahoe Plantation.** Serving as a working farm for 275 years, this home was built in 1712 by Thomas Randolph. The frame house and outbuildings remain in their original form, including the schoolhouse where Thomas Jefferson studied as a boy. Open during Historic Garden Week; otherwise, to groups by appointment. **Wickham–Valentine House.** John Wickham, who served as defense attorney in Aaron Burr's treason trial, built this fine example of architecture. It has splendid furnishings. Open year round. **Wilton.** Built in 1750, this stately Georgian mansion on a 2,000-acre James River plantation is remarkable for having paneled walls, floor to ceiling, in every room, hall, and closet! Lafayette made his headquarters here during the American Revolution. Open year round. **White House of the Confederacy.** Designed by Robert Mills, architect of the Washington monument, this 1818 house was the home of the Confederacy's president, Jefferson Davis, from 1861 until Richmond was evacuated in 1865. Next door, the Museum of the Confederacy contains the most impressive collection of Civil War artifacts in existence. Open all year. Advance information is available from Convention and Visitors Bureau, 300 E. Main St., Richmond, VA 23219; 804–782–2777.

McCormick's Birthplace, in Steele's Tavern, was the home of the man who revolutionized agriculture by inventing—at age 22—the mechanical reaper. He was born here in 1831 and nearly 100 reapers were built here in the blacksmith shop at Walnut Grove Farm until McCormick moved west in 1847 and set up a factory in Chicago that became International Harvester. Open year round. Call 703–377–2255.

McLean House, in Appomattox, where Gen. Robert E. Lee surrendered to Gen. Ulysses S. Grant on April 9, 1865, ending the Civil War. The house and surrounding village are restored to their 1865 condition, the whole area now constituting a national park offering guided tours. Closed major holidays.

Moore House. For a site of pure historical drama, it's hard to match this Yorktown house, for here, on October 18, 1771, General Cornwallis surrendered to George Washington and 7,500 British troops laid down their arms, ending the Revolution. This historic house is maintained by the National Park Service as part of the Yorktown Battlefield Tour. Open all year. For information contact Superintendent, Colonial National Historical Park, Box 210, Yorktown, VA 23690; 804–898–3400.

Booker T. Washington's Birthplace. Located in Hardy, near Rocky Mount, this is a typical small farm of the pre-Civil War era. Here, Booker T. Washington was born a slave in 1856, and here he lived until the war ended. Restored by the National Park Service, the tools, crops, and animals recreate the small farm of the time. Open year round. Call 703–721–2094.

These three dozen homes, dating from the earliest Colonial days through the Revolution and the Civil War, offer a three-century slice of American home life. Another three dozen outstanding homes scattered throughout Virginia are mentioned in later chapters.

CANOEING. Although visitors may be unaware of it, Virginia is rich in river resources. That means good canoeing, in every form—novice, intermediate, and expert. Since the state has three distinct regions—Mountain, Piedmont, and Coastal Plain—the canoeist has the option of paddling down powerful, demanding stretches of whitewater, gently falling Piedmont streams, or slow-flowing, cypress-lined waters of coastal rivers. All are within a day's drive of central Virginia.

Needless to say, the canoeing buff should make an honest appraisal of his skill, based on physical conditioning and previous experience, and choose a river appropriate to his ability. Safety, of course, is the paramount consideration. No one should take on any river without proper equipment. That means—as a minimum—a personal flotation device (life jacket) for everyone, gear firmly lashed down, two persons to a canoe, and two canoes in a party. Beginners should read up on canoeing techniques, and take lessons at their local Red Cross chapter before taking their first trip.

Virginia has 16 principal rivers for canoe trips. What follows is a capsule description of each, by region, containing: (1) river name; (2) terminal points; (3) distance; (4) difficulty rating.

Mountain Region. *James River*—Eagle Rock to Snowden, 48 miles, novice to intermediate. *New River*—North Carolina line to West Virginia line, 155 miles, novice to expert. *Clinch River*—Blackford to Tennessee line, 125 miles, novice to expert. *Smith River*—Woolwine to Philpott Reservoir, 21 miles, intermediate. *South Fork of Shenandoah River*—Luray to Front Royal, 46 miles, novice. *Passage Creek*—Elizabeth Furrace to Waterlick, 7 miles, expert.

Piedmont Region. *James River*—Bent Creek to Richmond, 111 miles, novice to intermediate (expert through city of Richmond). *Slate River*—Dianna Mills to James River, 9.5 miles, novice to intermediate. *Rappahannock River*—Remington to Motts Run, 29 miles, intermediate. *North Anna River*—Lake Anna to Carmel Church, 24 miles, novice to intermediate. *Nottoway River*—Rte. 609 in Brunswick County to Rte. 630 in Greensville County, 15 miles, novice.

Coastal Plain. *Mattaponi River*—Rte. 647 to Aylett, 35 miles, novice. *Pamunky River*—Rte. 301 to Rte. 360, 35 miles, novice. *Chickahominy River*—Rte. 609 at Roxbury to Providence Forge (Rte. 155), 6 miles, novice. *Blackwater River*—Rte. 603 to Franklin, 39 miles, novice. *Northwest River*—Bunch Walnuts Road to Rte. 168, city of Chesapeake, 5 miles, novice.

Clearly, this brief survey only outlines the possibilities and doesn't provide complete information for trip planning, such as water levels at different times of the year. Additional information is available from: "Boating Access to Virginia Waters" (map), Virginia Game Commission, Box 11104, Richmond, VA 23230; Coastal Highway Maps, Virginia Department of Highways, 1401 East Broad Street, Richmond, Virginia 23219; Coastal Canoeists (organization), Box 566, Richmond, VA 23204; Canoe Cruisers Association (organization), Box 572, Arlington, Virginia 22216; Canoe Union (organization), Box 6055, Suffolk, VA 23433.

SHELLFISHING. Virginia's tidal waters abound with clams, crabs, and oysters. These delicacies are yours for the taking in Chesapeake Bay and its tributaries and in the shallow waters of the Eastern Shore. Enough shellfish to satisfy even the most ravenous seafood lover can usually be gathered in half a day—in the right location. Here is some essential information on harvesting laws, suitable areas for each type, and the basic gear needed.

Crabbing. Blue crabs are found in Chesapeake Bay and in most of Tidewater Virginia. They are most common in shallow or near-shore waters during warm months, the peak season being mid-May to late September. Crabs can be taken with dip-nets, handlines, collapsible (wire) traps, or crab pots. While you can wade in shallow water near grass beds and scoop them up with a dip-net, jellyfish and stinging nettles may be plentiful during summer months, so it's wise to wear long pants to avoid their painful stings. Wear old sneakers to prevent cuts from broken shells on the bottom. One bushel of five-inch or larger crabs can be harvested daily for personal consumption. A bushel basket—with a cover to keep them in it—placed in an inner tube to keep them afloat and a "leash" to your belt is the handiest technique. Using a hand-line from the end of a dock is great fun for the kids. The baited line (chicken neck or fish head) is dangled in the water. This usually entices the crab within scooping range of the dip-net. Crab traps can be bought at bait-and-tackle shops, or rented at most public fishing piers. The trap is baited and allowed to sit on the bottom (where the sides fall open and lie flat). Haul it up periodically to see if you've been lucky. You're allowed to set one trap in deeper water—with a marker float—but not in marked channels used by boats.

Clamming. Both hard- and soft-shell clams are available. Unlike oysters, which attach themselves to something, clams only bury themselves a few inches in the sand or mud of tidal waters. The best areas are hard, sandy mud bottoms, with slightly coarse rock or shell. The simplest techniques for getting hard-shell clams is to wade in shallow water, "shuffling" your feet until you encounter one, then bend and pick it up with your hand or a clam rake. Soft-shell clams are trickier to find because they lie six to ten inches below the bottom. At extreme low tide, you must spot their pencil-sized, keyhole-shaped holes, often seen when they squirt water. You dig them out with a short-handled spade called a "sharpshooter," being careful you don't crush them. State laws permit you to harvest up to 250 clams a day without a license, *provided* you use only your hands or a clam rake and that you are on public grounds or have permission from private landowners.

Oystering. Harvesting oysters is permitted during the "open" season (October through March) from public grounds or in leased oyster grounds, provided you have permission from the lease holder. One bushel of three-inch or larger oysters per person is the limit. The best areas are those with firm sand and shell bottoms, near sea walls, dock pilings or bulkheads, and at the edge of marshes. Carry a bushel basket to ensure you don't gather more than the legal limit and avoid areas carrying yellow "Condemned" signs or are so marked on maps. Public grounds that are below low tide can be worked from a boat using oyster tongs. Many campgrounds and motels near the water either own or lease oystering grounds that are available for their guests. For additional information, write or call: Virginia Marine Resources Committee, P.O. Box 756, Newport News, VA 23607; (804) 245–2811.

SALTWATER FISHING. Out-of-state visitors who love salt-water fishing are often pleasantly surprised to learn that Virginia holds the all-tackle world-record catches for black drum, channel bass, speckled trout, and cobia. State waters also hold marlin, tarpon, dolphin, king mackerel, wahoo, tuna, jumbo bluefish, and striped bass. In all, 23 species of sport fish annually win trophies and citations for anglers fishing from Virginia boats, piers, and shores. These salt-water fishing grounds span wide areas—four great tidal rivers, the Bay itself (including the Eastern Shore), and the Atlantic Ocean's Gulf Stream and Labrador Current. These varied fishing areas produce and attract fish in such great number, variety, and size that the visitor stands a fairly good chance of catching a world-record fish.

Each year (since 1958) there has been a Salt-Water Fishing Tournament run by the state from May 1 through November 30 that awards 3,500 citation wall plaques for catches that meet minimum tournament standards. In 1984, for example, new state and world all-tackle records were set with a 21½-pound tautog boated off Wachapreague. To enter the tournament, the visiting angler need only catch a fish "in a sportsmanlike manner" and take it to one of the more than 100 official weighing stations, very possibly at the dock, marina, or pier from which you fish. If your catch qualifies, your citation will be mailed to you after November 30. There is no charge for entering the tournament. Full particulars are available from: Director, Virginia Salt Water Fishing Tournament, Suite 102, Hauser Building, 968 Oriole Drive South, Virginia Beach, Virginia 23451; (804) 428–4360. For general information about salt-water fishing in all Virginia waters, write: Virginia Division of Tourism, Department of Economic Development, 202 North Ninth Street, Suite 500, Richmond, VA 23219.

Many charter and head boats ply state waters (and there are fishing piers and small-boat rental stations) in the following locations: Hampton, Poquoson, Newport News, Deltaville, Gloucester Point, Greys Point, Cobbs Creek, Little Creek, Lynnhaven Inlet, Rudee Inlet, Norfolk, Virginia Beach, Portsmouth, Cape Charles, Chincoteague, Oyster, Quinby, Sanford, Wachapreague, Callao, Coles Point, Harryhogan Point, Lewisetta, Lottsburg, Reedville, and Warsaw. For extensive fishing information on these locations, send for the state pamphlet, "Salt Water Sport Fishing in Virginia," available from the Virginia Division of Tourism, address same as above.

STATE PARKS. Virginia maintains 23 recreational and six historical state parks, plus six "natural" areas. These are scattered throughout the state, with the heaviest concentration—25 of them—in the Piedmont and Coastal areas. Two more state parks are presently under development. Most state parks are open year-round, although they are generally geared to seasonal operation. The greatest activity is from Memorial to Labor Day. This period sees maximum use of swimming beaches, boathouses, boat and horse rentals, restaurants, refreshment stands, and stores (concession facilities). Note: Parking and admission fees are in effect during this "operating" season.

Copies of the rules and regulations are available at each park, and while you are expected to observe them, they are intended to ensure your safety and pleasure, not restrain your enjoyment.

In the "off" season, visitors still enjoy boating, fishing, hiking, bicycling, nature walks, picnics, and sightseeing. During the off-season months, fall to spring, you will of course encounter a wider range of weather—colder in the inland mountain regions and gradually warming as you pass eastward through the central Piedmont area to the coastal plain.

Hikers should note that 510 miles of the Appalachian Trail pass through Virginia (altogether, 2,000 miles long—from Georgia to Maine). Of this total, all parts of the trail that are not federally owned are now under the jurisdiction of Virginia's Division of State Parks, which administers and maintains 30 miles of the state-owned section.

Bike Tours. Beautiful countryside, historic sites, and good roads make Virginia a natural attraction to the cycling enthusiast. "Bike Virginia," Box 203, Williamsburg, Virginia 23187–0203, (804–253–2985) offers weekend, five-day, and two-week bicycle tours to six major areas, 12 months of the year. You "select the distance and degree of difficulty you desire and ride at your own pace. . . . A tour host rides the routes to provide assistance when needed." A van transports luggage on the five-day tour. Tours include: Williamsburg–Chesapeake, Prospect Hill, The Shenandoah, Vineyard Tour, Off-the-Road, and Winter Tours. A comprehensive brochure is available from the above address. *Safety.* To understand Virginia's laws and safety tips for cyclists, send for the brochure "Bicycling on Virginia Roads" from: State Bicycle Coordinator, Virginia Department of Highways, 1221 East Broad Street, Richmond, VA 23219.

Park Locations. Virginia's park system is so widespread and the activities and facilities so extensive—camping, hiking, swimming, showers, cabins, trailer parks, horse rentals, picnic areas, fishing, boat ramps, and rentals—that only a sweeping survey of places is possible here. It's enough, however, to whet the visitor's appetite and prompt a written request for the pamphlet, "Virginia State Parks," from: Division of Parks & Recreation, 1201 Washington Building, Capitol Square, Richmond, Virginia 23219. In the listing that follows, the words "state park" have been left out to save space. For the *precise* location of the parks, consult the pamphlet mentioned above. These lists are grouped by *region,* with a brief description to catch the flavor of each:

Mountain Region: *Claytor Lake*—472 acres near Dubbin, in Pulaski County; lake activities and hiking. *Clinch Mt. Wildlife Management Area*—25,000 wilderness acres on a high plateau west of Saltville; primitive camping. *Douthat*—4,500 acres of mountain scenery near Clifton Forge in Bath and Allegheny counties. *Goshen Pass Natural Area*—Spectacularly rugged terrain on Little North Mountain, in Rockbridge County, with elevations from 3,600 feet dropping sharply to 1,800 feet at the Maury River; picnicking, shelter, drinking water, toilet facilities. *Gray-*

son Highlands—Breathtaking alpine views (at over 5,000 feet elevation), between Damascus and Independence; hiking and horses permitted. *Hungry Mother*—Beautiful woodlands and a lake, near Marion, with elevations to 3,270 feet; boating and camping. *Lick Creek Natural Area*—836 acres on Carter and Brush mountains, 20 miles northeast of Marion, 6 miles of lakefront; hunting and fishing *not permitted* in natural area. *Natural Tunnel*—An 850-feet passageway through solid rock, cut by water over thousands of years, with both a stream and railroad tracks passing through it, north of Weber City; camping, picnicking, fishing, and swimming pool open "in season." *Shot Tower Historical*—A state landmark for 150 years, in southwest Virginia overlooking the New River; restrooms, picnicking, and hiking trails. *Sky Meadows*—1,132 acres of picturesque terrain in the Blue Ridge Mountains, 2 miles south of Paris; picnicking, hiking, overnight (primitive) campground for Appalachian Trail hikers. *Southwest Virginia Museum*—Exhibits and artifacts in a four-story mansion, relating the history of southwest Virginia, in Big Stone Gap; small admission charge.

Piedmont Region: *Bear Creek Lake*—In the heart of the Cumberland State Forest, 4.5 miles northwest of Cumberland; lakeside activities, campgrounds, hiking trails. *Fairy Stone*—168-acre lake in the foothills of the Blue Ridge Mountains, in Patrick and Henry counties; housekeeping cabins, tent and trailer campgrounds, sandy beach, pleasure boats, riding horses, bridle paths, and hiking trails. *Goodwin Lake–Prince Edward*—Picturesque country, on a lake southwest of Burkeville; swimming, picnicking, campgrounds, hiking trails, boating, and fishing. *Halliday Lake*—Deep in Buckingham–Appomattox State Forest, near Appomattox; wooded lakeside campgrounds, swimming beach, picnic areas, swimming, and fishing; *Lake Anna*—2,058 acres in Spotsylvania County, 22 miles southwest of Fredericksburg; 8.5 miles of lake shoreline for fishing, boat ramp, picnic area, hiking trails, and trailer parking. *Occoneechee*—On the John H. Kerr Reservoir, near Clarksville; campsites for tents and trailers, picnic area with shelters, launching ramp, and amphitheater for evening programs. *Pocahontas*—Within a large state forest, near Richmond and Petersburg; Swift Creek Lake available for boating, swimming, picnic area, playground, and bridle path. *Sayler's Creek Battlefield*—See Civil War Sites, above. *Smith Mountain Lake*—1,506 acres and 16 miles of lakefront in Bedford County near Lynchburg and Roanoke; boat ramp, fishing, picnic areas, and self-guided nature and hiking trails. *Staunton River*—For historical battlefield, see Civil War Sites, above; 1,287 acres of woods, meadows, and a long lake shoreline, in Halifax County, 10 miles from Scottsburg; swimming–wading pool, tent-trailer campgrounds, picnic areas, boat ramp, dock, playground, tennis courts, nature trails, and vacation cabins. *Tabb Mountain Historical*—On Rte. 609 in Amelia County, a marker stands on 1 acre of land to honor Father John B. Tabb, poet and philosopher.

Coastal Plain Region: *Caledon*—2,529 acres, under development and not yet open to the public. *Charles C. Steirly Heron Rookery Natural Area*—Located in a dense swamp, surrounded by timber, 5 miles north of Waverly, in Sussex County; heavy underbrush throughout, with boots recommended for bird watching; no camping allowed. *Chippokes Plantation*—1,400 acres of a working farm (still going strong after 300 years), on the James River directly opposite Jamestown; picnic tables and shelters, swimming pool, bicycle/hiking trails, and antebellum mansion tours.

False Cape—One of the few remaining undeveloped areas on the East Coast, south of Virginia Beach; potential visitors are urged to refer to the Division of Parks & Recreation (address above) for publications outlining regulations for using this bird sanctuary; hikers and bicyclists can enter through the Back Bay National Wildlife Refuge, and boaters through Back Bay to the dock at False Cape Landing. *Grist Mill Historical*—Originally owned by George Washington's family, this restored mill exhibits—with sound effects—how a grist mill operated; on Mt. Vernon Memorial Highway, 3 miles west of Mt. Vernon. *Leesylvania*—505 acres of parkland, under development in 1985 and not yet open to the public. *Mason Neck*—The newest addition to the park system, 1,804 acres 7 miles northeast of Woodbridge; hiking, picnic areas, visitors' center. *Parker's Marsh Natural Area*—A remote area bounded by Onancock and Back Creeks and Chesapeake Bay; bird watching; but no camping permitted. *Seashore*—2,770 acres of preserved natural area near Virginia Beach; hiking trails, housekeeping cabins, tent and trailer campsites, boat ramp, bicycle trails, picnic area, and grocery store. *Seashore Natural Area*—2,570 acres of preserved natural area (a National Landmark since 1965), lying between Broad and Linkhorn Bays near Virginia Beach; basically an environmental education center for group meetings, with a natural resource lab; 27 miles of hiking trails. *Westmoreland*—Faces Potomac River, 5 miles northwest of Montross; pool, bathhouse, boat ramp, hiking trails, picnic area, and refreshment stand with provisions. *Wreck Island Natural Area*—An offshore island, 7 miles east of Oyster, on the Delmarva Peninsula, about 3 miles long and only 20 percent of it "high ground" (10–12 feet above water); preserved as a wildlife refuge; no camping; accessible by boat from Oyster. *York River*—Midway between Richmond and Hampton Roads, 11 miles north of Williamsburg; part of the state's estuary system, a habitat for marine plant and animal life; fishing, boat ramp, picnic areas, and hiking trails.

Park Reservations: In Person. To reserve campgrounds, trailer sites, vacation cabins, etc. from Memorial Day to Labor Day, at Park Terminals (8:30–5); March 29–May 24 and September 3–December 1; Park Terminals open only on Fridays. *Terminals closed in winter and no out-of-state checks accepted. Also In Person:* At Division of Parks & Recreation Central Office, 1201 Washington Building, Capitol Square, Richmond, VA 23219; Year-round Monday–Friday, 8:30–4:30. *By Phone:* At Ticketron Reservation Center, (804) 490–3939, year-round, Monday–Friday 10–4 (except holidays). Note: Telephone reservations are *not accepted* at Central Office (above) or at Park Terminals. **By Mail.** Mail appropriate fees and reservation form to Ticketron Reservation Center (for list of centers and their addresses, call 804–490–3939. Mail requests must be accompanied by reservation application and certified check, money order, or bank draft, made payable to "Ticketron," in the correct amount for the accommodation fee. *Incorrect requests will be returned unprocessed.*

Foreign Visitors. If your check, money order, or bank draft is written in a foreign country, please write "U.S. Funds" after the amount.

Commercial Campsites. The Virginia Campground Association (VCA) is the state's private campground owners' association, and in addition to maintaining standards for "family camping" offers a brochure entitled "Virginia Campground Directory," available from: Virginia Campground Association, Route 1, Box 120, New Kent, VA 23124.

VIRGINIA VINEYARDS. Although a century ago Virginia enjoyed an international reputation for its claret wine, the state has not been known until recently for its vineyards. Many visitors will be surprised to learn of Virginia's rapid strides toward reestablishing that reputation. Thomas Jefferson was the state's original "wine pioneer" and has been called the "father of American wines" for his discovery that Virginia's climate and soils were very similar to those in European wine regions. A decline in grape growing and wine making resulted from a shift to other agricultural crops.

Then, about 10 years ago, Virginia planters began to return to this Colonial occupation and in only a decade Virginia has become one of the top 10 wine states in the United States. Virginia now claims 34 farm wineries and over 120 vineyards. Virginia's wine country runs in a broad band through the center of the state, generally from southwest to northeast, and mostly in the Piedmont region.

There are more than a dozen major wine events in the state—festivals, harvest celebrations, and open-house parties—each with wine tasting, of course. The range of wines produced (French and German types predominate) is astonishingly wide: Cabernet Sauvignon, Merlot, Riesling, Gewurztraminer, Chardonnay, Rose, Pinot Noir, Villard Blanc and Noir, Baco Noir, Seyval Blanc, Champagne, Claret, Vidal Blanc, Verdelet, Chambourcin, de Chaunac, Sauvignon Blanc, Chablis, Chelois, Semillon, and White Burgundy, plus an equally wide assortment of native types.

For more detailed information, especially on what types of wine are made at each winery, write for the pamphlet: "Vintage Virginia," available from: Virginia Department of Agriculture & Consumer Services, Division of Markets, P.O. Box 1163, Richmond, Virginia 23209. This pamphlet provides the full calendar of wine events for the current year. The latest guide is in preparation. Virginia's wine guide contains a fund of information about the state's wine industry.

What follows is a list of principal vineyards *by region,* with addresses and tour information. Note: Most of them are open for tours and tastings, but their hours and supplies of wine vary. It is advisable to call before visiting any of them.

Piedmont—Central and Southside. *Bacchanal Vineyards,* (804) 272–6937, in Afton; *tours,* seasonal April–October, Saturday and Sunday 8–4. *Barboursville Vineyards,* (703) 832–3824, in Barboursville; *tours,* Saturday 10–12 and 2–5; *please call in advance. Burnley Vine*yards, (703) 832–3874, Barboursville; *tours,* March–December, Friday, Saturday, and Sunday 11–5, other times by appointment. *Chermont Winery,* (804) 286–2211, Esmont; *tours,* by appointment only. *La Abra Farm & Winery,* (804) 263–5392, Lovingston; *tours,* daily 11–5, Sunday 12–5; closed Monday and Tuesday, January–March. *Montdomaine Cellars,* (804) 971–8947, Charlottesville; *tours,* April–October, Wednesday–Sunday 10–4; November–March, by appointment. *Oakencroft Vineyards & Winery,* (804) 296–4188 weekdays, (804) 295–4188 weekends, Charlottesville; *tours,* by appointment only. *Rose Bower Vineyard & Winery,* (804) 223–8209, Hampton-Sydney; *tours* (seasonal), April 1–May 15, July 1–August 15, November 1–December 20, Friday, Saturday, and Sunday only, sales 1–5, tastings 3 P.M. and by appointment.

Eastern Virginia. *Ingleside Plantation Vineyards,* (804) 224–7111, Oak Grove; *tours,* Monday–Saturday 10–5, Sunday 1–5, except major holidays.

Northern Virginia. *Meredyth Vineyards,* (703) 687–6277; Middleburg; *tours,* daily 10–4, groups over 10 by appointment. *Naked Mountain Vineyard,* (703) 364–1609, Markham; *tours,* March–December, Wednesday–Friday 12–5; Saturday, Sunday, Monday, and holidays 10–5; otherwise, by appointment. *Oasis Vineyard,* (703) 635–7627 or 635–3103, Hume; *tours,* daily 10–4. *Piedmont Vineyards & Winery,* (703) 687–5528, Middleburg; *tours,* Tuesday–Sunday 10–4. *Willowcroft Farm Vineyards,* Leesburg, (703) 777–8161; *tours,* by appointment only. *Dominion Wine Cellar,* (703) 225–8772, Free tours and tasting, year round, and *Rapidan River Vineyard,* (703) 399–1855, a German-style winery with daily tours, both in Culpeper.

Shenandoah Valley. *Guilford Ridge Vineyard,* (703) 778–3853 or (202) 554–0333, Luray; *tours,* by appointment only. *Shenandoah Vineyards,* (703) 984–8699, Edinburgh; *tours,* daily 10–6 all year. *Tri-Mountain Winery & Vineyards,* (703) 869–3030, Middletown; *tours,* January–March, Saturday and Sunday only 11–5. *Winchester Winery and Cedar Lane Vineyards.* (703) 877–1275. Vineyard and estate winery tours. Winchester.

Southwest Virginia. *Chateau Morrisette Winery,* (703) 593–2865; Meadows of Dan; *tours,* Wednesday–Sunday 10–4 or by appointment. *MJC Vineyard,* (703) 552–9083, Blacksburg; *tours,* Monday–Saturday 10–5.

POLO MATCHES. Polo as a spectator sport can now be enjoyed—spring through fall—in five Virginia locations: Goochland County, west of Richmond on I-64 (783–8950); Charlottesville, in the foothills of the Blue Ridge Mountains (979–0293); Middleburg, in Horse Country just west of Washington, DC (522–8325); Virginia Beach (428–8000); and Charles City County, between Richmond and Williamsburg (566–0342). For advance information and schedules, call: (800) 548–9797.

ARTS AND CRAFTS. The Virginia Commission for the Arts publishes an annual *Virginia Crafts Calendar,* which presents in detail each of the dozens of craft shows and festivals around the state. To obtain an advance copy, contact: Virginia Commission for the Arts, 17th Floor, 101 N. 14th St., Richmond, VA 23219.

TIME ZONE AND AREA CODES. Virginia is in the Eastern Standard Time Zone and goes on and off Daylight Savings Time in April and October—"*spring*ing ahead in the former, *fall*ing back in the latter." The state has two telephone area codes: (703) in the northern and western parts of the state, including the Shenandoah Valley and the Highlands, and (804) in most of Piedmont, Coastal, and Tidewater areas, including the Chesapeake Bay area south of the Potomac, Richmond, Petersburg, Lynchburg, and Danville.

AN INTRODUCTION TO VIRGINIA

by
ELEANOR LOUTTIT

It all started here.

America was born at the edge of the tide, her back to the mother country, her eyes on the distant blue mountains. Virginia is where it began.

Virginia still stands on the shore, where the Atlantic ripples or crashes, but now she embraces the Tidelands, America's "heritage country," the foothills of the Piedmont, the rugged heights of the Highlands, and the broad fertile valleys of the Shenandoah.

Virginia might be our favorite aunt. She's been there since the beginning; she knew all the old family members, the great and the not-so-great—even the rascals. She has a wondrous collection of relics to browse through; she is energetic or restful, whichever suits your fancy; she is never too busy to welcome you; and, like all favorite aunts, she is a delight to visit.

"Virginia is for lovers," they tell us.

True—but that's only part of the story; Virginia is for *everyone.* Few other states combine in almost perfect natural proportions all the best of America: sandy beaches, the old bricks of our past and the freshly poured concrete of our future, rolling green hills and shining cities, and—always—those distant blue mountains.

Whatever you want, Virginia has it. Try it. Savor it. Virginia is for lovers—and for all the rest of us.

Settlement and "That 'Noxious Weed"

When Walter Raleigh, the knight who had his clothes made of cloth-of-silver in order to appear "a shining knight" at court, approached his queen with the idea of colonizing the wilderness of the New World, he coupled the request for funds with the flattering request that he be allowed to name that fertile vastness between the Atlantic Coast and the Mississippi River in her honor. Elizabeth, Virgin Queen, probably the most able woman ever to rule and a coy coquette all her life, denied the funds but most graciously allowed the flattery. Virginia it became.

Raleigh made two attempts, failed at both, and succeeded in giving North Carolina a memorable mystery. When, in 1606, the new king, James I, was asked to help settle white men in the land where the Indians lived "in the manner of the golden age," he granted a charter to a private stock company, the Virginia Company. Shares were sold, colonists were recruited, and three small ships landed in the Chesapeake Bay after four and a half months of a weary sea voyage. They picked an unhealthy, swampy tidewater peninsula to settle on and two-thirds of them promptly died. The thirty or so who hung on until help came a year later could not have realized that they were the lone outpost of European civilization for a thousand miles in all directions.

Life was unimaginably difficult those first years. The precarious little settlement held out against disease, starvation, and Indian attack. It was saved by tobacco! The native plant and a West Indian variety were crossed in 1613 and produced a leaf that, when it was introduced in England, became the rage of all social levels. King James, that wily Scot, railed against its use as unnatural and ungodly but quickly saw its economic advantages. By 1620 the Virginia Company held a monopoly on tobacco sales in England. A short time later the Crown dissolved the Company and made Virginia a Crown colony.

As a Crown colony, Virginia began to prosper and to grow. And that, one might say, would be that if it were not for those not-too-noticeable little incidents that sprinkle history with fascinating "what-ifs." If an Englishman or his stock company would pay for the settlement of just 250 people, he would be granted thousands of acres on which to settle them—a "plantation," as it was called. It worked just like the old feudal system back home had, but, in this case, the serfs were not white Englishmen but black men from the unknown wilds of the dark continent who could be bought from traders making the Europe to Africa to West Indies run.

There were many opportunies for enterprising men to make a fortune. One of these, John Washington, gave up the sea in the middle of the century and bought some land in Virginia. It took him about 10 years to acquire 5,000 acres and to found a family at Wakefield from which would come a boy named George who, as legend would have it, would cut down a cherry tree on those very acres.

Revolution and Virginia Gentlemen

By the end of the seventeenth century a considerably smaller (reduced by the area of the Carolinas and Maryland) Virginia Colony boasted a population of nearly 100,000. Of these, only a few thousand were Indians; several more thousand were black slaves. People had spread westward slowly and hadn't bothered to go much farther than the inland reaches of the Atlantic shores and the coastal river basins. In the early years of the 1700s new settlers began to trickle in from the Pennsylvania Colony. They had already dealt with the mountains there and saw no particular drawback in settling Virginia's uplands. People began to spread over the colony like a flood. In 1750 young Daniel Boone opened the Cumberland Gap. It was to become a gate through which many thousands would flow in the search for an independence that those who stayed behind would soon fight for.

There were 13 colonies now and most of them had stable populations of at least second-generation families. The feeling for an independent America was rising; Massachusetts Colony was listening to the firebrands, Pennsylvania Colony was planning thoughtfully on how to arrange the necessary committee work, and Virginia Colony was mothering four of the first five future presidents of a new country. Washington, Jefferson, Madison, and Monroe were born and grew up in Virginia.

From the seven Virginians who signed the Declaration of Independence through those who accepted the surrender of Cornwallis at Yorktown to the signers of the Treaty of Paris, the men of Virginia helped force our own version of Magna Carta from an English king.

Gallantry and Grief

When Virginia voted on April 17, 1861, to secede from the Union, it doomed itself to become a major battleground of a war between North and South. It had not long to wait. On May 27, farmers living at Newport News Point, at the junction of Hampton Roads and the James River, saw troop-laden vessels approaching their shore. The Yankees had come! The peaceful farmlands of Virginia would be red with blood before peace finally came at Appomattox four years later.

As the potential cutting edge of the Confederacy, Virginia hoped for a lightning war. Like other southerners, Virginians had inordinate faith in the skill at arms of the South's outdoorsmen. Like South Carolina's Wade Hampton, they thought "Southern hotheaded dash, reckless gallantry, and spirit of adventure" would overwhelm the North. Only a few realists like Robert E. Lee understood what adverse odds the South faced.

Lee, who had declined the Army's offer of command of Union forces, resigned his federal commission to become commander of Virginia's forces. "Trusting in almighty God, an approving conscience, and the aid of my fellow citizens," he said, "I devote myself to the service of my native State, in whose behalf alone will I ever again draw my sword."

Unfortunately, Lee's sentiments were shared chiefly by eastern Virginians. In the trans-Appalachian northwest counties, slavery and secession were anathemas. At a meeting in Wheeling a few months later, western Virginia in turn "seceded" from Virginia and sought protection of the federal government. Thus the proud Old Dominion lost one-third of her territory and citizens.

Like the Revolution, the Civil War reached its climax in Virginia. After a succession of hapless Union commanders, Lincoln, in 1864, named Ulysses S. Grant, who at first suffered heavy losses in the Wilderness Campaign in Fredericksburg and Spotsylvania County in May and June 1864. Grant then moved more successfully against Lee at Petersburg, an important railhead and supply center. Grant's siege and destruction of food supplies led at last to Lee's evacuation of Petersburg and Richmond in April 1865.

After a five-year military occupation called Reconstruction, Virginia in 1870 was readmitted to the Union. Though its ex-Confederates swore allegiance, they retained their pride in the "lost cause" and in Lee, Jackson, Stuart, and other commanders. A Confederate Memorial Society was organized in Richmond, and a Confederate Memorial Day was observed at cemeteries and churches each May. Camps of Confederate veterans held frequent reunions in tented towns at Richmond and other southern cities. Civil War battlegrounds became national parks in Fredericksburg, Manassas, Petersburg, Appomattox, and elsewhere. Houses associated with the Confederacy were preserved in Richmond and Danville, and a Confederate Museum was created.

There was something to remember . . . more Americans died in that bloody travesty than in World Wars I and II combined. Fifteen thousand of the dead were Virginians.

Old South and New

In recapitulating the history of a particular area of the United States, one becomes aware of a process that began in Virginia in 1607 and that is just now beginning to end. Chronological history of America makes great geographical leaps and geographical history jumps time gaps as wide as a hundred years. Virginia had fostered revolution, produced eight presidents and would produce one more, suffered and bled the torment of civil war, then recovered quietly while history's spotlight swept the cowboys and Indians, the latter-day colonists through Ellis Island, and the doughboys in the trenches of France. After World War II and the middle of this century, 50 states became a real entity. Mobility, television, and a rising standard of living have enabled us to appreciate the nation as a whole, yet be proud of our state or our region. Thus, Virginia, where it all started, invites us to browse.

Today Virginia has an area of 39,700 square miles and a population of 5.3 million. Half of these citizens live in urban centers, some of which are inexorably growing into the megalopolis of the Eastern Seaboard and some are mushrooming in spots across the state. The other half of the population lives in rural areas in units as small as the single family isolated on a mountainside in the Highlands. Virginians still grow tobacco while rockets soar away from Wallop's Island. Women sit on wooden porches doing lap-quilting at the same time as other women research a new textile for NASA's next space men. A weekend sailor catches a Saturday afternoon breeze in the sails of his sloop on the Chesapeake to relax after his week's work on the latest Polaris submarine in a coastal shipyard. A forest ranger in the Blue Ridge cautions the camper to take care with his "fahr" in a dialect not far removed from Elizabethan times and a British sailor on leave from his ship at Norfolk struggles with the "English" of his counterpart who hails from the Bronx.

Virginia is diversity, marvelously proportioned. It begins in the sea where the Atlantic Barrier islands are wild and unspoiled as the Indians knew them. On Chincoteague and Assateague the first white men left some ponies and today wild ponies browse as if 400 years had not passed. Tidewater marshes and golden sands ring the bays and tidal rivers on the mainland to backlight the seaports and naval yards. A few miles inland Williamsburg is *then* and Busch Gardens is *now.* The land begins to rise slowly in the south, more quickly in the north. Modern highways provide access to sprawling farms, fox hunts, tobacco auctions, white water rivers, restored plantations, battlefields, and a feel of the "Old South." As the hills grow higher and threaten to turn into mountains, Charlottesville and Lynchburg become focal points: Lynchburg, a base from which to explore; Charlottesville, a place in which to discover.

America's first Renaissance man is the heart of Charlottesville. Thomas Jefferson's home at Monticello attracts visitors from all over the world. Jefferson leveled a mountain top to build this classic-style house and its grounds. But far from being just another nice old house, Monticello is unique in so many ways that it is possible to catch a glimpse of the complex man who lived in it. To give substance to that glimpse, forget the Declaration, the president, and the Virginia planter; visit the University of Virginia campus that he nurtured, as he would have a son.

Where the blue mountains are no longer distant, along the western reaches of Virginia, the pulse slows and the heartbeat steadies. Here it is tranquil. Old things matter more; not necessarily the historical old, certainly the traditional old. The rural culture patterns of small family farms and individual independence are deliberately maintained. Visitors are welcome to wave as they pass by, come and set a spell, or remark on the "quaintness" of local custom because it will hardly disturb the timelessness of the Virginia mountains.

Yes, Virginia is for lovers—lovers of mountains and of beaches, of sailboats and of horseflesh, of wilderness and of city, of our past, our pride, and our prospects. Welcome!

VIRGINIA'S EASTERN SHORE

by
RODNEY N. SMITH

Virginia's Eastern Shore, a 70-mile peninsula and secluded barrier islands, is one of the most fancifully beautiful places in America. It is a haven for herds of wild ponies. There are unspoiled beaches with rare and elaborate seashells, as well as charter boats to the islands, lazy lagoons, and quiet coves.

This is a region visited by Blackbeard the pirate and one adorned with romantic place names such as Nassawodox, Kiptopeke, and Pungoteague. Even the familiar names are colorful: Temperanceville, Birdsnest, and Modest Town.

One side of Virginia's Eastern Shore is bathed by the Atlantic and the other by the Chesapeake Bay. This favored location guarantees an epicurean feast of delicious and succulent seafood. There is even an annual local festival to honor it, with fresh oysters, fried eel, steamed clams, and chowder of unmatched quality and flavor.

The attractions of this area are unique and varied. Two of America's few preserved debtor's prisons are here, one at Eastville and one at Accomack. Tiny Tangier Island, accessible only by boat, has residents who still speak Elizabethan dialect. At Chincoteague and Assateague, each summer brings the famous Wild Pony Roundup. This is a day of carnivals and shows, good food, and high spirits; a time to retell the fascinating legends about the island ponies, descendants of horses that swam ashore from a wrecked Spanish galleon centuries ago.

A trip to the Eastern Shore is not complete without a close look at some of the beautiful craftwork created here. Eastern Shore duck decoys, for instance, are deservedly in demand nationwide. There is excellent salt-water fishing here, as well as canoeing in the marshes and hiking everywhere. Some particularly lovely natural areas are in the Chincoteague National Wildlife Refuge. The vigilant observer can spot numerous marsh and water birds, rabbits, raccoons, deer, otters, and muskrats.

Everywhere visitors go on Virginia's Eastern Shore they are aware of being in a very special and natural world. From the isolated fishing villages to the unspoiled beaches, this is what America was like in less complicated times when nature was lovely and vibrant, untouched by man's progress.

Virginia's Eastern Shore is bounded on the east coast by the wetlands and barrier islands of the Atlantic Ocean, and on the west by Chesapeake Bay. It was first visited by Europeans in 1608 when an exploring party led by Captain John Smith mapped the bayside and Chesapeake Islands. In 1614, the Jamestown government obtained the land from the Indians. The English came to the peninsula to stay in 1620. The settlement was called Accomack Plantation until 1634 when it became one of the eight original counties. In 1643, the name was changed to Northampton. Then, in 1663, the county was divided to form Accomack County in the north and Northampton County in the south. The area has been able to preserve much of its early charm because of the relative isolation it enjoyed until the Bay Bridge-Tunnel opened in 1965.

The people of Accomack organized early. There was a census in 1624, listing their names, their ages, and the ships on which they had arrived. In these two counties can be found the earliest continuous court records in the United States, dating from 1632.

Among other things, the records tell of the trial and acquittal in the case of a play, "The Bear and the Cub," in 1665, giving the Eastern Shore the distinction of having the first record of a dramatic performance in America. Tours of the two county seats include the Debtor's Prison in Accomack, and the Debtor's Prison, Court House, and Clerk's Office in Eastville.

Eastern Shore architecture is unique. Most early dwellings now standing are of frame construction with varying roof levels and two or more chimneys. The roofs are mostly of the A-type with small dormer windows on the front and back. Other houses are two full stories, some all brick, some with brick ends, and some all frame. A house with four different roof levels is often referred to as "big house, little house, colonnade, and kitchen." These houses can be explored all over the area.

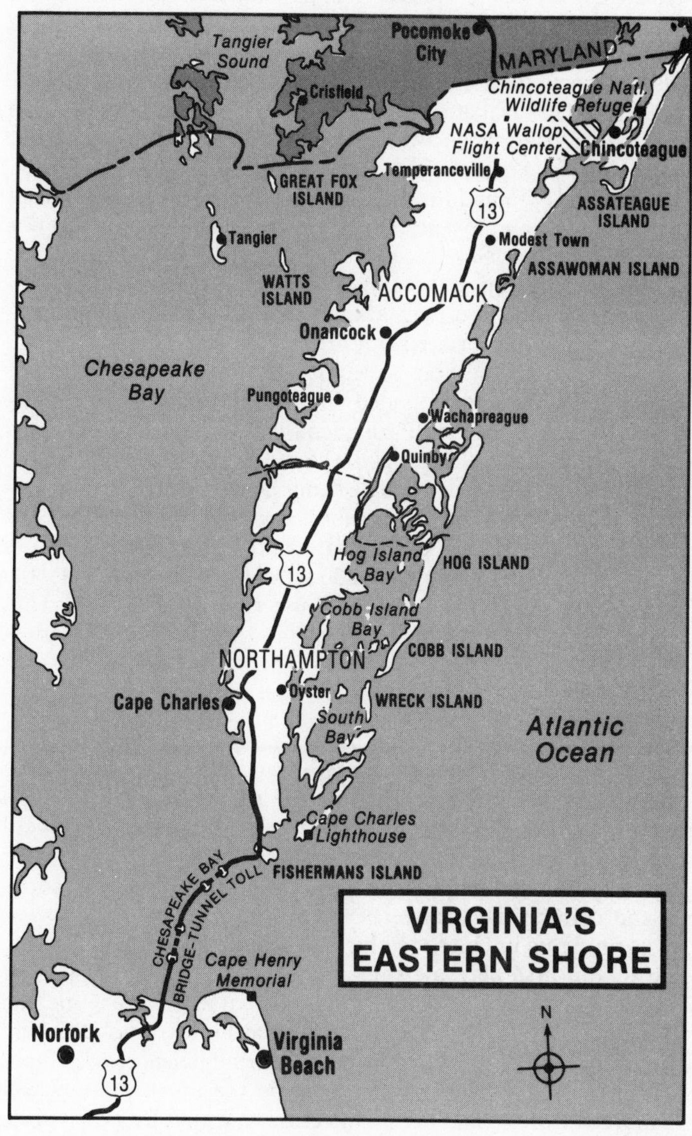
Tangier Sound
Pocomoke City
MARYLAND
Crisfield
Chincoteague Natl. Wildlife Refuge
NASA Wallop Flight Center
Chincoteague
Temperanceville
GREAT FOX ISLAND
13
ASSATEAGUE ISLAND
Tangier
Modest Town
ASSAWOMAN ISLAND
WATTS ISLAND
ACCOMACK
Onancock
Chesapeake Bay
Pungoteague
Wachapreague
Quinby
Hog Island Bay
HOG ISLAND
13
Cobb Island Bay
COBB ISLAND
NORTHAMPTON
Oyster
WRECK ISLAND
Cape Charles
South Bay
Atlantic Ocean
Cape Charles Lighthouse
FISHERMANS ISLAND
CHESAPEAKE BAY BRIDGE-TUNNEL TOLL
VIRGINIA'S EASTERN SHORE
Cape Henry Memorial
N
Norfork
Virginia Beach
13

Cape Charles

Cape Charles, where the Bay Bridge–Tunnel drops visitors, was established in 1884 when the New York, Philadelphia and Norfolk Railroad extended its service from Philadelphia to Norfolk. It is the largest town in Northampton County and offers excellent fishing, boating, and beaches. It is one of the few places on the East Coast where visitors can watch breathtaking sunsets over water.

Eyre Hall, for example, just south of Eastville, was built by Littleton Eyre in 1735 and has been in his family ever since. It boasts one of the oldest and loveliest boxwood gardens in America. It was enlarged by his son, Severn, in 1765 and furnished with handsome Queen Anne, Chippendale, and Hepplewhite pieces, family portraits, and Chinese export porcelain. In the cross hall is an interesting scenic wallpaper printed from French blocks designed by du-Four. Throughout the house are fine woodwork and paneling.

Eastville itself was not founded until 1766. Its County Court declared the Stamp Act of Parliament unconstitutional. The old Courthouse in Eastville contains the oldest court records in the United States, the first legible date being January 7, 1632. The preservation and survival of these records is all the more remarkable because they were housed in the homes of the court clerks for more than 100 years. Other sights include a Debtor's Prison (1644), the Clerk's Office (1719), the Court House (1730), and Parke Hall (1794). The nearby town of Oyster is famous for its seafood industries.

Onancock

Still farther north and on the Bay, Onancock is the home of the Eastern Shore Historical Society, housed in Kerr Place, which was originally built in 1790. Onancock's large, deep harbor offers well-protected docking facilities for pleasure craft of all sizes. The public dock and boat launching ramp are used by local and visiting sportsmen and commercial boats.

Historic sights in Onancock include the site of Fowkes' Tavern, home of the first play in America, and St. George's Episcopal Church, built in 1652. Sights from the twentieth century include the Town of Willis Wharf with its seafood industries and fishing facilities and the Virginia Institute of Marine Sciences.

Within a short radius of Accomack, in the north, visitors will find more restored Colonial architecture than in any other place in the United States except Williamsburg. Individual houses, however, are not opened to the public except when advertised or for Historic Garden Week. Places to visit include The Glade, The Little House (circa 1767), The Haven (1794), Ailworth House (1795), Roseland (1771), Seymour House and Ice House (1791), Court House Green, and the Debtor's Prison (1782).

The Eastern Shore, however, relies for income less on tourism than on agriculture, the biggest industry. The two counties together contain 120,000 acres of cropland. The Eastern Shore leads the state in the production of vegetables. The Irish potato is the most important crop, with 30,000 acres planted annually, but corn and soybeans are fast growing in importance. Sweet potatoes, snapbeans, tomatoes, cucumbers, and peppers are grown. Whether passing through or spending a vacation, visitors will want to stop at the roadside stands to sample and purchase the luscious local produce. There are also almost 150,000 acres of beautiful forestlands, with loblolly pine predominating.

More and more farmers are moving into the production of broilers, and two processing plants for chickens are in Accomack County.

Another important source of income for the Shore is the seafood industry. This includes oysters, hard-shell clams, sea clams, crab, and finfish. Oyster beds are cultivated on both bayside and seaside. Hard-shell clams, or quahog, are in great quantity. The largest clam-packing plant in the world is located on Chincoteague. The sea-clam industry is new to the Shore where both blue and soft-shell crabs are also abundant. The finfish industry is based on some 40 different species.

The Bay Bridge–Tunnel

The 17.6-mile Chesapeake Bay Bridge–Tunnel deposits northbound visitors from Virginia Beach, Norfolk, and Williamsburg on the southern tip of Virginia's Eastern Shore. One of the most incredible engineering feats in the world, the bridge proffers awesome vistas. It allows visitors to see the mighty surge of the Atlantic Ocean, the beauty of the Chesapeake Bay, and the soaring grace of an engineering marvel all from their cars. There is a scenic stop, a restaurant, and a fishing pier with bait and tackle available. Dipping from the bridge into one of the tunnels and under a massive, ocean-going freighter can take a visitor's breath away.

Virginia's Eastern Shore is bounded on the east by the wetlands and barrier islands of the Atlantic Ocean, and on the west by Chesapeake Bay. It was first visited by Europeans in 1608 when an exploring party led by Captain John Smith mapped the bayside and Chesapeake Islands. In 1614, the Jamestown government obtained the land from the Indians. The English came to the peninsula to stay in 1620. The settlement was called Accomack Plantation until 1634 when it became one of the eight original counties. In 1643, the name was changed to Northampton. Then, in 1663, the county was divided to form Accomack County in the north and Northampton County in the south. The area has been able to preserve much of its early charm because of the relative isolation it enjoyed until the Bay Bridge–Tunnel opened in 1965.

Chincoteague

Chincoteague Island, Virginia's only resort island, is perhaps the most beautiful of the many islands that dot Virginia's Eastern Shore. World famous for its oyster beds and clam shoals, this picturesque island is the gateway to the National Seashore and Chincoteague Wildlife Refuge. This serene fishing settlement, seven miles long and one-and-a-half miles wide, and abounding with history and natural beauty, welcomes visitors to explore its unique heritage.

The first colonists were humble sailors and herders who arrived in the early 1670s. With the exception of salvaging shipwrecks off Assateague Island, the inhabitants occupied themselves primarily with farming and livestock. Today, however, the surrounding waters are the main source of local income.

The island's famous salt oysters, sold since 1830, are cultivated on lease "rock" and public grounds that the watermen seed and harvest. Chincoteague is the home of many outstanding craftsmen and artists who produce some of the world's finest hand-carved duck decoys and wildfowl wood carvings.

Protecting Chincoteague Island from the Atlantic Ocean, Assateague Island boasts more than 37 miles of the widest and most beautiful beaches on the East Coast. This rare beauty is protected by the Assateague Island National Seashore and Chincoteague National Wildlife Refuge. A wide variety of nature activities and many miles of unspoiled beaches and sand dunes are there to explore.

Assateague Island

Assateague Island is well-known as a birdwatcher's paradise. Over 260 species are to be found, and as the days get colder, the arrival of the Canadian geese and snow geese and the whistling voices of the swans herald the onset of winter.

The most popular inhabitants of the Refuge, however, are the Chincoteague wild ponies, made famous in Marguerite Henry's book, *Misty of Chincoteague.* The legend has it that these island ponies are descendants of horses that swam ashore from a wrecked Spanish galleon centuries ago. The famous Wild Pony Round Up and Swim to Chincoteague are held annually in late July. It is a day of high spirits and good food.

In 1945, a launch site was established on Wallops Island by the Langley Research Center, then a field station of NASA. The site is on Route 13, the major north-south road to Chincoteague (Rte. 175 east to Chincoteague; Rte. 697 to Wallops). In the early years, research at Wallops was concentrated on obtaining aerodynamic data at transonic and low supersonic speeds. Wallops has been the launch site of over 150 unmanned spacecrafts and today is used primarily to obtain scientific data about the atmosphere and space. It continues to be an active part of the NASA unmanned space program. Tours can be arranged, and it is possible to make reservations to watch the launching of minor satellites.

The string of barrier islands running the length of the peninsula remain a natural wilderness. They are inaccessible except by boat and are privately owned by the Nature Conservancy or the government. Smith Island, the southernmost, was discovered by Capt. John Smith and named for himself. The Cape Charles lighthouse, the most powerful in Virginia, is on the island.

Tangier Island

Tangier Island in the heart of the Chesapeake can be visited by ferry from Reedville on Virginia's Northern Neck (U.S. 360). The island was discovered by Capt. Smith in 1608 and settlement was permanently established in 1686. There is no industry on the island and no cars are allowed. The population is only 800. The peace and quiet of the isolated village is a tonic after the hustle and bustle of the twentieth century. Transportation to the island is also possible via mail boat, leaving Crisfield, Maryland, at noon each day (Rte. 413 from U.S. 13).

PRACTICAL INFORMATION FOR VIRGINIA'S EASTERN SHORE

Note: The area code for the Eastern Shore is 804.

PLACES TO STAY

MOTELS AND INNS. There aren't many motels or inns on this stretch of the peninsula, but neither are there many towns of any real size. This is part of the charm of Virginia's Eastern Shore. But then, of course, Norfolk isn't all that far to the south and Salisbury (MD) is just up U.S. 13 to the north.

Channel Bass Inn. *Expensive to Deluxe.* 100 Church St., Chincoteague; 336–6148. 11 rooms, many furnished with antiques, near the wildlife sanctuary. Closed Dec. and Jan. AE, DC, MC, V.

America House. *Moderate.* On U.S. 13 at the entrance to the Chesapeake Bay Bridge–Tunnel; 331–1776. 79 rooms with balconies, a private beach, sail boats, picnic tables, and grills. Open all year. AE, DC, MC, V.

The Driftwood Motor Lodge. *Moderate.* Beach Rd. at Assateague Bridge, Maddox Blvd., Chincoteague; 336–6557. 52 rooms with private patios and balconies overlooking the shore at the entrance to Assateague National Seashore. AE, DC, MC, V.

Island Motor Inn. *Moderate.* 711 N. Main St., Chincoteague; 336–3141. 48 rooms, on the waterfront, some with balconies and boardwalk. Open all year. AE, MC, V.

Refuge Motor Inn. *Moderate to Expensive.* One block west of Assateague Bridge, Beach Rd., Chincoteague; 336–5511. 68 units with picnic tables and grills overlooking wildlife refuge. AE, MC, V.

Sea Shell Motel. *Moderate.* 215 Cleveland St., a short block south on South Main; Chincoteague; 336–6589. 40 rooms, including efficiencies. Pool. AE, MC, V.

Sunrise Motor Inn. *Moderate.* Chicken City Rd., Chincoteague; 336–6671. 24 units, some with kitchens. Closed Dec.–mid-Mar. Pool and picnic tables. Weekly seasonal rates. AE, MC, V.

Birchwood Motel. *Inexpensive.* 573 S. Main St., turn right when entering Chincoteague; 336–6133. Closed Dec.–Mar. 40 rooms. MC, V.

PLACES TO EAT

RESTAURANTS. There's something fishy about restaurants on Virginia's Eastern Shore—and that's hardly surprising; the quiet oyster and the noble crab reign supreme in the area. Restaurants tend to be modest and prices are often delightfully low. Finny fish is also abundant on the Eastern Shore.

Channel Bass. *Moderate to Deluxe.* 100 Church St., Chincoteague; 336–6148. Continental menu specializing in seafood Espagnol, back fin crab souffle, and oyster souffle. Elegant Colonial atmosphere. Major credit cards.

Beachway. *Inexpensive to Expensive.* Maddox Blvd., Chincoteague; 336–5590. Breakfast, lunch, and dinner. Closed Dec.–Feb. Full American menu in an English atmosphere. Beer and wine. AE, MC, V.

Hilda Crockett's Chesapeake House. *Inexpensive to Moderate.* On Main St., Tangier Island; 891–2331. Meals daily from Apr. 15 through mid-Oct. Crab—cakes, fritters, however. Worth the ferry ride. No credit cards.

THINGS TO SEE AND DO

FISHING. Virginia's Eastern Shore offers the best saltwater fishing to be found on the East Coast. A great variety of fish abound in the Chesapeake Bay and the Atlantic Ocean. The world's record for a black drum (111 pounds) is held jointly by two Eastern Shore residents, fishing in local waters. Many state records have been set here. The Virginia Salt Water Fishing Tournament can provide additional information (25th and Pacific Aves., Virginia Beach; 428–4360).

TOURS. The Eastern Shore Railroad, with its headquarters in Cape Charles, operates a unique 26-mile rail/barge ferry service between Cape Charles and Virginia Beach. Established in 1884, this line serves the ports of Hampton Roads and Cape Charles. It connects on the south with two giant railroads, the Norfolk-Southern and CSX and on the north with Conrail at Pocomoke City, Maryland. For information about the Cape Charles area, contact Chesapeake Bridge and Tunnel PR Dept., Box 111, Cape Charles 23310 (464–3511, ext. 46).

NORFOLK AND VIRGINIA BEACH

by
EDGAR and PATRICIA CHEATHAM

Norfolk

Site of the world's largest naval base and NATO's Atlantic headquarters, this seafaring city looks with pride to its waterfront. Stunning Waterside Festival Marketplace, designed by James Rouse Enterprises Development Corp. and boasting more than 100 boutiques, restaurants, lounges, and specialty shops, fronts on the Elizabeth River. So popular it is being doubled in size, Waterside has helped inspire the revitalization of downtown Norfolk. Neighboring Town Point Park is home each year to more than 230 free "Festevents"—concerts and events featuring ethnic foods, games, and live entertainment. Among Festevents are Summer's Eve Tuesday Night Concerts, June to August; Lunchtime Concerts, May and September; Wednesday Outdoor Movie Festival Series, June through August; TGIF Friday After-Work Concerts, June through October.

In downtown Norfolk, historic Selden and Monticello Arcades have been handsomely restored, as has a jewel-like landmark hotel, The Madison. Ghent and The Hague, attractive in-town neighborhoods, have been refurbished and renovated into a pleasing mix of traditional and contemporary decor.

Norfolk's waterfront also includes Ocean View, bordering Chesapeake Bay. This 14-mile stretch of sandy beaches and peaceful waters is ideal for family enjoyment. Ocean View is adjacent to the Norfolk end of the Bay Bridge–Tunnel.

Festivals have become a tradition in Norfolk. The April International Azalea Festival is followed by the May Ghent Arts Festival in Town Point Park and the lavish three-day June Harborfest celebration with fireworks, tall ship parades, boat races, luscious seafoods, and live entertainment. In mid-October the Renaissance Faire livens the Waterside with music, dance, strolling minstrels, poetry, and Shakespeare readings.

Virginia Beach

Virginia Beach, one of the Eastern Seaboard's most popular and attractive seaside resorts, boasts 29 miles of fine sand beaches, and offers superb surf swimming, waterskiing, boating, and fishing.

Atlantic Avenue, fronted by the city's famed boardwalk, has been revitalized and beautified as a pedestrian mall with greenery, benches, and public gathering spots. Free daily outdoor entertainment and Sunday fireworks are offered Memorial Day through Labor Day. Also free "Summer Sundays on the Beach" concerts are held at the Norwegian Lady statue, 25th Street and Oceanfront, and family fun is the focus of "Saturdays at the Park" at various city parks.

Popular seasonal events include the late June Annual Boardwalk Art Show, Shakespeare-by-the-Sea Festival, in late August at Pavilion Convention Center, and, the last weekend in September, the Virginia Beach Neptune Festival, with parades, dances, golf and tennis tournaments, arts and crafts, and seafood feasts. Throughout the summer, anglers can participate in a series of salt-water fishing tournaments for $15,000 in collective prize money.

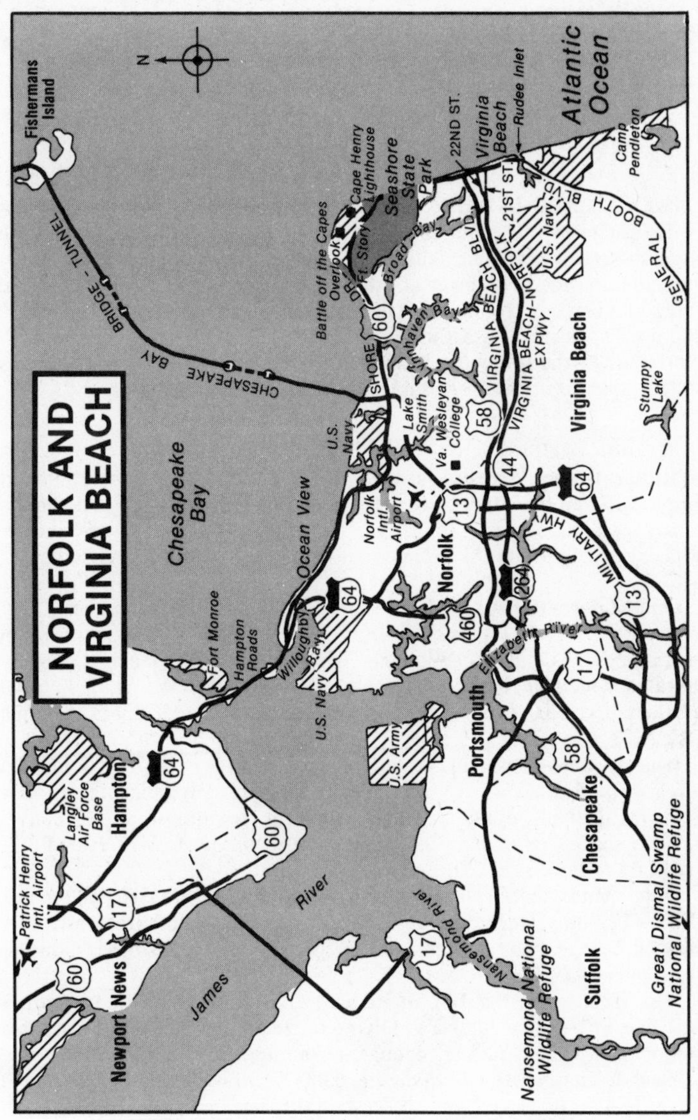
NORFOLK AND VIRGINIA BEACH
Chesapeake Bay
Fishermans Island
CHESAPEAKE BAY BRIDGE - TUNNEL
N
Battle off the Capes Overlook
Cape Henry Lighthouse
Ft. Story
Seashore State Park
SHORE DR.
Broad Bay
Lynnhaven Bay
22ND ST.
Virginia Beach
Rudee Inlet
Atlantic Ocean
21ST ST.
VIRGINIA BEACH BLVD.
VIRGINIA BEACH-NORFOLK EXPWY.
U.S. Navy
BOOTH BLVD
GENERAL
Camp Pendleton
Stumpy Lake
Virginia Beach
Lake Smith
Va. Wesleyan College
U.S. Navy
Ocean View
Norfolk Intl. Airport
Norfolk
MILITARY HWY
Elizabeth River
Portsmouth
U.S. Army
Willoughby Bay
U.S. Navy
Hampton Roads
Fort Monroe
Hampton
Langley Air Force Base
Patrick Henry Intl. Airport
Newport News
James River
Nansemond River
Nansemond National Wildlife Refuge
Suffolk
Chesapeake
Great Dismal Swamp National Wildlife Refuge
60
64
13
44
58
264
460
17

PRACTICAL INFORMATION FOR NORFOLK AND VIRGINIA BEACH

Note: The area code for Norfolk and Virginia Beach is 804.

PLACES TO STAY

HOTELS AND MOTELS. Most accommodations in Norfolk and Virginia Beach generally offer varied rate structures on a seasonal basis. Peak summer-season rates, particularly in the popular Virginia Beach resort area, are considerably lower at other times of the year. Here are general categories based on room rates per night, double occupancy: *Deluxe,* $100 and up; *Expensive,* $75–$100; *Moderate,* $40–$75; *Inexpensive,* below $40. Notations in the following listings indicate higher summer rates unless stated otherwise. Rates are subject to change without notice.

Norfolk

Hilton-Airport. *Expensive to Deluxe.* 1500 N. Military Hwy. at Northampton Blvd.; 466–8000. Color TV, outdoor pool, tennis courts, health center with indoor pool, sauna, gym, jacuzzi, lounge, specialty restaurant, coffee shop, nightclub. 28 *Deluxe* rooms in Concierge Tower. AE, CB, DC, MC, V.

Omni International Hotel. *Expensive to Deluxe,* year-round rates. 777 Waterside Dr. at St. Paul's Blvd. and I–264; 622–6664. Color TV, in-room movies, pool, valet parking, lounges, live entertainment, dancing, two restaurants, concierge, harborside location, convenient to Waterside Festival Marketplace. 57 *Deluxe* rooms and suites on Omni Classic floors. AE, CB, DC, MC, V.

Holiday Inn—Waterside Area, Downtown. *Expensive.* 700 Monticello Ave.; 627–5555. Color TV with movie channel, Olympic-size outdoor pool, racquetball, lounge, live entertainment, restaurant, shops, convenient to Scope Convention Center, free shuttle service to Waterside Festival Marketplace. AE, CB, DC, MC, V.

Hotel Madison. *Expensive.* Granby and Freemason Sts.; 622–6682. Color TV, sauna, steambath, hot tub, in-room continental breakfast, valet parking, lounge, two retaurants, concierge; an elegantly restored traditional hostelry. AE, CB, DC, MC, V.

Best Western Center Inn. *Moderate to Expensive,* year-round rates. 1 Best Sqe; 461–6600. Color TV, Olympic-size pool in courtyard, spa with indoor pool, sauna, Jacuzzi, lounge, restaurant. AE, CB, DC, MC, V.

Ramada Inn-Newtown. *Moderate.* 6360 Newtown Rd.; 461–1081. 140 rooms in a two-story motor inn. Restaurant, bar, room service, and pool. Near Naval Base and Norfolk International Airport. Major credit cards.

Days Inn-Military Circle. *Moderate.* 5701 Chambers St., U.S. 13 N. at I–264; 461–0100. 162 rooms. Color TV, pool, playground, gift shop, and 24-hour restaurant. AE, DC, MC, V.

Econo Lodge. *Inexpensive to Moderate.* 1850 E. Little Creek Rd.; 583–1561. 59 rooms. Color TV, pool, nonsmokers' rooms, guest laundry, and lounges. Restaurants nearby. AE, CB, DC, MC, V.

Virginia Beach

Best Western Oceanfront. *Expensive to Deluxe.* Atlantic Ave. and 11th St.; 422–5000. Color TV, in-room movies, heated outdoor pool, laundry and dry cleaning services, golf, and off-season packages. Some suites with hot tubs and water beds. Restaurant, lounge, and Beach Cabaret nightclub with entertainment. Open year-round. 152 rooms. AE, DC, MC, V.

Cavalier Hotel. *Expensive to Deluxe.* Atlantic Ave. and 42nd St.; 425–8555. 408 rooms. Cavalier Ocean Front is a restored vintage hostelry dating from the early years of the century; the Oceanside Tower is contemporary. Color TV, outdoor and indoor pools, playgrounds, platform tennis, valet parking, laundry services, family restaurant, patio dining, and lounge. Supper club for dining with entertainment; open year-round. AE, DC, MC, V.

Hilton Inn. *Expensive to Deluxe.* Atlantic Ocean at 8th St.; 428–8935. Color TV, heated indoor, outdoor, and kiddie pools, whirlpool, poolside cocktail and snack bars, marina, golf and tennis privileges, bridal rooms with mirrored ceilings, lounge with entertainment, and restaurant; open year-round. 124 rooms. AE, CB, DC, MC, V.

Holiday Inn on the Ocean. *Expensive to Deluxe.* 3900 Atlantic Ave. at 39th St.; 428–1711. Color TV, pool, lanai facing ocean, surfing, tennis, golf privileges, roof-top dining room, coffee shop, and lounge with entertainment; open year-round. 266 rooms. AE, CB, MC, V.

Ramada Oceanside Tower. *Expensive to Deluxe.* 57th St. on the ocean; 215 rooms in 17-story hotel. Pool, restaurant, bar, convention facilities, and concierge. Health club. Major credit cards.

Pavilion Tower—A Dunfey Resort & Conference Center. *Expensive to Deluxe.* 1900 Pavilion Dr., adjacent to Virginia Beach Pavilion Convention Center; 422–8900. Color TV, in-room movies, indoor pool, all-weather tennis courts, health spa and fitness center, and complimentary transportation to the beach. Lounge and restaurant. 298 rooms. AE, CB, DC, MC, V.

Princess Anne Inn. *Expensive to Deluxe.* Atlantic Ave. and 25th St., on the Ocean; 428–5611. 60 rooms. Color TV, in-room movies, heated indoor pool with automated sunroof for tanning in any weather, and giant sun solarium for natural tans, enclosed walkway from rooms to pool, whirlpool baths, dry sauna, oceanfront rooms with large glass-enclosed balconies, lounge, oceanside dining, and room service for all meals; outdoor cafe; open year-round. AE, CB, DC, MC, V.

Sheraton Beach Inn & Conference Center. *Expensive to Deluxe.* Oceanfront at 36th St.; 425–9000. Color TV, heated pool, golf, fishing and tennis nearby, recreation and game rooms, lounge with entertainment and dancing, and restaurants; open year-round. 203 rooms. AE, CB, DC, MC, V.

Ocean Holiday. *Inexpensive to Deluxe.* 2417 Atlantic Ave. at 25th St.; 425–6920. Color TV, indoor pool, lounge with entertainment, and restaurant; open year-round. Convenient to golf, fishing, and tennis facilities. 105 rooms. AE, CB, DC, MC, V.

Courtyard By Marriott. *Moderate to Expensive.* 5700 Greenwich Rd.; 490–2002. Restaurant, bar, heated pool, and meeting rooms. 146 rooms. Major credit cards.

Howard Johnson's Motor Lodge. *Moderate to Expensive.* 3705 Atlantic Ave. at 38th St.; 428–7220. Color TV, in-room movies, oceanside pool, and coin laundry. Convenient to dinner theaters, shops, golf, fishing and tennis facilities. Lounge, restaurant; open year-round. 177 rooms. AE, DC, MC, V.

Idlewhyle Motel & Efficiencies. *Moderate to Expensive.* Atlantic Ave. and 27th St.; 428–9341. Color TV, in-room movies, outdoor heated pool, oceanfront location, baby-sitting service. Restaurant nearby, coffee shop on premises. Open year-round. 46 units. MC, V.

Sea Gull. *Moderate to Expensive.* Atlantic Ave. at 27th St.; 425–5711. 38 rooms in a three-story motel. Pool. Restaurant nearby. AE, MC, V.

Days Inn Virginia Beach. *Moderate.* 4564 Bonny Rd.; use Exit 3B from Rte. 44 to Independence Blvd., north ¼ mile to Bonny Rd., exit east to Inn; 497–4488. Color TV, in-room movies, outdoor pool, lounge, and restaurant; open year-round. 144 rooms. AE, DC, MC, V.

Empress Motel. *Inexpensive to Expensive.* Atlantic Ave. at 28th St.; 428–3970. 38 rooms. Restaurant nearby. Pool. Balconies and patios. Major credit cards.

BED AND BREAKFAST. For information about bed-and-breakfast choices in Norfolk, Virginia Beach, and vicinity, contact: Bed & Breakfast of Tidewater Virginia, Box 3343, Norfolk, VA 23514, 804–627–1983 or 627–9409; call anytime, answering machine in use when coordinators are away from phone.

CAMPGROUNDS. Virginia Beach Campgrounds offer both seasonal or year-round facilities. Inquire about rates from individual establishments; pets on leash are accepted. Reservations advised, especially during peak summer vacation season. For further information, contact Virginia Division of Tourism, 202 N. Ninth St., Suite 500, Richmond, VA 23227; (804–786–4484). The following are available in the Virginia Beach area:

Best Holiday Trav-L-Park. 1075 General Booth Blvd.; 425–0249. Open year-round. Playground, 4 pools, 3 stores, LP gas, showers-restrooms, dumping station, water, electricity, sewer hookups, and tent sites. MC, V.

KOA Campground. 1240 General Booth Blvd.; 428–1444. Open seasonally, inquire. Playground, 3 pools, store, LP gas, restrooms-showers, dumping station, water, electricity, sewer hookups, and tent sites. MC, V.

North Bay Shore Campground. 3257 Colechester Rd.; 426–7911. Open Apr.–Oct. Playground, pool, store, LP gas, showers and restrooms, dumping station, water and electricity, and tent sites.

Seashore State Park. 2500 Shore Dr.; 481–2131. Open Apr.–Nov. Store, restrooms, and showers. Dumping station, but no water or electric hookups. Cabins available, additional fee for pets; reservations through Virginia State Parks or Ticketron, Mon.–Fri. 10–4.

Seneca Campground. 144 S. Princess Anne Rd.; 426–6241. Open year-round. Playground, pool, store, showers and restrooms, dumping station, water and electricity hookups.

Surfside at Sandbridge. 3665 Sandpiper Rd.; 426–2911. Open Mar.–Nov. Playground, store, showers and restrooms, dumping station, water, electricity, and tent sites.

PLACES TO EAT

RESTAURANTS. Fresh Chesapeake Bay seafood is the order of the day in many popular Norfolk and Virginia Beach restaurants, but steak lovers will find many seafood establishments cater to different tastes as well. Ask about Early Bird, daily specials, and child's plates. Those listed accept at least two major credit cards (MC, V). Estimated costs are per person excluding wine, cocktails, and tips. *Deluxe:* $25 or more; *Expensive:* $15–$25; *Moderate:* $7–$15; *Inexpensive:* under $7.

Norfolk

Le Charlieu. *Expensive.* 112 College Pl.; 623–7202. Intimate dining with a French touch, in restored downtown area. Lunch and dinner. Bar. Reservations. Coat and tie requested. AE, CB, DC, MC, V.

Esplanade. *Expensive.* Omni International Hotel, 777 Waterside Dr.; 623–0333. Elegant small gourmet dining room offers impeccable service and superb American and Continental cuisine. Dinner only, Mon.–Sat. Bar. Reservations. Jacket and tie requested. AE, CB, DC, MC, V.

Lockhart's of Norfolk. *Moderate to Expensive.* 8440 Tidewater Dr.; 588–0405. One of area's oldest and most popular restaurants for seafood and prime ribs. Nautical decor, with antiques. Family proprietors grow their own vegetables. Bar. AE, CB, DC, MC, V.

The Ships Cabin Seafood Restaurant. *Moderate to Expensive.* 4110 E. Ocean View Ave.; 583–4659. This very popular award-winning seafood restaurant serves mesquite-grilled fresh fish and choice steaks. Good choice of Virginia and California wines. Dinner only. Bar. AE, CB, DC, MC, V.

Phillips Waterside. *Moderate.* 333 Waterside Dr., inside Waterside Festival Marketplace; 627–6600. Airy, gardenlike setting overlooks bustling Elizabeth River. Specialties include crab delicacies, grilled tuna, other local seafoods. Lunch and dinner. Evening piano bar, acoustic guitar, ragtime band entertainment. Bar. AE, DC, MC, V.

Il Porto of Norfolk. *Moderate.* 333 Waterside Dr.; 627–4400. Taverna setting, Italian specialties; overlooks harbor. Bar. Wine list. Evening ragtime piano. AE, MC, V.

Szechuan Garden Chinese Restaurant. *Inexpensive to Moderate.* 123 W. Charlotte St.; 627–6130. Authentic Szechuan cuisine; friendly, personalized service; locally popular. Lunch and dinner. Reservations requested. DC, MC, V.

Virginia Beach

Orion's Roof. *Expensive to Deluxe.* Top of the Cavalier, Atlantic Ave. at 42nd St.; 425–8555. Continental menu, live entertainment, and dancing in a sophisticated supper club. Bar and wine list. AE, DC, MC, V.

Blue Pete's. *Moderate to Expensive.* 1400 N. Muddy Creek Rd.; 426–2278. Casual seafood restaurant, locally popular. Noted for sweet-potato biscuits and fresh vegetables. Outdoor lounge, live entertainment. AE, DC, MC, V.

The Lighthouse. *Moderate to Expensive.* Rudee Inlet at 1st St. & Atlantic Ave.; 428–9851. Maine lobster and Eastern Shore seafoods, with its own bakery. Sunday brunch. Bar. Outdoor dining in season. AE, CB, DC, MC, V.

39th Street Seafood Grille. *Moderate to Expensive.* Holiday Inn-on-the-Ocean. 39th & Atlantic Ave.; 428–1711 or 428–2411. Skytop restaurant and lounge. Seafoods, steaks, and lavish salad bar. AE, CB, MC, V.

Wesley's. *Moderate to Expensive.* 32nd St. & Holly Rd.; 422–1511. Creole-accented steaks and seafood; menu changes weekly. Peanut butter cheese cake a specialty. Extensive wine cellar. Bar. AE, MC, V.

Captain George's Seafood Restaurants. *Moderate to Expensive.* Two Virginia Beach locations: 1956 Laskin Rd., 428–3494, and 2272 Pungo Ferry Rd., Intracoastal Waterway, 721–3463. Both noted for gourmet seafood and nautical decor. Mixed drinks and children's menu. Open daily. AE, MC, V.

Ocean Crab House. *Moderate.* 15th St. & Oceanfront; 428–6186. Seafood buffet, à la carte service. Home-baked desserts. CB, DC, MC, V.

Sir Richard's. *Inexpensive to Moderate.* 21st St. & Atlantic Ave.; 428–1926. Prime rib, steaks and seafoods; daily specials. Live entertainment. AE, MC, V.

Caesar's Restaurant. *Inexpensive.* 2312 Atlantic Ave.; 422–3232. Veal, seafood, Italian cuisine. Early Bird specials. Live entertainment. Extensive wine list. Local following. MC, V.

Fogg's. *Inexpensive to Expensive.* 415 Atlantic Ave.; 426–3644. Seafood and prime beef in four dining areas. Bar and wine list. Oceanside dining, with children's plates. Reserve for dinner. Open daily except Christmas; lunch and dinner. Major credit cards.

THINGS TO SEE AND DO

Norfolk

GARDENS. *Norfolk Botanical Gardens.* Located on Airport Rd., Norfolk's 175-acre botanical gardens are site of International Azalea Festival and one of nation's top Rose Display Gardens. Open daily. Seasonal boat, mini-train tours, picnicking, restaurant, and gift shop. Call 441–5386.

HISTORIC SITES. *Moses Myers House,* 323 E. Freemason St. (622–1211), classic Georgian structure; *St. Paul's Episcopal Church,* 201 St. Paul's Blvd. (627–4353), sole survivor of British bombardment of 1776, with a cannonball still embedded in one wall; *Willoughby-Baylor House,* 601 E. Freemason St. (622–1211), fine period furnishings, and charming herb and flower garden. All closed Mon., some holidays.

MUSEUMS. *Chrysler Museum.* Olney Rd. and Mowbray Arch (622–1211). Among the Nation's top 20 museums. Notable for its ancient collections and major European and American art. Decorative Arts collection and home of Chrysler Institute of Glass. This major world collection includes Tiffany Sandwich glass. Closed Mon., major holidays. Branch at Seaboard Center, 235 E. Plume St., offers several exhibits for downtown visitors, Mon.–Fri.

The Hermitage Foundation Museum. 7637 North Shore Rd. (423–2052), English Tudor mansion on garden grounds fronting Lafayette River. Displays rare Oriental and Western art treasures. 10–5 Mon.–Sat., 1–5 Sun. Closed major holidays.

Douglas MacArthur Memorial. Plume and Bank Sts. (441–2965), in historic 1850 City Hall. The final resting place of General MacArthur. Extensive exhibits and film chronicling his life. Open daily. Free.

Hampton Roads Naval Museum. Pennsylvania Bldg., Naval Base, Norfolk; 444–2243 or 444–3827. Official Naval museum, open daily, 9–4.

NATIONAL PARKS. *Dismal Swamp National Wildlife Refuge.* Located approximately 24 miles southwest of Norfolk, via I–64 and U.S. 17 S., is rare geographic area of peat bogs and thick forest, laced by man-made canals. Refuge for migratory birds, waterfowl, and black bears, Dismal Swamp was surveyed by George Washington in 1763. In its center is Lake Drummond, which can be explored by boat tours along the Dismal Swamp Canal. Call 986–3705.

ZOOS. *Virginia Zoological Park.* 3500 Granby St. (441–5227), on 55 wooded acres beside the Lafayette River. The zoo houses animals in natural habitat environments. Children's petting zoo. Open daily except major holidays.

SPECIAL INTEREST. *Norfolk Naval Station.* 9809 Hampton Blvd. (444–7955). The Naval Station is home port for more than 123 ships and aircraft squadrons, plus shore-based military activities. Tours of ships every weekend, year-round; base tours Mar.–Nov. *Waterside.* 333 Waterside Dr., with easy exit from I-264. More than 100 shops and restaurants in a "festival marketplace." See Places to Stay and Places to Eat, above. Phone 627–3300 for information.

LIVELY ARTS. Norfolk is witnessing a cultural boom. *Virginia Opera Assoc.* (623–1223), one of nation's top regional companies, performs at Center Theater; *Virginia Symphony Orchestra* (623–2310) appears at Chrysler Hall, Scope Cultural and Convention Center; *Feldman String Quarter* (489–2271 or 625–4137) offers seasonal performances in Chrysler Museum Theater; the *Virginia Stage Company* (627–1234) performs at historic Wells Theater; *Riverview Playhouse* (623–7529), community theater of Old Dominion University, presents classic traditional, avant-garde fare; *Tidewater Dinner Theatre* (461–2933) on the grounds of Lake Wright Resort Complex, 6270 Northampton Blvd., offers buffet dinner and professional theater, Wed.–Sat.; and *Little Theatre of Norfolk* (627–7551) is one of nation's oldest amateur groups.

WATER SPORTS. *Charter Fishing:* Cobbs Marina, 4524 Dunning Rd. (588–5401).

Cruises: American Rover Sailing Tour. Suite 15B, Harbor Tower, Portsmouth, (627–7245). Memorial Day–Labor Day.

Fishing Piers: Harrison Boathouse & Pier, 414 W. Ocean View Ave. (588–9968); Sea Gull Fishing Pier, Chesapeake Bay Bridge Tunnel (464–4641); and Willoughby Bay Marina, 1651 Bayville St. (583–8223).

Fresh-Water Fishing: Lakes Prince and Smith; rental boats, and launching ramps.

Sailing: Charters, Rover Marine Inc., 1651 Bayville St. (627–SAIL).

SPECTATOR SPORTS. Norfolk's Met Park is scene of minor league baseball games between the Tidewater Tides (New York Mets affiliate) and other AAA teams.

STATE PARKS. *False Cape,* accessible only by a five-mile walk, bicycle ride, or boat trip through Back Bay Wildlife Refuge, has maritime forests and natural dunes along the Atlantic Shore. *Seashore,* located at Cape Henry on U.S. 60, has visitor center, guided walks, and biking over 27 miles of nature trails. The first English colonists in Virginia landed on Cape Henry in 1607.

TOURING INFORMATION. Most of Norfolk's attractions are located on or near the water. This is a seaport town that has rediscovered its nautical heritage. The tours below reflect a renewed interest in Norfolk's magnificent harbor.

By Auto: Follow Norfolk Tour signs to attractions.

By Boat: Various seasonal excursions aboard *Carrie B* riverboat replica (393–4735); *New Spirit* launch (627–7771); *American Rover* topsail schooner (627–SAIL).

By Bus: Tours of world's largest naval base Mar.–Nov. Tickets, departure at The Waterside, Naval Base Tour Office (444–7955 or 444–2163.)

By Guided Tour: For list of companies, also complete sightseeing information, contact Norfolk Convention & Visitors Bureau, 236 E. Plume St., Norfolk, VA 23510, (441–5266 or 800–368–3097.) Or drop by Bureau Visitor Centers: Ocean View, W. End of 4th St., off I–64, (588–0404); or The Waterside, second level, "Ask Me" booth, (588–0404).

Virginia Beach

Virginia Beach's Boardwalk runs three-and-a-half miles along the resort's magnificent broad and sandy beach from Rudee Inlet at 2nd St. northward to 38th St. The area is covered by lifeguards, and rental folding chairs, floats, and beach umbrellas are available.

HISTORIC SITES. *DeWitt Cottage* (1895). The Cottage, which reflects early beach life, can be viewed from Boardwalk at 11th St.; *First Landing Cross (Cape Henry Memorial),* within Fort Story Military Reservation, marks the spot where Jamestown colonists first touched New World shores on April 26, 1607; *Old Cape Henry Lighthouse* (1791) is adjacent to the entrance to Chesapeake Bay; *Lynnhaven House* (ca. 1680) is known for its fine masonry, and decorative arts, open Apr.–Nov., Tues.–Sun., 12–4 (460–1688); *Adam Thoroughgood House* (1636) is believed to be the nation's oldest brick home, open 10–5 Tues.–Sat. Apr.–Nov., 12–5 Dec.–Mar., closed holidays (460–0007); *Princess Anne Courthouse* (1824), 9 miles southwest via Rtes. 615 and 149, in Princess Anne, stands beside the impressive and beautifully landscaped *Municipal Center,* open 9–5 Mon.–Fri.

MUSEUMS. *Virginia Beach Arts Center,* 18th and Arctic Ave. (425–0000), with changing exhibits, moves in 1986 to site across from the Pavilion, off Rte. 44, Virginia Beach Expressway; *Virginia Beach Maritime Historical Museum,* 24th & Oceanfront (422–1587), in 1903 Seatack Lifesaving Station, houses ship models, artifacts, and shipwreck mementos; open daily Memorial Day–Oct., closed Mon. rest of year; *Virginia Museum of Marine Sciences,* 717 General Booth Blvd. (422–3814), has unique hands-on marine exhibits, Finny habitats, 100,000-gallon aquarium. The Museum offers simulated deep ocean dive; *Royal London Wax Museum,*

1606 Atlantic Ave. (425–3823), with over 100 life-size figures in realistic settings. Open year-round.

SPECIAL INTEREST. *Association for Research and Enlightenment, Inc. (ARE),* 67th & Atlantic (428–3588), ESP exploration center, offers free daily lectures, films, and tours, based on works of Edgar Cayce, history's best-documented psychic; *Little Creek Amphibious Base* (passes at Main Gate, Shore Dr.; 464–7761) welcomes visitors to museum and weekend ship open houses; *Norwegian Lady,* 9-foot bronze statue at 25th & Oceanfront, commemorates 1891 sinking of Norwegian ship *Diktator,* was gift from sister city of Moss, Norway; *Oceana Naval Air Station,* Oceana Blvd., offers take-off and landing views of advanced Navy aircraft; *Wildwater Rapids,* General Booth Blvd. (425–1080), family-oriented water park that features splashy slides, wave pools, and inner-tube rides.

LIVELY ARTS. *The Virginia Symphony Orchestra* presents four annual concerts at Pavilion Theater (428–8000), which is also site of the *Virginia Symphony Pops* series, performances by *Tidewater Ballet Association.*

SPORTS. The emphasis, of course, is on the water and water-related activities, but Virginia Beach also has a full measure of fun-in-the-sun participant sports.

Boating Ramps: free at Owl Creek, General Booth Blvd., Munden Point Park, Munden Point Rd.

Charter Boat Deep Sea Fishing: Bubba's Marina, 3323 Shore Dr. (481–3513); D&M Marina, 3311 Shore Dr. (481–7211); Virginia Beach Fishing Center, 200 Winston-Salem Ave. (422–5700).

Fishing Piers: Little Island, Sandbridge, Atlantic Ocean; Lynnhaven Inlet, Starfish Rd., Chesapeake Bay; Rudee Inlet Fishing Site, south end; Sea Gull, Chesapeake Bay Bridge–Tunnel; Virginia Beach, 15th St. & Oceanfront.

Golfing: On six championship courses—challenging new Hell's Point, Red Wing, Bow Creek, Stumpy Lake, Kempsville Meadows, Lake Wright.

Oceanfront Cruising: 200 Winston-Salem Dr. (422–5700); 90-minute narrated ocean cruising, three times a day. Memorial Day–Labor Day.

Paddle-Boating. Mount Trashmore, a 162-acre park with two lakes. Fishing and picnicking. Phone 497–2157 for information.

Scuba, Snorkeling: Lessons, gear, trips from Lynnhaven Dive Center, 1413 Great Neck Rd. (481–7949); Scuba Ventures, 2247-B N. Great Neck Rd. (481–3132).

Tennis: On 156 courts, most lighted, including Owl Creek Municipal Tennis Center, considered one of nation's 50 best such complexes, 928 S. Birdneck Rd. and General Booth Blvd. (422–4716).

SHOPPING. Virginia Beach has become one of the nation's fastest-growing centers for off-price shopping, with well over 125 stores discounting designer fashions and name brand items. Major centers with a 15-minute drive of the oceanfront include *Great American Outlet Mall; Lynnhaven Mall,* with 140 stores, including six major department stores; *Pembroke Mall; Military Circle;* and *Pacific Place* with quality designer wear, collector and decorative art works, jewelry, china, crafts. The *Virginia Beach Maritime Historical Museum* (see above) has an outstanding gift shop featuring nautical items, clocks, brasses, prints, and jewelry.

TOURING INFORMATION. Virginia Beach is an ocean resort and most of its touring attractions are located at or near the surf and the Boardwalk.

By Auto: Self-guided tour follows prominent road signs to major landmarks and attractions. (See address and phone below.)

By Bicycle: Rentals available along the Boardwalk for ocean-front trail.

By Trolley: Tidewater Regional Transit Authority (TRT) vehicles run mid-May–summer from Rudee Inlet to 42nd St., and Redwing Park to the Civic Center (The Dome). Call 428–3388. Shuttles also run to Lynnhaven, Pembroke Malls and there's service to Norfolk and back via the Oceanside/Waterside Express (428–3388), which runs between The Dome and Waterside. TRT also offers tours to Norfolk Naval Station, downtown Norfolk.

By Boat: Cruises aboard *Miss Virginia Beach* from Rudee Inlet daily, Memorial Day through Sept. Call 422–5700.

For Sightseeing Information: Virginia Beach Visitors Bureau, Box 200, Dept. MTB, Virginia Beach, VA 23458, 425–7511. or call toll-free 800–446–3038; calls are answered from 9 to 5 seven days a week. The Center provides a free continuous audio-visual presentation about the beach and the resort's attractions.

TIDEWATER VIRGINIA

by
RODNEY N. SMITH

Tidewater Virginia is the oldest part of America, a romantic land of elegant plantations and horse-drawn carriages, historic churches, and famous battlefields. It is a place of unspoiled beaches, Colonial taverns, and some of the finest nautical and space museums in the country.

In the beginning there was only Jamestown. In 1607 America's first permanent English settlement was struggling on Jamestown Island. The "feel" of Jamestown is recaptured today in the Old Church Tower and reconstructed church and the early foundations and unearthed streets of this first settlement. At nearby Jamestown Festival Park there are full-scale replicas of James Fort and the three tiny ships that brought those first English settlers to the shores of the New World—*Susan Constant, Godspeed,* and *Discovery.*

Tidewater Virginia is also the home of Colonial Williamsburg, the largest restored eighteenth-century town in America. Here visitors will find charming old taverns, Colonial homes, and stately public buildings such as the Colonial Capitol and the seventeenth-century Wren Building on the campus of the College of William and Mary. Between the College and Colonial Williamsburg, up and

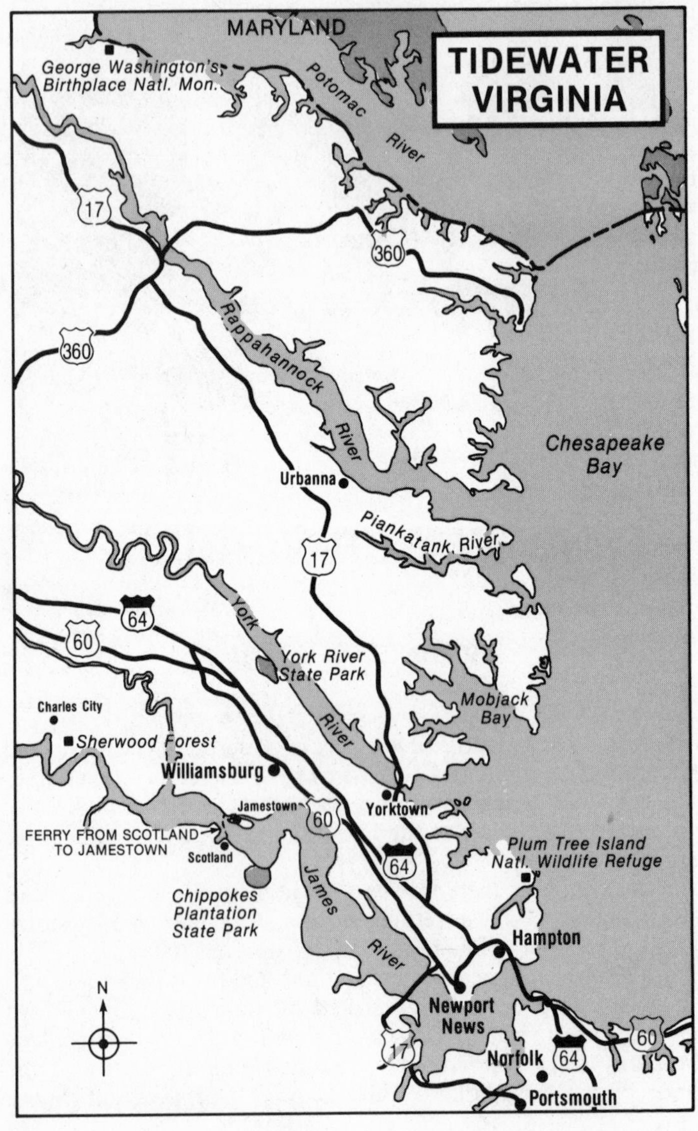
TIDEWATER VIRGINIA
MARYLAND
George Washington's Birthplace Natl. Mon.
Potomac River
Rappahannock River
Chesapeake Bay
Urbanna
Piankatank River
York River
York River State Park
Mobjack Bay
Charles City
Sherwood Forest
Williamsburg
Jamestown
Yorktown
FERRY FROM SCOTLAND TO JAMESTOWN
Scotland
Plum Tree Island Natl. Wildlife Refuge
Chippokes Plantation State Park
James River
Hampton
Newport News
Norfolk
Portsmouth
N
17
360
64
60

down the length of Duke of Gloucester Street, every byway thrills and delights us. A fife and drum corps marches past, a beautiful garden comes into view, or an expert artisan demonstrates his skill, producing a barrel, a basket, a candle, or a silver bowl. Many of these hand-made "Colonial" wares can be bought in the charming shops about the village.

From Williamsburg, the beautiful Colonial National Parkway leads the visitor to Yorktown, where the Revolutionary War ended and a new nation had won its right to be born. Visitors should see the Yorktown Victory Center and National Park Visitors Center, the picturesque village, and the famous battlefield. They should also try the little seafood restaurants beside the Bay, for Yorktown is home to some of America's finest fresh seafood.

Tidewater Plantations

Of all landmarks and monuments northwest of Norfolk, nothing better recaptures antebellum American life than the majestic plantations along the James. Tidewater Virginia has been amply blessed with some magnificent survivors. These marvelous mansions flourished along the James River from Williamsburg to Richmond and throughout the Tidewater and Northern Neck regions. Their legends are a delight. Rolfe-Warren House stands on land given to John Rolfe by his father-in-law, Chief Powhatan. Other plantations are the ancestral or actual homes of presidents. George Washington was born here on the banks of Pope's Creek and Berkeley Plantation is said—by Virginians—to have been the site of America's first Thanksgiving in 1619, a year before the Pilgrims *landed* at Plymouth Rock.

Tidewater Virginia is the oldest part of the state, but it also glitters brightest. Visitors can find lively golden beaches, such as world-famous Virginia Beach. Popular for its sun, surf, and seafood, Virginia Beach is celebrated as one of the country's outstanding ocean resorts for fun-filled family vacations, while its neighbor, Norfolk, has rediscovered itself and its magnificent harbor.

Nearby are the harbor towns, with attractions as varied as Portsmouth's Naval Shipyard Museum; Norfolk's Chrysler Museum and Scope Convention and Cultural Center; and Hampton's old St. John's Church, historic Fort Monroe, and the Hampton Coliseum.

Busch Gardens

Here too is the fantastic world of family fun at Busch Gardens' "The Old Country," which has thrilling rides and exciting shows, fascinating shops and stirring oompah bands. Busch Gardens has something for every age in four tasteful European flavors.

A Tidewater vacation in the Chesapeake vacationland can range between a visit to one of the best theme parks in the world to a day in the sun on a wide stretch of golden sand, or from the pleasures of the moment to an appreciation of the past.

Exploring Williamsburg

Colonial Williamsburg is the site of one of the most extensive restorations ever undertaken. Visitors experience life as it was lived in George Washington's day in this small Colonial village. History lives again in Williamsburg's functioning shops, its craftspeople at work at their specialties, and in authentic taverns serving food and drink that would have been offered in the eighteenth century when this town was the capital of English Virginia.

The 173-acre Historic Area is centered on Duke of Gloucester Street, which runs about one mile from the College of William and Mary where Thomas Jefferson studied, to the Capitol where Patrick Henry denounced King George III's stamp tax. The streets are lined with old homes, taverns, stores, and craft shops.

In addition to the buildings open to the public and the shops, visitors can enjoy dining in one of the village's authentic Colonial taverns. There the rich variety of food offered in the eighteenth century has been carefully recreated, as it has been also in the many restaurants located in and around this historic area. Shopping is another fascinating aspect of a Williamsburg visit, and tempting souvenirs of your trip abound in craft shops, gift shops, and stores in the Virginia Peninsula.

All this is part of the Colonial experience in Williamsburg, which three centuries ago was the capital of England's largest colony in America. As such, Williamsburg played a vital role in the struggle for the freedom and representative government that we now enjoy.

Williamsburg became the second capital of Virginia in 1699. It replaced Jamestown, the first permanent English settlement in the New World, where colonists had battled Indians, fire, famine, and pestilence since 1607. The Virginia Assembly selected Middle Plantation for the new capital and renamed it Williamsburg in honor of their English king.

The new city was already the site of the second college in America. Six years before, in 1693, a royal charter was granted for an institution to be named in honor of the British sovereigns, King William and Queen Mary. The royal governor and the Assembly carefully set about raising a new and well-ordered capital, one of the first planned cities in America.

An old horseway running the length of the settlement was straightened, widened, and renamed Duke of Gloucester Street. At the east end, facing the handsome Wren Building a mile away, the first government building in America to be given the dignified name of Capitol was built. Midway between the College and the

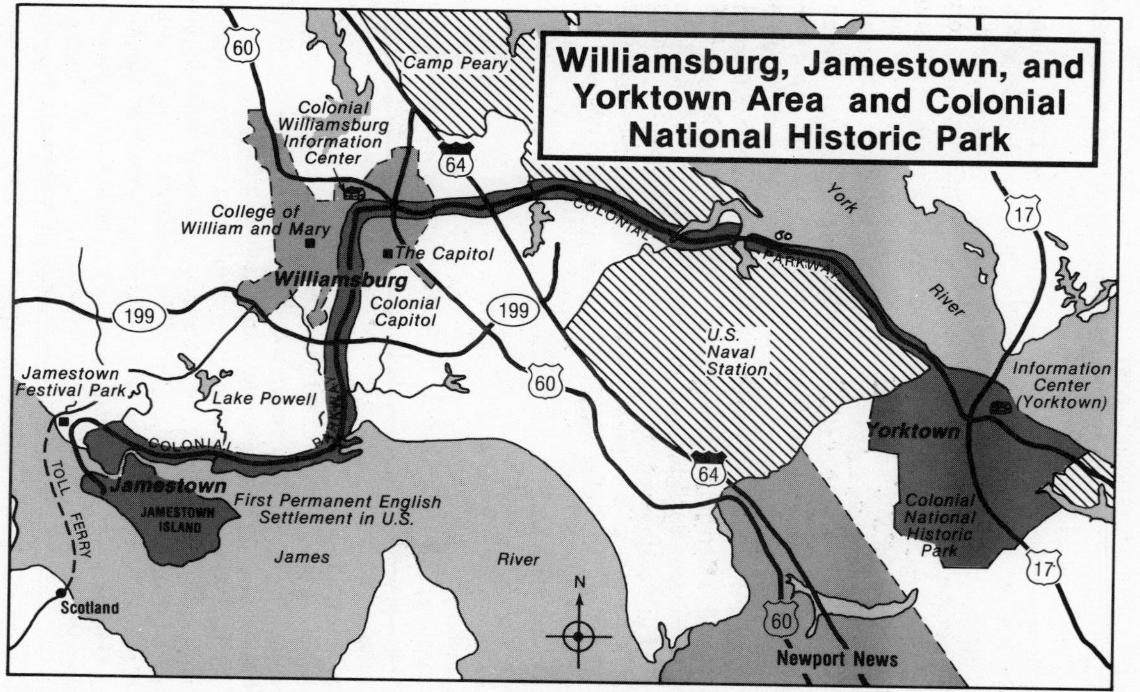
Williamsburg, Jamestown, and
Yorktown Area and Colonial
National Historic Park
60
Camp Peary
Colonial
Williamsburg
Information
Center
64
College of
William and Mary
The Capitol
Williamsburg
Colonial
Capitol
199
199
COLONIAL
PARKWAY
York
River
17
U.S.
Naval
Station
60
Jamestown
Festival Park
Lake Powell
Information
Center
(Yorktown)
Yorktown
COLONIAL
64
Jamestown
JAMESTOWN
ISLAND
First Permanent English
Settlement in U.S.
TOLL
FERRY
Colonial
National
Historic
Park
James
River
17
N
Scotland
60
Newport News

Capitol, a residence for the royal governor was completed in 1720. This mansion became known as the Governor's Palace. It was in time occupied by seven royal governors and the first two governors of the Commonwealth of Virginia, Patrick Henry and Thomas Jefferson (who moved the capital to Richmond in 1780 because of the threat of a British attack).

Many weathered landmarks survived to the twentieth century. The Rev. W.A.R. Goodwin, then rector of Bruton Parish Church, recognized the significance of these remaining structures. Through the minister's efforts and enthusiasm, John D. Rockefeller, Jr., became interested, and in 1926 the first steps were taken to preserve and restore the city's Historic Area.

The two men began a modest project to preserve a few of the more important buildings but, as the worked progressed, it expanded to include the major portion of the Colonial capital. Today approximately 85 percent of eighteenth-century Williamsburg is encompassed by the undertaking. Rockefeller gave the project his personal leadership until his death in 1960, and it was his generosity and uncompromising ethic of excellence that guided and dominated its development. The old city today appears much as it did when Patrick Henry thundered his defiance of King George III and Virginia burgesses voted their historic resolution for independence.

Carter's Grove

Nearby Carter's Grove Plantation, located seven miles from Williamsburg on the banks of the James River, has a mansion that has been called "the most beautiful house in America. It was the bread basket of Williamsburg in Colonial times. One of the great plantation homes of Colonial Virginia, Carter's Grove stands majestically on 600 acres of rolling countryside. Stretching 200 feet from end to end, this Georgian mansion was completed in the 1750s. It was renovated in 1929 by Mr. and Mrs. Archibald McCrea.

Remains of seventeenth-century Wolstenholme Towne have been discovered by Williamsburg archeologists and, aided by their investigations, the development of the gardens and the disclosure of the Wolstenholme Towne are ongoing projects that should in time enhance our understanding and appreciation of Colonial America.

Not everything about a Williamsburg visit is tied to our Colonial past; Busch Gardens, a modern theme park in 360 acres of beautiful Virginia forest, is only a few miles away. Its theme, *The Old Country,* is presented in sections that recreate the romance, atmosphere, and architectural highlights of the British Isles, France, Germany, and Italy. Keyed to the four themes are live entertainment, shops, and restaurants. Among the most thrilling rides at Busch Gardens is the sensational Loch Ness Monster. Some of the biggest and brightest stars of today's entertainment world appear at Busch Gardens on special dates.

PRACTICAL INFORMATION FOR THE WILLIAMSBURG AREA

Note: The area code for Williamsburg is 804.

PLACES TO STAY

HOTELS AND MOTELS. There is no shortage of good accommodations in the Williamsburg-Busch Gardens area, but you may not believe that, if you neglect to book well ahead during the peak summer touring season. Although space limitations restrict the length of the following list, we have attempted to provide a representative *selection,* keeping convenience, personal tastes, and the traveler's pocketbook always in mind. In general, but *only* in general, our categories follow the same price ranges that appear elsewhere in this guide: *Deluxe,* $100 and up; *Expensive,* $75 to $100; *Moderate,* $40 to $75; and *Inexpensive,* under $40. All are based on double occupancy. For details about accommodations at Colonial Williamsburg, including Colonial houses, contact Colonial Williamsburg Foundation, Box B, Williamsburg, VA 23187; 229–1000 or 800–HISTORY. Foundation accommodations require a deposit. AE, MC, V accepted.

Williamsburg Inn. *Deluxe.* S. Francis St., Colonial Williamsburg; 229–1000 or (800) 446–8956. 102 rooms, plus 85 in 26 Colonial houses and taverns, some more than 200 years old. All in the Historic Area. The Inn is elegantly furnished in Regency style; the houses are restored buildings with eighteenth-century decor. Restaurant, golf, and tennis. AE, MC, V.

Hilton Inn Williamsburg. *Expensive to Deluxe.* 50 Kingsmill Dr., 2½ miles east on U.S. 60, I–64 exit Busch Garden; 220–2500. 300 rooms with Williamsburg and Busch Garden plans. Some units with private patios and balconies. Restaurants, bar, room service, and pool. All major credit cards.

Royce Hotel. *Expensive to Deluxe.* 415 Richmond Rd., two blocks west of the Historic Area. 313 rooms, with lounge, bar, restaurant and pool in former Williamsburg Hospitality House. Concierge and valet parking. Golf and tennis privileges; 229–4020. Major credit cards.

Williamsburg Lodge. *Expensive to Deluxe.* S. England St., near the Inn; 229–1000 or (800) 446–8956. 314 rooms at the edge of the Historic Area. Beautiful gardens. Restaurant. AE, CB, DC.

Fort Magruder Inn & Conference Center. *Expensive.* 6945 Pocahontas Trail; 220–2250. 304 rooms with local entertainment, lighted tennis and golf privileges. Some rooms with private patios and balconies and some outside dining. AE, CB, DC, MC, V. Full convention facilities.

The Motor House-Williamsburg. *Expensive.* 1 mile southeast of I–64, opposite the Information Center; 229–1000 or (800) 582–8976. 164 rooms with golf and tennis plans. Tennis and golf privileges, putting green, lawn games, and miniature golf. AE, MC, V.

Holiday Inn–East. *Moderate to Expensive.* 804 Capitol Landing Rd., a short drive east on Rte. 5; 229–0200. 136 rooms near the Visitors Center. Restaurant. Major credit cards.

Ramada Inn-East. *Moderate to Expensive.* 351 York St., 2 blocks east on U.S. 60E. 229–4100. 201 rooms in a convenient location. Restaurant and pool. Major credit cards.

Quality Inn—Colony. *Moderate to Expensive.* 309 Page St., at junction of U.S. 60E and VA 162; 229–1855. 59 rooms. Restaurant and pool. Major credit cards.

Sheraton Patriot Inn. *Moderate to Expensive.* 3032 Richmond Rd., 3 miles west on U.S. 60; 565–2600. 160 rooms. Restaurant, pool. AE, CB, DC, MC.

Best Western Patrick Henry Inn. *Moderate to Expensive.* York and Page sts., Rte. 60E, 2 blocks east of the Colonial Capitol; 229–9590. 301 rooms. Convenient location and golf privileges. Restaurant. Major credit cards.

Quality Inn—Lord Paget. *Moderate.* 901 Capitol Landing Rd., 1½ miles east on Rte. 5; 229–4444. 88 rooms on a resort location with a small lake. All major credit cards.

Governor's Inn. *Moderate.* 506 N. Henry St., 3½ blocks north on Rte. 132; 229–6605. 72 rooms. Golf privileges. Pool. Major credit cards.

Days Inn. 902 Richmond Rd.; 229–5060. 100 rooms with golf privileges. Downtown location. Restaurant. Major credit cards.

Comfort Inn-West. *Moderate.* 5611 Richmond, Rd.; 253–0999. 80 rooms. Pool and restaurant. Major credit cards.

Econo Lodge—York Street. *Moderate.* 505 York St., Rte. 60E; 220–3100. 100 rooms. Pool. Morning coffee. AE, MC, V.

George Washington Inn. *Moderate.* 500 Merrimac Trail, 1½ miles east on Rte. 143; 253 rooms. 220–1410. All major credit cards.

Governor Spottswood Motel. *Moderate.* 1508 Richmond Rd., northwest about 2 miles on U.S. 60W; 229–6444. 74 rooms. Picnic tables on a shaded lawn. All major credit cards.

John Rolfe Motel. *Moderate.* 1313 N. Mount Vernon Ave., ¾ mile from Williamsburg off Richmond Rd.; 220–1710. 28 rooms with kitchen units available. Pool. AE, DC, MC, V.

Minuet Manor. *Moderate.* 1408 Richmond Rd., slightly more than 1 mile northwest on U.S. 60W; 220–2367. 180 rooms with tennis. Restaurant. Major credit cards.

Quarterpath Inn. *Moderate.* 620 York St., 1½ miles east on Rte. 60E; 220–0960 or (800) 446–9222. 140 rooms, with a restaurant. All major credit cards.

Williamsburg Westpark. *Moderate.* 1600 Richmond Rd.; 229–1134. 181 rooms in two and three-story motel. No elevator. Bar, restaurant, and bell hops. Room service. Major credit cards.

King William Inn. *Inexpensive to Moderate.* 824 Capitol Landing Rd., ½ mile northeast on Rte. 5; 229–4933 or (800) 446–1041. 183 rooms, some with balconies. MC, V.

Quality Inn—Mount Vernon. *Inexpensive to Moderate.* 1600 Richmond Rd., slightly more than 1 mile northwest on U.S. 60; 229–2401. 65 rooms on spacious grounds AE, CB, DC, MC, V.

PLACES TO EAT

RESTAURANTS. Dining in and around Williamsburg should be a joy, hopefully never traumatic. As is true in any major touring center, restaurants—even the most expensive—tend to be crowded during the summer tourist season and we strongly recommend that you make reservations if at all possible. The following selection of restaurants is not meant to be all-inclusive; there are simply too many fine places to eat in the Colonial National Historical Park area. We've tried to tailor this list of *selections* to a variety of tastes and pocketbooks, but if you discover "a very special place" that we've neglected or overlooked, we'd be delighted to hear about it. General price categories for dinner, excluding drinks, tips, and taxes, are: *Deluxe,* $25 or more; *Expensive,* $15–$25; *Moderate,* $7–$15; *Inexpensive,* under $7. For Historic Area restaurants, call 229–2141.

Christiana Campbell's Tavern. *Expensive.* Waller St. just across the lawn from the Colonial Capitol; 229–2141. Another of the authentic Colonial taverns still in operation. House specialties include spoon bread, seafood, and the special fruit sherbet. George Washington ate here often, but in the private rooms. AE, MC, V.

Josiah Chowning's Tavern. *Expensive.* Duke of Gloucester St. at Queen St.; 229–2141. One of the Colonial taverns of Williamsburg, featuring Brunswick stew and Welsh rabbit in beer. Ale house atmosphere. AE, MC, V.

King's Arms Tavern. *Expensive.* Duke of Gloucester St.; 229–2141. The most genteel of the eighteenth-century taverns. Specialties include Colonial game pies, scalloped oysters, and Sally Lunn bread, in a Colonial atmosphere, of course. AE, MC, V.

Kingsmill. *Expensive.* 100 Golf Club Rd., 2½ miles east of U.S. 60E exit off I–64, Busch Gardens; 253–3900. Continental menu featuring escalope de veau, duck, and fresh seafood. Contemporary decor. AE, MC, V.

Lafayette. *Expensive.* 1203 Richmond Rd.; 229–3811. Continental fare specializing in rack of lamb, shrimp, and lobster. Reservations recommended. AE, DC, MC, V.

Regency Room, Williamsburg Inn. *Expensive.* Francis St. 229–2141. Fine dining in an elegant setting. Continental menu, with rack of lamb and veal with morrel sauce as specialties. AE, MC, V.

Trellis. *Expensive.* Duke of Gloucester St., Merchant's Square. Adjacent to the Historic Area; 229–8610. Continental menu, with fresh seafood. Homemade ice cream and pasta. Dinner reservations suggested. AE, MC, V.

Le Yaca. *Expensive.* 1915 Pocohantas Trail in the Kingsmill Shops, U.S. 60E; 220–3616. French cookery with a good wine cellar. Open-spit rack of lamb and Le Yaca's own special pastries. An elegant dining room. All major credit cards.

Aberdeen Barn. *Moderate to Expensive.* 1601 Richmond Rd.; 229–6661. Rustic atmosphere with an open-hearth grill. Specializes in roast prime rib, seafood, and steak. Major credit cards.

Captain George's Seafood. *Moderate to Expensive.* 5363 Richmond Rd.; 565–2323. Seafood the specialty, but also steaks and veal. Salad Bar and children's portions. Bar. AE, MC, V.

Cascades at Motor House. *Moderate to Expensive.* Near Information Center, east of Historic Area; 229–1000. Specializes in seafood and beef. Pleasant atmosphere. Favored by locals. AE, MC, V.

Lobster House. *Moderate to Expensive.* 1425 Richmond Rd.; 229–7771. Specializing in lobster, seafood, and steak in a nautical ambience. Major credit cards.

Whaling Company. *Moderate to Expensive.* 494 McLaw Circle; 229–0275. Continental menu specializing in mesquite grilling and fresh seafood. AE, MC, V.

Williamsburg Lodge. *Moderate to Expensive.* S. England St.; 229–1000. Offers a Chesapeake buffet Fridays and Saturdays. A pleasant garden cocktail lounge. Major credit cards.

THINGS TO SEE AND DO

There is a lot to see and do in Williamsburg. Not all of it is in the Historic Area, but that is where most visitors start.

Visitors to Colonial Williamsburg should stop first at the Visitors Center, where they can buy tickets and get sightseeing information; the Center can also help with food and lodging reservations and suggestions. There is a cafeteria and a bookstore at the Center, as well as an orientation film. This is where the free buses start that take visitors around the extensive restored site.

HISTORIC AREA. The Capitol at the east end of Duke of Gloucester Street is probably the most important building in the Historic Area. The General Assembly met here from 1704 to 1709 and it was here that Patrick Henry delivered his famous fiery "Caesar-Brutus" speech in 1765. The Capitol is also the site of the Resolution for Independence in 1776.

The Public Gaol is north of the Capitol across Nicholson St. It is the building in which debtors, pirates (including Blackbeard's crew), and criminals were jailed.

A few steps west and back on Duke of Gloucester Street is the Raleigh Tavern, which stood firmly in the forefront of life in the Colonial capital. Raleigh Tavern was a frequent meeting place for Washington, Jefferson, Henry, and other Revolutionary patriots and was for a time the social center of the Virginia Colony. It is open to the public but no longer offers food or lodging. Wetherburn's Tavern, one of the most popular of the period, is directly across the street.

The Governor's Palace and gardens at the north end of the Palace Green was the home of seven royal governors and Virginia's first two governors, Henry and Jefferson. One of the most elegant buildings in Colonial America, it is set in 10 acres of beautifully restored formal gardens.

Just southeast of the Palace is Brush-Everard House, the home of one of the early mayors. It has a hand-carved staircase and beautiful boxwood gardens. Peyton Randolph House (1716) is just to its southeast. This was the home of the president of the First Continental Congress and headquarters of General Rochambeau prior to the Battle of Yorktown.

Southwest of that is James Geddy House, once the home of a prominent silversmith. The site includes a working silver shop and pewter foundry. Across Palace Green at the corner of Prince George Street is Wythe House, the home of George Wythe, America's first law professor. Wythe taught Jefferson, Clay, and Marshall. Wythe House served as Washington's headquarters before the siege of Yorktown and Rochambeau's afterward. The house, dependencies, and gardens form a miniature plantation layout.

Back on Duke of Gloucester Street, a block east of the Palace, is the Magazine, the arsenal of the colony. Authentic arms are exhibited and demonstrated there today.

James Anderson House contains extensive exhibits on Williamsburg archaeology and gives visitors a more thorough understanding of what has been accomplished here. Basset Hall on York Street, southeast of the Capitol, is an eighteenth-century house that served as local residence of Mr. and Mrs. John D. Rockefeller, Jr.

Bruton Parish Church on Duke of Gloucester Street, just west of Palace Green, is one of America's oldest Episcopal churches. It has been in continuous use since 1715. Nearby is the Public Hospital, the first public institution in the English colonies devoted exclusively to the treatment of mental illness. The DeWitt Wallace Decorative Arts Gallery, adjoining the hospital is a modern museum featuring decorative arts of eighteenth-century America.

TOURS. Tickets to various tours can be bought at the Courthouse of 1770. The carriage ride through the Historic Area is one of the most popular. The two-and-a-half hour Tricorn Hat Tour for children ages 7 to 11 is also popular. Once Upon a Town is designed for children 4 to 6. The Townsteader Program offers an opportunity for 8 to 14-year-olds to try eighteenth-century domestic crafts. Lanthorn Tour offers guided tours of craft shops by candlelight. The Escorted Tour, a two-hour guided tour through the Historic Area, is the most popular in Williamsburg. Call 229–1000 for information.

College of William and Mary. Outside the Historic Area, visitors will want to make sure they take in the College of William and Mary (1693) at the west end of Duke of Gloucester St. It is the second oldest college in America and it initiated the honor system, elective system of studies, a school of law, and one of modern languages. It was the second American institution to have a school of medicine. The Phi Beta Kappa Society was founded here in 1776.

Certainly the most commanding building on campus is the Wren Building (1695, restored 1928) the oldest academic building in America. Earl Gregg Swem Library, housing the College Museum and Gallery of Colonial Art, and the President's House (1734), the oldest such residence in continuous use in the United States, are also both on the William and Mary campus.

Outside the Historic Area are the Abby Aldrich Rockefeller Folk Art Center (307 South England Street), which houses American folk painting, sculpture, decorative useful wares, and gardens and the Craft House, the sales center for approved Williamsburg reproductions. These are located at the Williamsburg Inn and at Merchants Sqe.

Merchants Square. A pleasant, shaded shopping area between the College of William and Mary and Historic Colonial Williamsburg. Merchants Square is bisected east–west by Duke of Gloucester Street. There are more than 50 shops and services, from ice cream and handcrafted sweets to pewter, old prints, and antique furniture. Restaurants in the Square include A Good Place to East and Trellis, see above.

COLONIAL PARKWAY. An attraction in its own right, this 23-mile scenic drive links Jamestown with Williamsburg and Yorktown. Access at either end, Williamsburg, or Rte. 199, east and west of Williamsburg. There are no service stations along the parkway, which curves gently through wooded hills and skirts the James River to the west and York River to the east. Markers, overlooks, and picnic areas at Great Neck (south of Williamsburg) and Ringfield (midway between Williamsburg and Yorktown). Speed limit: 45 m.p.h.

SHOPPING. Approved Williamsburg reproductions are available at two locations in the Historic Area: off S. England St., adjacent to Williamsburg Inn, and the corner of Henry and Duke of Gloucester Sts., Merchants Square. Gift shops in the area include *DeWitt Wallace Decorative Arts Gallery,* Bus Stop 7A, S. Henry St.; *Carter's Grove* (above), and in the lobbies of the *Williamsburg Inn* and *Williamsburg Lodge,* or at the Motor House Cafeteria or Cascades Restaurant at the *Visitors Center.*

STATE PARK. York River State Park has another flavor. Eight miles northwest of Williamsburg on I-64 at the Croaker exit, and north one mile along VA 607 to VA 606E, York River State Park is a 2,491-acre natural preserve along the river and its marshes. It offers fishing, canoe trips, boat launch, hiking trails, picnicking, and nature walks.

THEME PARK. And then there is Busch Gardens—"The Old Country." Located three miles east of Williamsburg on U.S. 60, Busch Gardens is a theme park on 360 acres. The Old Country features an "Oktoberfest" in a recreated German village plus English, French, Italian, and Scottish villages. Each area has rides, shows, live entertainment, and national restaurants. There is transportation around the grounds by monorail, sky lift, paddleboat, and steam train. Not to be outdone by its splashy neighbor, Water Country USA, Busch Gardens in 1988 opened its Roman Rapids water ride. Visitors shoot the rapids for ⅓ mile in a 6-passenger inflatable boat. The 3-minute ride is very wet but very popular. Other attractions include animal acts, musical reviews, and magic shows, a reproduction of the Globe Theatre, 30 rides (including the super-thrill "Loch Ness Monster" and "da Vinci's Cradle"), arcade, antique carousel, concerts, brewery tour by monorail, miniature of Le Mans racetrack, "Rhine River" boat ride, and the "Grimm's Hollow" ride for small children. For further information, call 253–3350 or write: Busch Gardens, The Old Country, Drawer F.C., Williamsburg, VA 23187.

THE HISTORIC TRIANGLE. Colonial Williamsburg is the star, but your visit to the Virginia Peninsula should include the other two major attractions—Jamestown and Yorktown. The three together are a trilogy—the beginning, middle, and end of America's Colonial Experience. Here, in a relatively small setting, is the nation's heritage: 175 years of Colonial life between the landing at Jamestown in 1607 and the climatic battle of Yorktown in 1781.

Exploring Jamestown

In mid-May 1607, a small band of apprehensive English settlers landed on a swampy peninsula near Chesapeake Bay and founded the first permanent English settlement in the New World. Three small ships, *Susan Constant, Godspeed,* and *Discovery,* brought those first colonists to the place that is Jamestown after landing briefly at Cape Henry near the mouth of the Chesapeake. (The three vessels were recreated and put on display at Jamestown in 1959. *Godspeed* was built again in 1985 after the first replica rotted.)

Jamestown in those early years was anything but an English rose garden. Hostile Indians and voracious mosquitoes plagued the settlers, and there was seldom enough to eat. This was "the Starving Time." Much credit is given to Captain John Smith for holding it all together during those early bad years; if the London Company, patron of the colony, was stubborn but inept, Smith was stubborn but capable. Most historians acknowledge his efforts, for although only a few score settlers survived the first dreadful winter, Jamestown, like Roanoke (North Carolina) might have become another Lost Colony if the remarkable Smith hadn't been there.

But survive it did, and by 1612 Jamestown was producing commercial crops of tobacco, and the colonists were soon producing glass, bricks, and clapboards, fishing nets, pottery, and a variety of implements and tools. The New World's first representative legislative body was established in Jamestown in 1619, only nine years after Lord De La Warr visited the dispirited colonists and persuaded them to hang on. That same year—1619—the first African blacks in the Western Hemisphere arrived aboard a Dutch warship. Like many white new arrivals, they were probably indentured servants who paid for their passage with their labor. Although the English arrived first and established the colony, they were followed in later years by Dutch, French, Scots, Germans, Irish, Welsh, and Italians. Each newcomer brought to the New World a "national" character that would in time be woven into the fabric of Virginia.

When Jamestown became a royal colony in 1624, her colonists were already feeling the first stirrings of a new and fierce independence. There was open revolt in 1676 and the village was burned. It was partly rebuilt, but decline was inevitable because of the damp, unhealthy climate. The statehouse was burned in 1698; the government moved to Williamsburg the following year. By the time of the American Revolution, Jamestown was no longer an active community. At about the same time, the James River eroded the sandy isthmus and the peninsula became an island.

Nothing of the seventeenth-century settlement remains above ground except for the Old Church Tower; however, archaeological exploration by the National Park Service since 1934 has made the outline of the old town clear. Further careful excavation has uncovered foundations, streets, monuments, ditches, hedge rows, and fences. Markers, recorded messages, and monuments have been strategically placed to guide Jamestown visitors.

PRACTICAL INFORMATION FOR JAMESTOWN

Note: The area code for Jamestown is 804.

HOW TO GET THERE. Jamestown Island in the James River is located about five miles southwest of Colonial Williamsburg as the crow flies, approximately 10 miles by car (via Colonial Parkway). Use Rte. 199 off I-64 if you're driving north from Norfolk. There is also a toll ferry from Scotland on the south bank of the James River to Jamestown Festival Park, adjacent to the old town, on Powhatan Creek.

PLACES TO EAT

Mermaid Tavern Restaurant. *Inexpensive.* Jamestown Festival Park; 229–2756. Family-oriented, reasonably priced, fast-food service. Hot and cold sandwiches, fried chicken, and fish 'n' chips. Breakfast and lunch served daily. Box lunches available by advance order. Open to 5 P.M.

THINGS TO SEE AND DO

TOURING JAMESTOWN. There is a Visitor Center just past the Entrance Station. From there it is possible to walk to all the sights. Starting with "New Towne," the area where Jamestown expanded about 1620, visitors walk along "Back Street" and other original streets. In this area are the sites of Country House and Governor's House and the homesites of Richard Kemp (builder of one of the first brick houses in America), Henry Hartwell (a founder of William and Mary), Dr. John Pott, and William Pierce (who led the "thrusting out" of Gov. John Harvey in 1635).

Visitors can take in the place that has been fixed by tradition as the point on the James that was the First Landing Site. It was also probably the site of the first fort. The Old Church Tower is the only standing ruin of the seventeenth-century town. It is believed to be part of the first brick church in America (1636). Memorial Church adjoins the tower. This church was built in 1907 by the Colonial Dames of America over the foundations of the original. Within are foundations said to be those of the earlier church. The foundations of a brick building have also been discovered near the river. These are believed to have been those of the First Statehouse.

There is the Tercentenary Monument near the Jamestown Visitor Center, built in 1907 to commemorate the 300th anniversary of the colony's founding. Other monuments include Captain John Smith statue, Pocahontas Monument, and House of Burgesses Monument (listing members of the first representative legislative body).

There is also a Confederate Fort, built in 1861, near the Old Church Tower, one of several Civil War fortifications on the island. Visitors can enjoy a five–mile trail that makes the entire area easily accessible. Finally, visitors can see the Glasshouse, where colonialists first made glass in 1608. There are glass-blowing demonstrations daily.

Jamestown is open to visitors daily from mid-June through Labor Day, 9 to 7; after Labor Day through October and from Apr. till mid-June to 5:30, and Nov. through Mar. till 5. Closed Christmas.

FESTIVAL PARK. The Jamestown Festival Park area was built in 1957 adjacent to Jamestown to commemorate the 300th birthday of the first permanent English settlement in the New World. Its recreation of early seventeenth-century Jamestown includes full-scale replicas of the *Susan Constant, Godspeed,* and *Discovery;* wattle-and-daub buildings in reconstructed James Fort of 1607, and Powhatan's "Indian Village", which has a pottery-making exhibit. The Old World Pavilion presents Virginia's English heritage, while the New World Pavilion traces Virginia's history as a colony and later as a state. Both feature audio-visual displays and costumed guides. A Settlement Celebration commemorates the arrival of the first settlers each year on May 12. For information, call 229–1607.

Exploring Yorktown

The third treasure of American heritage on the 15-mile wide strip of land known as the Virginia Peninsula is Yorktown. Here, in 1781, American independence was won. Yorktown was first settled in 1630 when free land on the south bank of the York was offered those adventurous enough to move out of Jamestown. The Assembly authorized a York River port in 1691 and the town grew quickly, soon becoming a major Colonial shipping center. Its prosperity peaked about 1750 and the port declined when Tidewater Virginia's tobacco trade declined.

Yorktown is most famous as the site of the British surrender in 1781, ending the American Revolution. British commander Cornwallis, after raiding the Virginia countryside almost without resistance, was ordered to establish a port for the winter. The French fleet lying off the capes blocked the British fleet, however, while Washington's troops bottled up the British army on land. The Americans shelled the British from October 9 to October 17, when Cornwallis requested terms. He surrendered two days later while his pipers played "The World Turned Upside Down."

Yorktown today is still an active peninsula community but many surviving and reconstructed Colonial structures affect an air of the eighteenth-century America. Yorktown Battlefield, the third point of the Colonial National Historical Park triangle, surrounds this Virginia town.

PRACTICAL INFORMATION FOR YORKTOWN

Note: The area code for Yorktown is 804.

HOW TO GET THERE. Yorktown is easily accessible by car from Williamsburg, Newport News, or Norfolk. The Colonial Parkway curves east along the York River from Williamsburg, while I-64, then Rte. 238, comes north from Norfolk, and U.S. 17 crosses the York (north–south) close to town and the battlefield.

TOURIST INFORMATION. First-time visitors to Yorktown should stop first at the modern and spacious Yorktown Victory Center. In one entertaining hour, they will experience the entire spectacle of the Revolutionary War and the decisive victory at Yorktown by George Washington and our French allies over Lord Cornwallis. The Center is open daily year-round (except Christmas), 8:30–6, mid-June through Labor Day. Phone 887–1776.

A strikingly realistic film sets the stage for visitors by showing the American Colonies just before the Revolutions. A stunning series of multi-media exhibits and artifacts displays recreate the sights and sounds of the Revolution from Bunker Hill through Saratoga, Trenton, and Valley Forge, and, finally, to Yorktown. A dramatic, award-winning film, *The Road to Yorktown,* concludes the experience.

PLACES TO STAY

MOTELS. Visitors to Yorktown, one of the three major historical sites in Colonial National Historical Park, may very well base themselves in or around Williamsburg. Here is a brief list of "local" Yorktown accommodations:

Duke of York. *Moderate.* 508 Water St. on Rte. 238, 1 block east of the bridge; 898–3232. 57 rooms with balconies. The Duke of York is opposite a beach and overlooks the York River. MC, V.

Thomas Nelson Motel. *Moderate.* 2501 George Washington Highway, U.S. 17, 3 miles south of Yorktown; 898–5436. 26 units with kitchenette. Pool. AE, MC, V.

Tidewater Motel. *Moderate.* 4 miles north of Yorktown (over York River Bridge, Rte. 17); 642–2155 or 642–6604. 33 rooms. Pool. Restaurants nearby. Picnic area. Major credit cards.

Yorktown Motor Lodge. *Inexpensive to Moderate.* 2 miles south of the bridge on U.S. 17; 898–5451. 52 rooms, some with private patios. AE, MC, V.

PLACES TO EAT

Nick's Seafood Pavilion. *Moderate.* Rte. 238 and Water St. at the Bridge; 887–5269. Wide variety of excellent fresh seafood, but also beef and chicken. Open daily 11 A.M.–10 P.M. Closed Christmas. No reservations, so join the queue. Major credit cards.

Duke's Den Dining Lounge. *Inexpensive to Moderate.* 100 Water St., Duke of York Motor Hotel; 898–3232. Modest dining room with superb view of the York River. Breakfast and lunch, 7:30 A.M.–2 P.M.; dinner hours vary with season. V.

THINGS TO SEE AND DO

COLONIAL NATIONAL HISTORICAL PARK. Located on the bluffs above the York River at the eastern end of Colonial Parkway, about 13 miles from Colonial Williamsburg and 23 miles from Jamestown. Access from Colonial Parkway, Rte. 238 (Williamsburg Rd.), or U.S. 17, which spans the York River from Yorktown to Gloucester Point. Battlefield and Encampment tours begin at the National Park Service Visitor Center (extreme eastern terminus of the Parkway), but those touring the *total* area are advised to first visit the Yorktown Victory Center (see the last listing below). There are walking tours and 7-mile and 9-mile loop drives of the Battlefield and Encampment area, respectively. The *Visitor* Center, not to be confused with the Yorktown *Victory* Center, features Revolutionary War artifacts and exhibits, and an outdoor terrace overlooking the Battlefield. For a full appreciation of one of the most stirring events in American history, visit **Moore House,** where the "articles of capitulation" were drafted, and **Surrender Field,** where a defeated British army laid down its arms. Open daily except Christmas. Phone 898–3400.

HISTORIC SITES. In town visitors will discover the *Monument to Alliance and Victory* at the east end of Main Street. It is an elaborately ornamented 95-foot granite column memorializing the American–French alliance in the Revolution.

Swan Tavern, at Main and Ballard streets, is a reconstructed eighteenth-century tavern, now an antique shop. The original was destroyed by a gun powder explosion in 1863. *The York County Courthouse,* across the street from the tavern, was reconstructed in 1955 to resemble the original 1733 courthouse. The town clerk's office has records dating from 1633.

The *Nelson House* at Nelson and Main streets is an original restored mansion built by "Scotch Tom" Nelson in the early 1700s. It was the home of his grandson, Thomas Nelson, Jr., one of the signers of the Declaration of Independence and is an impressive example of Georgian architecture.

Grace Episcopal Church at Church St. was originally built in 1697. It was damaged in 1781 and gutted by fire in 1697; nevertheless, the original 1649 Communion service is still in use.

Visitors should also see the *Virginia Research Center for Archaeology* at the Victory Center. It is presently conducting one of the most ambitious archaeological projects in North America under the York River, just three blocks from the Victory Center. There lies one of General Cornwallis's ships, sunk during the Battle of Yorktown. Ultimately, a specially constructed pier will allow visitors to walk from the shore to watch divers as they carefully excavate the hull and bring its contents to the center. The artifacts will be placed on exhibit in the *Gallery of the American Revolution* at the Victory Center. The gallery already offers a growing collection that includes the table used by Cornwallis on this southern campaign in America, along with art works and loaned exhibits.

Waterman's Museum. Housed in a Gloucester County manor house, barged to Yorktown's waterfront, the museum is dedicated to the men and women who have worked Virginia's waterways for more than three centuries. For details, write Box 631, Yorktown, VA 23690. Phone 898–3180.

Exploring Hampton and Newport News

Hampton claims to be the oldest English-settled community in the United States. (Jamestown is a park, not a town.) The settlement began in 1610 at a place called Kecoughtan with the building of two stockades as protection against the Kecoughtan Indians. In the late eighteenth century, Hamptonians were harassed by pirates until the notorious "Blackbeard" was killed by Captain Henry Maynard. Piracy came to an end here when Blackbeard's pirates were jailed in Williamsburg.

Hampton was shelled in the Revolution, burned by the British in the War of 1812, and burned again by its own citizens in 1861 to prevent occupation by Union forces. Just five houses survived the last conflagration. Commercial fishing and defense are now the major industries.

Newport News, adjacent to Hampton and closer to Williamsburg, is one of three cities that make up the Port of Hampton Roads. The third is Norfolk. Settled in 1619, Newport News has the world's largest shipbuilding company, the Newport News Shipbuilding Company, which employs 25,000 workers. Hampton Roads, 14 miles long and 40 feet deep, is formed by the James, York, Elizabeth, and Nansemond Rivers as they pass into the Chesapeake Bay. It is one of the world's finest natural harbors. It sits at the inland end of the historic Virginia Peninsula.

PRACTICAL INFORMATION FOR HAMPTON AND NEWPORT NEWS

Note: The area code for Hampton and Newport News is 804.

PLACES TO STAY

HOTELS AND MOTELS. Visitors to Colonial National Park sometimes find it advantageous to seek accommodations in Hampton or Newport News. The two cities, across Hampton Roads from Norfolk, are convenient to most of the peninsula's Colonial sites and are easily accessible from I-64, Norfolk to Richmond. In general, accommodations in the area may be slightly less expensive than those closer to Colonial Williamsburg or to the south in Norfolk.

Hampton

Radisson. *Expensive.* 700 Settlers Landing; 727–9700. 174 rooms in a new 9-story hotel. Valet parking, pool, restaurant, bar, room service, and concierge. Shopping arcade. Airport transportation. All major credit cards.

Sheraton Inn—Coliseum. *Moderate to Expensive.* 1215 W. Mercury Blvd., Exit 8 off I-64; 838–5011. 187 rooms in an 8-story inn. Indoor pool and cafe-bar with entertainment. Meeting rooms. Transportation to terminals. Suites in *Deluxe* category. Major credit cards.

Holiday Inn. *Moderate.* 1815 W. Mercury Blvd., Exit 8 off I-64; 838–0200. 325 rooms in a two-story inn. Pool, bar, and room service. Some suites and meeting rooms. Game room. Golf privileges. Major credit cards.

Newport News

Holiday Inn. *Expensive.* 6128 Jefferson Ave.; 826–4500. 162 rooms in a 5-story inn. Playground and restaurant. Room service. Bar entertainment. Major credit cards.

Ramada Inn. *Moderate.* 950 J. Clyde Morris Blvd., Jct. U.S. 17, I-64; 599–4460. 180 rooms with lighted tennis, 24–hour restaurant. AE, CB, DC, MC, V.

Econo Lodge. *Inexpensive.* 15237 Warwick Blvd.; 874–9244. 48 rooms. TV and sundries. AE, MC, V.

Regency Inn Motel. *Inexpensive.* 13700 Warwick Blvd.; 874–4100. 48 rooms. Major credit cards.

PLACES TO EAT

Port Arthur. *Moderate to Expensive.* 11137 Warwick Blvd., Newport News; 599–6474. Chinese-American menu, lunch and dinner. Bar and wine list. Closed Thanksgiving and Christmas. Weekend guitarist. Most major credit cards.

Seafood House at Wharton's Wharf. *Inexpensive to Moderate.* 915 Jefferson Ave., Newport News; 380–5408. Seafood in a nautical setting, overlooking the harbor and adjacent to the wharf. Lunch and dinner. Bar. MC, V.

THINGS TO SEE AND DO

Hampton

HISTORIC SITES. In Hampton, *Hampton Monument,* ½ mile south on the grounds of the VA Medical Center, marks the approximate spot it is believed the first settlers landed in 1607. *St. John's Church and Parish Museum* on W. Queen's Way and Court St. dates to 1728. Its Bible dates to 1599.

Hampton Institute, E. end of Queen St., was founded in 1866 by Union General Samuel Champion, chief of the Freedman's Bureau, to prepare the youth of the South, regardless of color, for the work of organizing school teaching in the South. Many blacks and Indians were educated here. Today, it is Virginia's only coeducational, nondenominational private four-year college. *Ft. Monroe Casemate Museum.* This museum is located at Ft. Monroe, a National Historic Landmark on the shore at Hampton Roads. Phone 727–3973 for details.

SPECIAL-INTEREST TOURS. NASA has a major presence in Virginia; its *Langley Research Center* is three miles north of Hampton on VA 134. It offers a self-guided tour of the history of flights, aeronautics research, and space exploration. Space artifacts include moon rock, the Apollo Command Module, and a space suit worn on the moon. Phone 865–2855.

The Big Bethel Battlefield commemorates the first "regular" battle of the Civil War. *The Syms-Eaton Museum* at 418 W. Mercury Blvd. exhibits Hampton's history. Phone 727–6248. *The Kecoughton Indian Village* at 418 W. Mercury Blvd. is a reproduction of an early Indian village. Phone 727–6248. *Bluebird Gap Farm* at 60 Pine Chapel Rd. is a 15-acre farm with a barnyard zoo, indigenous wildlife, including black bears, deer, wolves, and antique and modern farm equipment. It offers picnic and playgrounds. Phone 727–6347. *Aerospace Park,* at 413 Mercury Blvd., has jet aircraft and missile exhibits. (Open daily.) Phone 727–6108. The park is adjacent to Hampton Tourist Information Center, same telephone. *Fort Monroe,* three miles southeast of Hampton, near I-64, stands on the site of a 1609 Stockade. The *Casemate Museum* is at the fort, which was completed about 1834. Free. Closed major holidays. Phone 727–3973.

BEACHES. *Buckroe Beach* on VA 351 offers swimming, boating, and fishing on the Chesapeake Bay. It has a 12-acre amusement park.

TOURING INFORMATION. Hampton Visitors Center, Settlers Landing Rd. and Eaton St., 727–6108. Brochures and maps are available. Also cruises of Hampton Roads Harbor, Fort Wool, and Norfolk Naval Station. Open daily except major holidays, 9 A.M.–5 P.M.

Newport News

MUSEUMS. The premier attraction in Newport News is the *Mariners Museum* at the junction of U.S. 60 and Clyde Morris Blvd. 595–0368. It features a collection of international scope devoted to maritime history in the broadest sense, including inland navigation. Exhibits include the Hall of Steamships, Chesapeake Bay Gallery, Gibbs Gallery, small craft, ships' carvings, ship models, Crabtree Collection of Miniature Ships, marine decorative arts, marine paintings, seapower, and temporary special exhibits. There is a research library and a 550-acre park with a 167-acre fishing lake and picnic area.

Since the beginning of time, the sea has captured the imagination of men. The many who were inspired to explore her waters could not have done so were it not for the craftsmen who built their vessels. It is to these craftsmen that the Mariners Museum is dedicated.

The War Memorial Museum of Virginia at 9285 Warwick Blvd. offers a comprehensive display of more than 30,000 artifacts, including weapons, uniforms, vehicles, posters, insignia, and accoutrements relating to every major American military involvement from the Revolution to Vietnam. Phone 247–8523.

Virginia Living Museum. 524 J. Clyde Morris Blvd.; 595–1900. Living animals and plants in natural outdoor habitats. Also indoor exhibits, aquariums, planetarium, natural history, and aviary. Open Mon.–Sat., 9 A.M.–5 P.M.; Sun 1–5 P.M.; Thur. evening, 7–9.

Fort Eustis. Headquarters of U.S. Army Transportation Center, the fort is located on Mulberry Island, northwest section of the city. The *Army Transportation Museum* is located here. Open daily except Christmas and Jan. 1. Free. Phone 878–1109.

HARBOR CRUISE. *Wharton's Wharf Harbor Cruise* aboard the *American Patriot* leaves the boat harbor, at the south end of Jefferson Ave. at 12th Street, for a two-hour narrated cruise on Hampton Roads, the world's largest natural harbor. Also Intercoastal Waterway and evening cruises. Apr.–Oct. Call 245–1533 for prices and schedules.

OTHER ATTRACTIONS. *Peninsula Nature and Science Center,* at 524 J. Clyde Morris Blvd., in Deer Park, offers exhibits on natural science. Open daily; call 599–6800. Finally, the *Peninsula Fine Arts Center* on Museum Drive exhibits the Tidewater's and Virginia's artists and craftsmen. Closed Mon. and holidays. Call 596–8175. Free.

PARK. *Newport News Park,* more than 8,000 acres located a mile north of Rtes. 105 and 143, has canoes, paddleboats and rental boats, nature trails and rental bikes, fresh-water fishing and golf, and supervised campsites. Open year round. Call 877–5381 for park information, or Virginia Peninsula Tourism Council, 838–4184, for general area information.

Exploring James River Plantations

Historic plantations dot the banks of the James River from Williamsburg to Richmond. Three of the most important along Rte. 5 begin with *Sherwood Forest,* 20 miles from Williamsburg, the plantation home of John Tyler, tenth president of the United States. It was also owned by William Henry Harrison, the ninth president. This is the longest frame house in America, the same length as a football field. Still in the Tyler family, it includes magnificent furnishings and stands on 12 acres of grounds with 80 varieties of trees. Sherwood Forest dates from 1730.

Berkeley, three miles from Shirley (below), has no peer among the James River plantations as a center of historic interest. It is a beautifully restored example of the mansions that graced Virginia's "Golden Age." This was the site of what Virginians say was the first official Thanksgiving in 1619. Berkeley was also the birthplace of Benjamin Harrison, a signer of the Declaration of Independence, and William Henry Harrison, the ninth president. It was the ancestral home of President Benjamin Harrison and the headquarters for General McClellan. "Taps" was written there in 1862. It was built in 1726, and today, it is in outstanding condition with exceptionally fine period antiques.

Finally, *Shirley,* (1723) 20 miles from Richmond, has no rival in Queen Anne architectural style. A complete set of eighteenth-century brick buildings form a Queen Anne forecourt, unique in this country. The mansion, on the banks of the James River, has been the home of the Carters since 1723. The original family portraits, silver, furnishings, superb paneling, and carved walnut staircase are there to see. Shirley was the home of Anne Hill Carter, mother of Robert E. Lee, and is owned and operated by the ninth generation of Carters.

Plantations that may be visited by the public are well marked along Rte. 5, a pleasant 51-mile drive along the James River between Williamsburg and Richmond. For information, fees, and visiting times, phone Sherwood Forest (829–5377) or Shirley (795–2385). There are fees for these and other plantation tours. (See also **Carter's Grove** in the Williamsburg section, above.)

TOURING INFORMATION. For details and advance information about the Peninsula, call or write: Virginia Peninsula Tourism & Conference Bureau Center, Patrick Henry International Airport, Newport News 23602, (800) 558–1818 outside Virginia, or (800) 237–5606; Hampton Dept. of Conventions & Tourism, 710 Settlers Landing Rd., Hampton, VA 23669, (804) 727–6108; or Williamsburg Area Tourism & Conference Bureau, Drawer GB, Williamsburg, VA 23187, (804) 253–0192.

THE PIEDMONT

by
PATRICIA and EDGAR CHEATHAM

Soon after Tidewater plantations and townsites were developed, demands for new land became apparent as Virginia's Colonial population increased. Settlements then advanced into the Piedmont province lying south of the James River, Richmond, and Charlottesville to the North Carolina border, thence westward to Lynchburg, Chatham, and Danville. Undulating landscapes, forests, meadows, and riversides in this south-central region often possess a quiet, mellow beauty, immensely comforting and appealing. Thomas Jefferson built his stately Monticello mansion atop a "little mountain" near Charlottesville. And his political adversary, Patrick Henry, chose to spend his last years in a modest frame dwelling at Red Hill in the vicinity of Lynchburg. Some folks brought Tidewater grace and manners with them; others arrived with an abiding sense of independence.

Thus the Piedmont province has become Virginia's heartland. Here a vivid past and vibrant present seem to coexist harmoniously. A network of busy interstate highways, convenient federal and state routes, some lesser traveled byways, and a few watercourses offer numerous opportunities to explore the Old Dominion's rich and rewarding Piedmont. Between Charlottesville and Richmond,

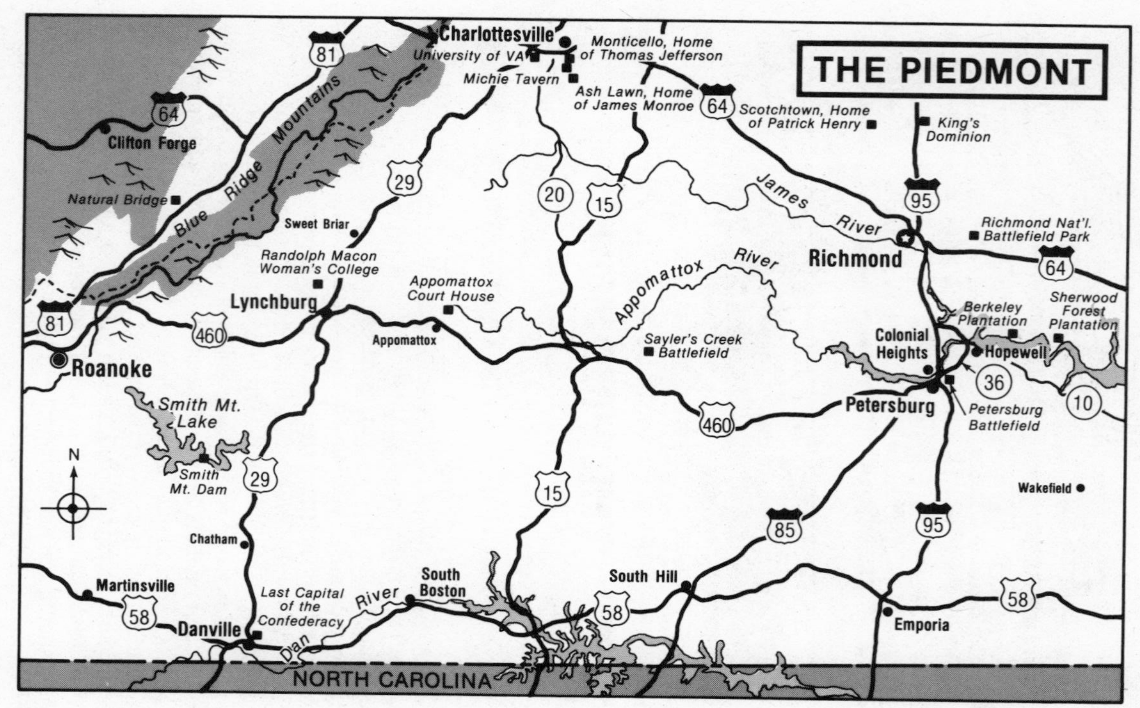
THE PIEDMONT
Charlottesville
University of VA
Monticello, Home of Thomas Jefferson
Michie Tavern
Ash Lawn, Home of James Monroe
Scotchtown, Home of Patrick Henry
King's Dominion
Clifton Forge
Blue Ridge Mountains
Natural Bridge
Sweet Briar
Randolph Macon Woman's College
Appomattox Court House
James River
Richmond
Richmond Nat'l. Battlefield Park
Appomattox River
Lynchburg
Appomattox
Sayler's Creek Battlefield
Berkeley Plantation
Sherwood Forest Plantation
Colonial Heights
Hopewell
Roanoke
Petersburg
Petersburg Battlefield
Smith Mt. Lake
Smith Mt. Dam
N
Wakefield
Chatham
Martinsville
Last Capital of the Confederacy
Dan River
South Boston
South Hill
Emporia
Danville
NORTH CAROLINA

I-64 is the northern limit of the heartland. Northward from the Tar Heel State, I-95 and I-85 converge at Petersburg, from which VA 36 then leads eastward about eight miles to Hopewell and its historic district at City Point. Here, in 1613, a covey of colonists founded the second oldest permanent English settlement in Virginia (Jamestown came first) atop tall bluffs overlooking the confluence of the James and Appomattox rivers, an ideal location for a deep-water inland harbor.

Other remnants from these earliest days of English settlement linger along the southern shore of the James River at sites easily reached on side roads branching off VA 10. Founded in 1618 on land granted to Governor George Yeardley and named for his wife's family in Norfolk, England, Flowerdew Hundred survived Indian attacks, became a prosperous tobacco plantation, but declined and all but disappeared in later years. Since 1971 it has been an archaeological treasure trove, yielding thousands of artifacts from Indian, Colonial, and Civil War times. A short distance away, the Rolfe–Warren House, built in 1652, stands on land that powerful Indian chief Powhatan presented as a wedding gift in 1614, when his daughter Pocahontas married John Rolfe, the young English colonist who pioneered cultivation of tobacco as a profitable staple. And at nearby Chippokes Plantation State Park, vintage buildings stand on a continuously working farm dating from the 1600s.

Civil War

Some of the most dramatic events in the last agonizing months of the Civil War occurred in the Piedmont. The Union established a massive arsenal and supply depot at City Point, where General Ulysses S. Grant also had his headquarters. From here supplies were sent to troops that lay siege to Petersburg for over 900 days and finally forced General Robert E. Lee's Army of Northern Virginia to move toward the west. By early April 1865, his army diminished, disheartened, and virtually surrounded, Lee sought terms of surrender from Grant. On April 9, the two generals met at McLean House in the remote town of Appomattox Court House and reached a gentlemen's agreement that effectively ended the bitter conflict.

During the years after the Civil War, amid an arduous national reunification, economic and cultural recovery came about slowly in the Virginia heartland. Petersburg, a flourishing antebellum manufacturing and social center, suffered severely during the long wartime siege. Today, though, an influx of diversified industries, commerce, business enterprises, increasing tourism, and continuing restorations in the Historic District have brought about considerable regional prosperity.

Appomattox Today

Though historically revered, the little village of Appomattox Court House languished and almost died. Since no bloody battle was fought there the states declined to construct lavish monuments as they had at various carnage-soaked Civil War sites. The court house burned in 1892 and the following year McLean House was dismantled with intent of reconstructing it as a Civil War Museum in Washington,D.C. This never materialized and the piles of timber and bricks disintegrated. By the 1930s, the stunning restoration of Colonial Williamsburg inspired Congress in 1935 to authorize a similar small-scale effort at Appomattox Court House. Construction accelerated after World War II and on April 6, 1954, the site was officially designated Appomattox Court House National Historical Park. It appears today much as it did in 1865.

At the western perimeter of Virginia's heartland, U.S. 29, a four-lane divided route, often resembles a pleasant parkway as it passes through scenically beautiful countryside. Situated on the southern end of the highway, Danville, a major textile and tobacco marketing center, sprawls among low-lying hills beside the Dan River. Other industries range from manufacturing of shoes and furniture to glass and chemicals. Confederate President Jefferson Davis held his last cabinet meeting here at the time of Lee's surrender and somehow seemed strangely oblivious to the hopelessness of the southern cause.

Lynchburg, about 67 miles north along U.S. 29, stands on high bluffs overlooking the James River. This remarkably diverse city dates from 1786 and has flourished as an industrial, commercial, and educational center. Lynchburg is justifiably proud of its notable accomplishments in the fine and performing arts.

Northward, 69 miles via U.S. 29, Charlottesville nestles in the northwestern corner of the heartland. Undeniably among the Old Dominion's loveliest cities, it has an eloquently restored downtown Historic District. The aura of Mr. Jefferson's restrained good taste is reflected in his Monticello home, the stately Rotunda and classic Student Ranges at the University of Virginia. For his friend James Monroe he designed Ash Lawn, a surprisingly simple home beautifully restored with original family furnishings. Nearby, Historic Michie Tavern, originally built on land granted to Patrick Henry's father, was a favorite partying place for such luminaries as Jefferson, Madison, Monroe, and Lafayette. During a ball at the Tavern, Jefferson caught his eldest daughter Martha participating in a scandalous new dance called the waltz. Outraged, he immediately dispatched his errant offspring back to Monticello where she was ignominiously sent to bed.

Exploring the Piedmont

Appomattox

Following the Civil War, the present-day town of Appomattox, built around a station on the Norfolk and Western Railroad, attracted a considerable population. When the original court house, three miles north, burned in 1892, the county seat was moved to the new community, which lies astride U.S. Highway 460. During the second weekend in October, the annual Historic Appomattox Railroad Festival, centered at the N&W Depot and along Main Street, highlights such lively happenings as a parade, street dancing, 10K (kilometer) foot race, karate match, chain saw competition, firemen's drills, helicopter rides, and fireworks. There's also good country cooking at the Depot, one-of-a-kind arts and crafts, an antique show, exhibitions, and music from the "Good Ole Days."

Charlottesville

Charlottesville, at the foot of the scenic Blue Ridge Mountains, reflects a singular statesman's devotion to his homeland. Describing the panoramic vistas from its gently rolling hills, Thomas Jefferson wrote, "These mountains are the Eden of the United States." Here Thomas Jefferson's Virginia remains alive and well.

To visit Charlottesville is to be caught up in the best of eighteenth-century tradition blended with twentieth-century buoyancy. Several annual events heighten the experience. They include Dogwood Festival, mid-April; Garden Week, late April; Fourth of July celebrations, with picnics, band concerts, carnivals, fireworks; Court Days in Old Charlottesville, early October; Yuletide Traditions celebrations, December; and First Night/Virginia, New Year's Eve, in the Historic Downtown District.

Danville

Gently rolling meadowlands and cattle-dappled hillsides surround Danville and a city limits sign welcomes visitors to the "World's Best Tobacco Market." The handsome city on the Dan River is home to the world's largest single-unit textile mill named, fittingly, Dan River Mills. It is also a major southside Virginia educational center. Just outside town are Chatham Hall and Hargrave Military Academy.

An aura of history pervades the city's tranquil, leafy streets. Here was the last capital of the Confederacy, home (April 3–10, 1865) to President Jefferson Davis and his cabinet after Richmond was evacuated. Famed Lady Astor, first female member of the British

Parliament, was born Nancy Langhorne in Danville in 1879. Her cottage birthplace, privately owned, stands at 117 Broad Street.

Visitors are welcome to attend seasonal tobacco auctions in nine warehouses of the nation's second largest tobacco sale center, mid-August–November. The World Tobacco Auctioneering Championship is a popular event of the annual four-day early October Harvest Jubilee; also offered are live family entertainment, a farm equipment show, youth activities, a shrimp fest, clogging, fireworks, and a harvest ball.

Lynchburg

Lynchburg, central Virginia's cultural and industrial capital, sits proudly on its seven hills overlooking the scenic James River Valley. It is an educational center, home to five liberal arts colleges including one of the South's best known—Randolph Macon Woman's College. Twelve miles north at Amherst is Sweet Briar, another renowned women's liberal arts college.

Dotted with handsome Victorian-era homes—many extensively restored—the downtown area has also undergone a $40-million revitalization in the central business district.

Founded as a ferry crossing by John Lynch, the city grew steadily throughout the seventeenth century. During the Civil War it was second only to Richmond as an ammunition supply center. In the war's latter days, Confederate General Jubal A. Early saved Lynchburg from destruction by running empty rail cars continuously along the tracks, convincing Union forces that heavy reinforcements were arriving.

A year-long series of events during 1986 will commemorate Lynchburg's Bicentennial. A high spot, planned to become an annual happening, is *Thomas Jefferson's Tomatoe Faire,* slated August 1–3, with stage shows, exhibits, street entertainers, period symphonic and choral music, "tomatoe" cooking, and recipe contests. It was at Lynchburg, legend tells, that Jefferson, a frequent visitor, became the first person to eat a "love apple" (tomato), which was at that time considered poisonous. Other annual events include Lynchburg Garden Day, third Tuesday in April, with distinctive homes and gardens open to visitors, and Kaleidoscope, a gala fall festival (September 13–28, 1986) with art, music, concerts, food, crafts, and the Virginia Ten Miler, one of the South's best known road races.

Petersburg

Founded as Fort Henry, a 1645 frontier fort and trading post, Petersburg reached full flower in the 1850s. Foundaries thrived, as did the cotton and tobacco trade. Commercial success stimulated cultural and educational vibrance.

Likely no southern city was more touched by the Civil War's last ravages. In the summer of 1864, General Robert E. Lee's struggle against General Ulysses S. Grant was played out as Petersburg lay under siege for 10 months. Finally, in April 1865, Lee's supply routes were cut and he was forced to evacuate, surrendering a week later at Appomattox Court House.

Today, there is a heartening effort to restore Olde Towne Petersburg, where railroad buildings and warehouses, many dating from 1815, are being turned into apartments, shops, antique stores, and cafes. Other major annual events include Nostalgiafest Celebration, first full weekend in October, Olde Towne, bluegrass, jazz, gymnastics, choirs, puppetry, symphony performances, historic homes tour; An Old Towne Christmas, first Friday in December; Christmas Homes Tour, Saturday before Christmas; Historic Garden Week, last full week in April.

PRACTICAL INFORMATION FOR THE PIEDMONT

Note: The area code for the Piedmont is 804.

PLACES TO STAY

HOTELS AND MOTELS. Accommodations in Virginia's Piedmont heartland span a wide range of costs and lodging amenities. Here are general categories based on room rates for double occupancy: *Deluxe,* $60 and up; *Expensive,* $50–$60; *Moderate,* $40–$50; and *Inexpensive,* below $40. Rates are subject to change.

Appomattox

Traveler's Inn Motel. *Inexpensive.* On U.S. 460, near junction with VA 24; 352–7451. Color TV, pool, playground, restaurant nearby, convenient to Appomattox Court House National Historical Park. Advance reservations advised during peak summer vacation season. 20 rooms. AE, MC, V.

Charlottesville

Boar's Head Inn. *Deluxe.* U.S. 250 west, 2 miles from junction U.S. 29, on Ivy Rd.; 296–2181. Color TV, 3 pools, health club, driving range, putting green, golf-tennis privileges, lawn games, horseback riding stable nearby, bicycles, lounge, entertainment, dancing, restaurants. Full-scale vacation and conference center in a beautiful rural residential setting. 175 rooms. AE, CB, DC, MC, V.

Wintergreen Resort. *Deluxe.* West of Charlotte on U.S. 250, VA 6 and VA 151S; 325–2200. 325 units, with full mountain-resort facilities. Excellent restaurant, serving breakfast, lunch and dinner. Reservations for dinner. Three pools, health club, and shops. AE, MC, V.

Omni International Hotel. *Deluxe.* 235 W. Main St. in Downtown Historic Charlottesville; 971–5500. Color TV, indoor-outdoor pool, health club, saunas, whirlpool, 65-foot atrium lobby, multi-level restaurant, bi-level cocktail lounge, lobby lounge. 209 rooms. AE, CB, DC, MC, V.

English Inn of Charlottesville. *Expensive.* U.S. 29 N. and U.S. 250 By-pass at 2000 Morton Dr.; 971–9900. Color TV, indoor pool, exercise room, sauna, tennis, squash, rental bicycles, country breakfast included in lodging, lounge, restaurant. 90 rooms and 21 suites. AE, CB, DC, MC, V.

University Hilton—Charlottesville. *Expensive.* 2350 Seminole Trail; 973–2121. 252 rooms, 4 suites, with 2 restaurants, 2 lounges, and indoor/outdoor pool. The hotel overlooks the Rivanna River. Convention facilities. Major credit cards.

Holiday Inn South. *Moderate to Expensive.* Junction I–64 and 5th St., Exit 23; 977–5100. Color TV, in-room movies, pool, tennis, golf privileges at Lake Monticello Golf Club, home of PGA Virginia Open; lounge, restaurant. 130 rooms. AE, DC, MC, V.

Howard Johnson's Motor Lodge. *Moderate to Expensive.* On U.S. 250 Business route, 13th and West Main sts.; 296–8121. Color TV, pool, parking garage, 24-hour restaurant, lounge. 126 rooms. AE, DC, MC, V.

Best Western Cavalier Inn. *Moderate.* Located at the junction of U.S. (Bus.) 29 and 250; 296–8111. 118 rooms in a five-story motor hotel. Restaurant, bar, pool, and room service. Opposite University of Virginia. Major credit cards.

Best Western Mount Vernon. *Moderate.* Junction U.S. 29 and 250 By-pass; 296–5501. Color TV, pool, some rooms in French Provincial decor, others in contemporary style, restaurant adjacent. AE, DC, MC, V.

Quality Inn. *Moderate.* Junction U.S. 250 and I–64, Exit 25; 977–3300. 100 rooms. Color TV, miniature golf, pool, lounge, entertainment, restaurant. AE, DC, MC, V.

Ramada Inn. *Moderate.* 1901 Emmet St., U.S. 29N, with access to U.S. 250 E & W; 977–7700. Restaurant and heated pool. 179 rooms. Major credit cards.

University Lodge Motel. *Inexpensive.* U.S. 29 N. and U.S. 250 Business route; 293–5141. Color TV, restaurant adjacent. 40 rooms. AE, CB, DC, MC, V.

For information about bed-and-breakfast accommodations—many in historic homes and estate cottages—contact Guesthouse Bed & Breakfast, Inc. Reservation Service, Box 5737, Charlottesville, VA 22905; 979–7264 or 979–8327; call between 12 noon and 5 P.M. weekdays.

Danville

Holiday Inn. *Moderate.* 2500 Riverside Dr., On U.S. 58, just east of junction with U.S. 29; 793–2731. Heated pool, playground, whirlpool, color TV, lounge, restaurant. 165 rooms. AE, DC, MC, V.

Howard Johnson's Motor Lodge. *Moderate.* 100 Tower Dr., On U.S. 58 west of U.S. 29; 793–2000. Color TV, pool, lounge, restaurant. 120 rooms. AE, DC, MC, V.

Econo-Lodge. *Inexpensive.* U.S. 20 N. at 1390 Piney Forest Rd.; 797–4322. Color TV, in-room movies, phones. 48 rooms. AE, MC, V.

Emporia

Holiday Inn. *Moderate.* Junction I–85 and U.S. 58 E., Exit 3A; 634–4191. Color TV, pool, lounge, entertainment, restaurant, nonsmoking rooms. 144 rooms. AE, CB, DC, MC, V.

Days Inn. *Inexpensive.* On U.S. 58 at junction with I–95; 634–9481. Color TV, pool, playground, restaurant. 121 rooms. AE, DC, MC, V.

Hampton Inn. *Inexpensive.* I–95 and U.S.58; 634–9200. 155 rooms. Shoney's Restaurant adjacent. Pool and free Continental breakfast. Major credit cards.

Quality Inn Belco. *Inexpensive.* U.S. 301 and I–95, Exit 2; 634–4181. Color TV, in-room movies; pool, playground, lounge, restaurant. 42 rooms. AE, CB, DC, MC, V.

Lynchburg

Hilton Lynchburg Hotel. *Expensive to Deluxe.* 2900 Candler's Mountain Rd.; 237–6333. Sauna, indoor pool, color TV, lounge, restaurant. 168 rooms. AE, CB, DC, MC, V.

Radisson Hotel. *Expensive.* 601 Main St., in downtown business district; 528–2500. Outdoor pool, inside sun terrace with whirlpool, color TV, restaurant, lounge. 243 rooms. AE, CB, DC, MC, V.

Days Inn. *Moderate.* U.S. 29 Expressway at 3320 Candler's Mountain Rd.; 847–8655. Pool, playground, color TV, 24-hour restaurant, gift shop, across from River Ridge Mall shopping center. 131 rooms. AE, DC, MC, V.

Holiday Inn. *Moderate.* U.S. 29 South Expressway at Odd Fellows Rd.; 847–4424. Pool, color TV, lounge, restaurant. 260 rooms, some suites. AE, CB, DC, MC, V.

Sheraton Inn. *Moderate.* U.S. 29 South at Odd Fellows Rd.; 847–9041. Pool, color TV, lounge, restaurant. 124 rooms, 4 suites. AE, CB, DC, MC, V.

Howard Johnson's Motor Lodge. *Inexpensive to Moderate.* Off U.S. 29 North Expressway; 845–7041. Pool, color TV, restaurant. 72 rooms, some with patios and balconies. AE, CB, DC, MC, V.

Travel Inn. *Inexpensive.* 1500 E. Main St.; 845–5975. Pool, game room, color TV, complimentary coffee, lounge, restaurant. 120 rooms. AE, CB, DC, MC, V.

For information about bed-and-breakfast accommodations in Lynchburg and vicinity, contact The McAlisters, Sojourners Bed & Breakfast, 3609 Tanglewood Lane, Lynchburg, VA 24503; 384–1655; call before 10 A.M. or after 6 P.M. Mon.–Sat., or all day Sun.

Petersburg

Best Western of Petersburg. *Moderate.* Off I–85 at Washington St.; 733–1776. 124 rooms. Pool, playground, color TV, in-room movies, lounge, restaurant. AE, CB, DC, MC, V.

Camara Inn. *Moderate.* Off I–95 on Crater Rd.; 861–3930. 138 rooms. Pool, color TV, restaurant. AE, MC, V.

Holiday Inn I–85 North. *Moderate.* I–95 at Exit 3, Wythe St., and Washington St.; 733–0730. Pool, color TV, lounge, restaurant, convenient to Ft. Lee. 226 rooms. AE, CB, DC, MC, V.

Holiday Inn South. *Moderate.* I–95 at VA 35-U.S. 301-Courtland Exit 12; 733–1152. Pool, playground, color TV, lounge, restaurant. 112 rooms. AE, CB, DC, MC, V.

Howard Johnson's Motor Lodge. *Moderate.* 530 E. Washington St., Exit 3, Wythe, I–95; 732–5950. Pool, color TV, in-room movies, lounge, restaurant. 113 rooms. AE, CB, DC, MC, V.

Ramada Inn. *Moderate.* East of I–95 Exit 3; 733–0000. Color TV, pool, lounge with entertainment, beauty salon, gift shop, restaurant. 200 units, some suites. AE, CB, DC, MC, V.

Comfort Inn West. *Inexpensive to Moderate.* I–95 at U.S. 301 N.; 732–2000. 98 rooms. Pool, color TV, in-room movies, playground, jacuzzi. Lounge and restaurant nearby. AE, CB, DC, MC, V.

Quality Inn—Steven Kent. *Inexpensive to Moderate.* I–95 and U.S. 301, Exit 13; 733–0600. Color TV, Olympic pool, game room, kiddieland, tennis, fitness course, putting green, shuffleboard, gift shop, lounge, coffee shop, restaurant. 138 rooms. AE, CB, DC, MC, V.

Econo Lodge-South. *Inexpensive.* I–95 and VA 35, Courtland Exit; 862–2717. Color TV, in-room movies, pool, lounge, restaurant. 96 rooms. AE, MC, V.

South Hill

Holiday Inn. *Moderate.* Junction U.S. 58 and I–85, Exit 58 South Hill; 447–3123. Color TV, pool, game room, lounge, entertainment, restaurant. 152 rooms. AE, CB, DC, MC, V.

Econo Lodge. *Inexpensive.* 623 E. Atlantic St., east of town at U.S.58 and I–85; 447–7116. 53 rooms, with a restaurant.

Suffolk

Econo Lodge. *Inexpensive.* 1017 N. Main St., U.S. 460; 539–3451. 80 rooms, some small suites.

Wakefield, Sussex County

Wakefield Inn. *Inexpensive to Moderate.* On U.S. 460, 2 blocks north of town; 899–3841. Color TV, 10 guest rooms, lounge with entertainment, restaurant. MC, V.

CAMPGROUNDS. Piedmont campgrounds offer seasonal or year-round facilities as indicated. Any rates noted are approximate. Check with individual property for up-date rates and any seasonal changes. Inquire also about pets. Reservations are advised, especially during peak summer vacation season. For a keyed map/brochure of Virginia campsites, contact The Virginia Travel Council, Box 15067, Richmond, VA 23227.

Charlottesville

Cambrae Lodge KOA. On VA 708 between U.S. 20 and VA 20 S.; 296–9881. Open Mar. 15–Nov. 15. 90 sites. Reservations accepted. Outdoor pool, store. MC, V.

Lake Reynovia. 1770 Avon St. Extended (VA 742); 296–1910. 100 sites. Open Apr. 5–Oct. 31. Reservations accepted in season. Lake swimming, snack bar during summer. No credit cards.

Charlottesville's Jellystone Park. Half a mile west of I–64 on U.S. 250, Crozet Exit, 13 miles west of Charlottesville, and seven miles east of Skyline Dr.; (703) 456–6409. 90 sites. Open year-round. Reservations accepted.

South Hill

Americamps Lake Gaston. I–95 Exit 1, 5 miles east on VA 903; (804) 636–2668. Open year-round. 245 sites. Reservations accepted.

PLACES TO EAT

RESTAURANTS. Piedmont Virginia's friendly downhome ambience is reflected in hearty southern cooking. Prices, even the most elegant establishments, are often surprisingly modest. Those listed accept at least two major credit cards (MC, V). Area code: 804. Estimated costs are per person, excluding wine, cocktails, tips. *Expensive,* $15–$25; *Moderate,* $7–$15; and *Inexpensive,* under $7.

Charlottesville

Old Mill Room. *Moderate to Expensive.* The Boars Head Inn, Rte. 250 W., 1 mile west of jct. U.S. 29 & 250 Bypass; 296–2181. Breakfast, lunch, Continental and American dinner specialties. Child's plates, lavish Sunday brunch. Handsomely furnished in Jeffersonian decor. Reservations suggested, jacket required. AE, CB, DC, MC, V.

Aberdeen Barn. *Moderate to Expensive.* 2018 Holiday Dr.; 296–4630. Seafood and beef, with a bar and wine list. Pleasing decor, with an open charcoal hearth. AE, MC, DC, V.

C & O Restaurant. *Moderate to Expensive.* 515 E. Water St.; Exit VA 20N off I–64; 971–7044. Typically nouvelle French-American, the C & O closes for late-Aug. holidays. Jackets required for dinner upstairs. A bar and a decent wine cellar. AE, MC, V.

Le Snail. *Moderate to Expensive.* 320 W. Main St.; 295–4456. Fine dining by candlelight in serene ambience of beautifully restored vintage home; white linen, gracious service. Continental menu. Chef owned. Reservations, jacket requested. AE, CB, DC, MC, V.

Historic Michie Tavern. *Moderate.* VA 53, Monticello Mountain, conveniently located en route to Monticello; 977–1234. Colonial fried chicken, black-eyed peas, green bean salad, homemade biscuits, apple cobbler, local wines, in 200-year-old tavern. Luncheon only, buffet service. No credit cards.

The Ivy Inn. *Moderate.* 2244 Old Ivy Rd.; 977–1222. Ivy Inn seafood kettle and home baking are specialties in handsomely restored historic home. Closed Sun., also serves lunch Tues.-Fri. MC, V.

Lord Hardwick's. *Moderate.* 1248 Emmet St.; 295–6668. Casual but full-service dining, featuring steak, seafood, and pub sandwiches. Open daily, noon on Sun. MC, V.

Ken Johnson Cafeteria. *Inexpensive.* Barrack Rd. Shopping Center; 293–9324. Home-style cooking, served cafeteria style. Open daily, lunch and dinner. MC, V.

Danville

Baron's Restaurant. *Moderate to Expensive.* 671 Woodlawn Dr.; 822–0120. 31 entrees—lamb, veal, beef, and seafood—in an elegant woodland setting. Seating for 85; reservations recommended. Dinner only after 6; closed Sun. Major credit cards.

The Bistro. *Moderate.* Holiday Inn, 2500 Riverside Dr., on U.S. 58 just E. of jct. with U.S. 29; 793–2731. Barbecue, seafood, veal, poultry, steaks, imaginative salad bar, home-made desserts, exotic dessert coffees. Handsome brass chandeliers, Old English prints, smooth, friendly service. Great local favorite. Live entertainment in The Bistro Lounge. AE, MC, V.

Ashley's Family Restaurant. *Inexpensive.* 2818 Riverside Dr., (58 W.); 797–3888. Pay one price all-you-can-eat family fare. Open daily 11 A.M.; lunch and dinner only. No credit cards.

Fork Union

Wagon Wheel. *Inexpensive to Moderate.* U.S. 15, south edge of town in Fork Union Shopping Center; 842–3400. Casual and friendly in twin dining rooms. Hearty roast beef sandwiches, fried chicken, and steaks. Country music Sat. nights, seafood buffet Wed. AE, MC, V.

Lynchburg

Jefferson's Dining Room and Lounge. *Expensive.* The Radisson Hotel, 601 Main St.; 528–2500. Crabmeat Chesapeake, breast of chicken Jefferson, other specialties, in serenely elegant setting. Lavish, moderately priced Sunday brunch. Adjoining Jefferson's Lounge has nightly entertainment, cozy fireplace. AE, CB, DC, MC, V.

Emil's Le Chalet. *Moderate to Expensive.* Boonsboro Shopping Center, 7 miles northeast on U.S. 501, 8 miles north of U.S. 460, Fort Ave. exit; 384–3311. Continental specialties, also regional seafoods. Large selection of fine wines. Chalet decor, Swiss owner-chef. Reservations requested. Moderately priced luncheon in adjoining Emil's Cafe. Closed Sun. AE, DC, MC, V.

Repast at St. Paul's. *Moderate to Expensive.* 7th and Church Sts.; 528–3133. Dine in historic structure where Robert E. Lee attended 1868 convention of the Episcopal Diocese as a lay delegate. Choice entrees include beef, seafood, game. Lunch and dinner. Valet parking. Closed weekends. AE, MC, V.

Crown Sterling. *Moderate.* 6120 Fort Ave.; 239–7744. Rainbow trout, aged western beef broiled over live charcoal. Breakfast, lunch, and dinner. Mon.–Fri.; dinner only Sat.; closed Sun. Bar and wine list. Colonial decor. AE, DC, MC, V.

Jeanne's Restaurant. *Moderate.* 5 miles east of U.S. 460, en route to Appomattox; 993–2475. Lobster, shrimp, steaks, burgers, salad bar, child's plates. Regionally popular; attractively landscaped setting overlooks lake. Open daily, dinner only Sat. AE, DC, MC, V.

Charley's. *Inexpensive to Moderate.* G-330 River Ridge Mall, 237–5988. Local favorite highlights fettuccine, quiche, chicken Kiev, veal, steaks, scampi. Also in Danville, Roanoke, Virginia Beach. AE, MC, V.

Clayton's Restaurant. *Inexpensive.* 3311 Old Forest Rd.; 385–7900. Breakfast and lunch daily, dinner Wed., Fri. Good home-style cooking. MC, V.

The Farm Basket. *Inexpensive.* 2008 Langhorne Rd.; 846–0477. Light lunches—melted gouda cheese biscuits, Swiss apple quiche are specialties—in charming setting with tables tucked amid wares of kitchen boutique. Box lunches to go. Virginia crafts, gift items sold on premises. MC, V.

Petersburg

Steak and Ale Restaurant. *Moderate to Expensive.* 500 E. Wythe St.; 861–5993. Hearty prime ribs, steaks, seafood. Old English decor, background music. Open daily; dinner only Sat. AE, DC, MC, V.

Steven Kent Restaurant. *Moderate to Expensive.* Quality Inn Steven Kent, I–95 & U.S. 301, Exit 13; 733–0600. Southern specialties include plantation fried chicken, Virginia ham. Entertainment, dancing. AE, CB, DC, MC, V.

The French Betsy. *Moderate.* 20 W. Old St.; 732–1553. Good American cooking blended with some Continental specialties. Lunch and dinner; breakfast Sat. Mon.–Sat. in handsomely restored old Appomattox Iron works.

Annabelle's Restaurant and Pub. *Inexpensive to Moderate.* 2733 Park Ave.; 732–0997. Beef, chicken, prime rib, seafood, unlimited salad bar. Lunch time favorites served all day. Friendly service, pleasant setting of hanging baskets, Tiffany style windows. Open daily, noon on Sun. AE, MC, V.

THINGS TO SEE AND DO

TOURS AND TOURING INFORMATION. For information about the Appomattox Railroad Festival and community, contact Appomattox County Chamber of Commerce, Box 704, Appomattox, VA 24522; phone 352–2621.

Free brochures, including a Charlottesville walking tour guide, travel assistance, and local reservation service, are available at Thomas Jefferson Visitors Center, VA 20 S.; 977–1783. Here a free exhibit, "Thomas Jefferson at Monticello," offers insights into statesman's remarkable career. Open 9 A.M.–5:30 P.M., Mar.–Oct. 31, 9–5 winter. Also contact: Thomas Jefferson Visitors Bureau, Box 161, Charlottesville, VA 22902; 293–6789.

For free brochures and a Danville walking tour guide, contact City of Danville Visitor Center, Box 330 (National Tobacco-Textile Museum, 614 Lynn St.) Danville, VA 24541; (804) 797–9437 or (804–799–5149.

For Petersburg Civil War sites, contact: Petersburg Dept. of Tourism, Siege Museum, 15 West Bank St., Petersburg, VA 23804; (804) 733–2400.

Appomattox

HISTORIC SITE. *Appomattox Court House National Historical Park,* three miles north of the town of Appomattox on VA 24, commemorates the first step in reuniting a nation torn by tragic civil conflict. Here on Palm Sunday, April 9, 1865, Confederate General Robert E. Lee surrendered his beleaguered Army of Northern Virginia to Union General Ulysses S. Grant. The dignified ceremony took place in the spacious parlor of Wilmer McLean's home.

Today much of the small village, authentically restored and reconstructed, reflects these dramatic events in the spring of 1865. Pedestrian pathways, delightful for leisurely strolling, lead to historic highlights. The reconstructed Court House serves as a visitor center with museum displays, orientation slide programs, and an information desk where descriptive literature and pictorial maps are available. Park Service rangers at McLean House, rebuilt and furnished in period, explain in fascinating detail the momentous meeting of Lee and Grant. Auxiliary buildings—the kitchen, servants' quarters, ice house, and a 40-foot well surrounded by an ornate gazebo—reveal aspects of mid-nineteenth-century daily life in Virginia's heartland.

When Appomattox County was formed in 1845, its only town, Clover Hill, subsequently renamed, became the county seat. An appropriate hall of justice was built the following year. A few merchants, lawyers, artisans, and agrarians established themselves in the little community, which served as a stopping-off point for travelers on the Richmond-Lynchburg Stage Road. Even by 1865, though, the town boasted scarcely more than 150 inhabitants. Remnants of their everyday lives may be seen at Francis Meek's Store, which also functioned as post office and pharmacy, and at John Woodson's Law Office in a small building next door. Clover Hill Tavern, dating from 1819 as the oldest structure in the village, flourished to such an extent that a subsidiary guesthouse, extensive kitchen, and servant's quarters were later added. An attractive gift shop in the former Tavern kitchen stocks books, prints, memorabilia, and souvenirs of the Civil War era.

The restored Isbell House, built in 1849–50, and the antebellum Peers House, among the more imposing homes in the village, may be viewed from outside, but are closed for public visits. In the three-story brick County Jail, begun in 1860 and completed a decade later, the sheriff maintained his office and residence on the first floor and prisoners' cells on the top two. Among less pretentious restorations are the Mariah Wright House, dating from the early 1820s, residence of a widow, and the Lorenzo Kelly House, built after 1845 as the home of a local carpenter. Both of these modest clapboard-sided houses have chimneys of brick and stone distinctive to this particular region. On April 12, 1865, family members and local inhabitants gathered about the Kelly House, facing Surrender Triangle, to watch as 28,231 Confederate soldiers furled their battle flags and stacked arms in the presence of victorious Union troops. This event took place four years to the day after the firing upon Fort Sumter in the harbor of Charleston, South Carolina, ignited the Civil War.

In the Park area outside the village, markers along VA 24 indicate headquarter sites of Grant and Lee, a monument honoring North Carolina troops, and the minuscule cemetery where 19 Confederates and one Union soldier lie at rest in tragic testimony to the last day of fighting on April 9. Interpretive cultural and historic programs, exhibitions, and demonstrating craftspeople are presented during spring and summer visitor seasons. The National Historical Park is open daily except December 25 from 9 A.M. to 5 P.M. Admission $1 per car April through October. For additional information contact: The Superintendent, P.O. Box 218, Appomattox, Virginia 24522; phone (804) 352–8782.

MUSEUM. A former jail in Jeffersonian architectural style is now home of *Appomattox County Historical Museum* showcasing a one-room school, vintage doctor's office, numerous Civil War artifacts, and relics from the past including a renovated prison cell. Inquire locally for hours.

LIVELY ARTS. *Hampden-Sydney Music Festival* is held annually, two weeks in mid-to-late June, at Hampden-Sydney College for Men, about 33 miles east of Appomattox via U.S. 460, U.S. 15, and VA 133. Highlights include chamber ensemble, vocal and instrumental concerts by internationally renowned artists, a musicians' coaching program, and music lovers' weekends. Accommodations and meals available on campus. For further information, contact Hampden-Sydney Music Festival, Hampden-Sydney College, Hampden-Sydney, VA 23943; phone (804) 223–4381.

Charlottesville

Court Square Historic District, downtown, is site of original *Albemarle County Court House* (1803), focal point of self-guided walking tour that passes historic spots, including *Jackson Park* with famous *equestrian statue of Stonewall Jackson.* Court House open Mon.–Sat., closed holidays. Pick up free walking tour brochure at Thomas Jefferson Visitors Bureau (see Tours and Touring Information).

Historic Michie Tavern, VA 53, Monticello Mountain, is restored 1700s structure with authentic facilities and furniture, wine cellar, keeping hall, Colonial bar. Outbuildings include General Store, Meadow Run Grist Mill, home of Virginia's Wine Museum. Open 9–5 daily, closed holidays. Fee. Call 977–1234.

Monticello, VA 53, 2 miles southeast, Thomas Jefferson's mountaintop home, is one of the nation's architectural masterpieces. House and gardens were designed by Jefferson over a period of 40 years; original furnishings, paintings, Jefferson's inventions are displayed. Restoration, excavation is ongoing. East portico has been restored to original sand-painted finish. Open daily 8–5, winter hours 9–4:30 (Nov.–Feb.). Guided tours of restored gardens, orchards, vineyards, spring–fall. Fee. Call 295–8181.

The University of Virginia, U.S. 29 and 250 Business, was founded by Thomas Jefferson, who designed its imposing Rotunda; graceful serpentine walls; Student Ranges, whose residents have included Edgar Allan Poe, Woodrow Wilson; other prominent sites. Free tours daily except two weeks at Christmas. Call 924–7969 to confirm times.

Ash Lawn–Highland, off I-64, 2½ miles beyond Monticello, is the 550-acre tobacco plantation of James Monroe, impeccably restored with many family possessions. Picnic sites, spinning, weaving demonstrations late June–mid-Aug. Special events include operas, concerts, plays, Colonial crafts weekend. Open daily 9–6 Mar.–Oct., 10–5 Nov.–Feb. Fee. Call 293–9539.

MUSEUMS AND GALLERIES. *Baley Art Museum,* Rugby Rd., University of Virginia, (924–3592), has European, American paintings; Oriental, contemporary, Jefferson period art. Open Tues.–Sun. 1–5; free.

George Rogers Clark Museum, 1 mile north of Charlottesville, via U.S. 250E, VA 20, is an old pioneer house relocated, restored on foundation of Clark's birthplace. Furnishings and housewares are from 1720–1840 period. Picnic sites, free spring water. Open Apr.–Oct., 10–5.

Western Virginia Visitor Center, VA 20S, just south of I-64 exit, has displays of Colonial exploration. An imaginative exhibit, "Thomas Jefferson at Monticello," highlighting the statesman's domestic life, displays over 400 artifacts, many excavated at Monticello. Open daily except major holidays, 9–5:30 Mar.–Oct. 31, 9–5 winter. Free. Call 977–1783. Sells "Presidential Pass" for combination visits to Monticello, Michie Tavern, Ash Lawn.

LIVELY ARTS. *Second Street Gallery,* 116 Second St., N.E., (977–7284), presents films, lectures, readings, displays contemporary artwork.

McGuffey Art Center, 201 Second St., N.W., (295–7973), houses studios where visitors may view artists, craftsfolk at work.

The University of Virginia ballet, theater, and symphony series are open to visitors. Call 924–3984.

SPORTS. Boating at Lakes Albemarle (296–4731), Chris Greene (296–5844), Reynovia (296–1910), and Montfair Resort/Farm (823–5202 or 5234).

Canoeing offered by James River Runners, Scottsville (286–2338).

Fishing at above lakes, also Mint Springs, Beaver and Totier Creeks, (296–5844), Sugar Hollow Reservoir (985–7293).

Golfing: 9-hole courses at McIntire Park, Pen Park (977–0615).

Horseback Riding: Foxfield (973–4886); Montfair Stables (823–5202 or 5234);The Barracks (293–6568); Hickory Ridge Equestrian Center (973–9292).

Tennis: McIntire and Pen Parks (295–7170); Montfair Resort Farm (823–5202 or 5234).

Danville

HISTORIC SITES. Historic Chatham, 16 miles north of Danville via U.S. 29, is a charming town with antebellum *Court House* dating from 1853. Nearby **Town Hall** is home of Pittsylvania Historical Society Museum, open Sun. 2–5 May–Oct. and by appointment. Here visitors can pick up self-guided walking tour brochure to explore historic county seat, founded in 1777.

"Millionaires' Row," 8 blocks containing one of the South's best collections of beautifully preserved Victorian architecture, may be viewed in a leisurely walking tour along Main Street and side streets. Pick up free tour brochure at city Visitor Center, 614 Lynn St.

"Wreck of the Old 97," marker, Riverside Dr. between N. Main and Locust Lane overpass, commemorates the site of the 1903 train wreck that inspired the folk ballad.

MUSEUMS AND GALLERIES. National Tobacco Textile Museum, 614 Lynn St., (797–9437 or 799–5149), is the city Visitor Center; also displays equipment, looms, extensive collections pertaining to the tobacco and textile industries. Open Mon.–Fri., 10–4. Closed holidays. Fee.

The Sutherlin House, 975 Main St., (793–5644), now home of The Danville Museum of Fine Arts and History. The museum shop stocks original work of over 150 area craftsfolk. Open 10–5 Tues.–Fri., Sun. 2–5. Closed holidays. Free.

Museum of Natural History. Danville Community College; 797–3553, Ext. 291. A new 5,000-square-foot museum that houses two major natural history collections—the Johnny Westbrook bird collection and the Walter Grant big game mammal collection. Open Sun., 2–5.

PARKS. *Ballou Park,* Park Ave., has nature trails, forest playground, joggers' health loop, tennis, picnic sites.

SHOPPING. *Dan River Mills Outlet Store,* 1000 Block W. Main St., across from mill, offers good buys in first quality towels, designer sheets, pillowcases and coverlets, some sportswear and gift items. Open Mon.–Fri. 8–5, Sat. 9–5.

Lynchburg

SCENIC ATTRACTIONS. *Blackwater Creek Natural Area,* center of town, off Cranehill Dr. Rd., offers six-mile Creekside Nature Trail, bicycling trails, 115-acre Ruskin Freer Preserve, sanctuary for native plants, animals. Athletic area has lighted ball fields, pavilion, picnic tables. Part of the national trail system. Open daily, free.

HISTORIC SITES. *City/Confederate Cemetery,* Fourth St., has graves of early settlers, Confederate soldiers, on land donated by John Lynch; and *Fort Early,* Fort Ave. at Memorial Ave., includes restored fort and breastworks that were focal points in Confederate General Jubal A. Early's defense of Lynchburg. Open by appointment.

Carter Glass (Montview Farm) Home, now Visitors Center and Executive Offices of Liberty University, was home of Senator Carter Glass where he wrote the Federal Reserve Act. Open free to visitors during college hours; (804) 237–5961, ext. 782.

Miller–Claytor House, Riverside Park, is restored 1791 house where Thomas Jefferson reputedly ate the first "tomatoe." Open by appointment; (804) 847–1459. Fee.

Point of Honor, 112 Cabell St., atop Daniel's Hill on a bluff overlooking the James River, sits on dueling ground site. The fine Federal-style mansion, built by Dr. George Cabell, Sr., personal physician of Patrick Henry, has unique octagonal bay facade, magnificent interior woodwork. Open daily 1–4; (804) 847–1459. Fee. Closed major holidays.

Mr. Jefferson's Poplar Forest, just outside the city limits in neighboring Bedford County, is favorite hideaway retreat Jefferson designed at peak of his architectural maturity. Under major restoration, it is open by appointment only. For directions, hours, phone (804) 847–1732.

Red Hill, 35 miles south via U.S. 501 to Brookneal, then 3 miles east via VA 40, 2 miles south on VA 600, 619, is Patrick Henry's beloved last home and burial site. Main house, which burned, has been reconstructed on original foundation, along with some outbuildings. Henry's law office, with his desk and document cabinet, is on the grounds. Visitor center museum houses personal belongings of the "voice of the Revolution" and his descendants. Open daily 9–5, to 4 Nov.–Mar. Closed Christmas Day. Phone (804) 376–2044. Fee.

Quaker Meeting House, 5810 Fort Ave., adjacent to Quaker Memorial Presbyterian Church, was completed in 1798, replacing original structure built by city founders, the Lynch family. Free admission. Phone (804) 239–2548 in advance.

Anne Spencer House & Garden, 1313 Pierce St., house, garden, and garden cottage, "Edankraal," contain artifacts and memorabilia of internationally recognized black poet of the 1920s Harlem Renaissance period. Open by appointment; (804) 845–1313, or 846–0517. Fee.

MUSEUMS AND GALLERIES. *Maier Museum of Art,* campus of Randolph-Macon Woman's College, 2500 Rivermont Ave., has fine collections of nineteenth-, twentieth-century American art. Open. Tues.–Sun., 1–5, free; (804) 846–7392; and *Old Court House Museum,* 901 Court St., built in 1815, former court house is beautifully restored example of Greek Revival architecture, with original courtroom restored to early appearance. Other rooms' exhibits trace Lynchburg history. Open daily 1–4, closed major holidays; (408) 847–1459. Fee. Leading up to the structure from Church St. is much photographed 139-step *Monument Terrace,* memorial to Lynchburg citizens killed in American wars.

LIVELY ARTS. *Liberty University* (582–2000) and *Sweet Briar College* (381–6100) present annual musical and theatrical programs, including touring productions, which are open to the public.

Lynchburg Symphony Orchestra (845–6604) performs Nov.–May in the Lynchburg Fine Arts Center, which is also stage for a yearly series of comedies, dramas, musicals, appearances of *Lynchburg Regional Ballet Theatre* and nationally known dance companies.

Joseph Nichols Tavern Players, dinner theater troupe, present several plays annually in restored Western Hotel, Fifth and Madison Sts. Structure open other times by appointment; 528–3305.

Virginia Center for the Creative Arts, (946–7236) at Mt. San Angelo, adjacent to Sweet Briar campus, is year-round artist colony offering music, painting, sculpture, photography, poetry readings, concerts, a spring opera, by leading artists.

SPORTS. Several private clubs have pools, golf courses, racquetball, and tennis courts. Inquire locally about reciprocal privileges. The YMCA and YWCA have full schedules of activities. The city operates playgrounds, community centers, pools, tennis courts, and eight parks—Peaks View, the newest, northwest off VA 291, provides nature study, picnicking, tennis, basketball, playgrounds, football, soccer fields.

SPECTATOR SPORTS. *Baseball:* City Stadium hosts summer games of the Lynchburg Mets, Class A farm club of New York Mets; *college sports:* football, offered by the Liberty Baptist University Flames, a highly competitive team that fields a tough schedule; the Flames basketball team plays 15 home games. Lynchburg College has nationally ranked baseball, soccer, women's field hockey, and lacrosse teams; *golf:* Fox-Puss Golf Tournament, annually at Boonsboro Country Club, draws top amateur golfers; *tennis:* top Middle Atlantic players compete in Central Virginia Invitational Tournament, June, Oakwood Country Club.

SHOPPING. Lynchburg has a number of factory outlet stores offering good buys in clothing, shoes, and linens. These include *Consolidated Shoe Co.,* 460 W. Timberlake Rd.; *Craddock–Terry Shoe Corp.,* 3100 Albert Lankford Dr.; *Dale Garment Co.,* 14th & Kemper Sts.; *Dress House,* 1700 12th St.; *Imperial Reading Outlet,* The Plaza; *Quality Towel & Linen Outlet,* Rte. 221: *Williamson–Dickie Factory Outlet,* 15th & Kemper Sts. For complete listing, consult "A Visitors' Guide to Lynchburg." (See Tours and Touring Information).

TOURS AND TOURING INFORMATION. City-Scape Tours, Ltd., offers customized step-on-motorcoach tours for groups. Information: P.O. Box 3424, Lynchburg, VA 24503; phone 384–8699 or 384–1794. For a variety of tours, also contact Brockman Tour and Travel, 2316 Alterholt Rd., Suite 204, Lynchburg, VA 24501; 846–3012.

For "A Visitors' Guide to Lynchburg," free brochures detailing self-guided historic Lynchburg tours, assistance with reservations for dining and lodging, as well as travel directions, contact: Visitors Information Center, Box 60, 12th and Church Sts., Lynchburg, VA 24505; 847–1811.

Petersburg

HISTORIC SITES. *Blandford Church and Interpretation Center,* 321 S. Crater Rd. (732–2230), built in 1735, abandoned, restored as Confederate shrine, has 15 stained glass windows personally designed by Louis Comfort Tiffany. Here, Memorial Day originated. Open Mon.–Sat. 9–5, Sun. 12:30–5. Fee.

Centre Hill Mansion, Centre Hill Ct. (732–8081), is beautifully restored 1823 Federal mansion with fine marble mantels, chandeliers, antique furnishings. Open Mon.–Sat. 9–5, Sun. 12:30–5, closed major holidays. Fee.

Courthouse, N. Sycamore between E. Bank, E. Tabb sts. (732–7013), elegant 1839 structure with graceful clock tower is city's symbol. Open seasonally. Free.

Farmer's Bank and Visitors Center, 19 Bollingbrook St. (733–2400), town visitor center, has banking memorabilia, marks beginning of Historic Petersburg Tour. Open daily, 9–5; closed major holidays.

St. Paul's Episcopal Church, 110 N. Union (733–3415), 1856 structure where Lee worshipped during siege; admission at adjacent parish house.

Trapezium House, Market and Banks sts. (733–7690), built in early 1800s by eccentric bachelor, has neither right angles nor parallel sides. Open Mon.–Sat., 10–4, Sun., 12:30–4. Fee.

Violet Bank, at Colonial Heights, across the Appomattox River, was Lee's headquarters during part of the siege. Federal period house is now a Civil War museum, open Apr.–Oct. Mon.–Wed., Fri.–Sat., 10–3, Sun. 1–5. Free. Call 520–9395.

NATIONAL PARKS. *Petersburg National Battlefield Park,* off VA 36 adjoining city (732–3531), is site of Lee's last stand before retreat to Appomattox. Self-guided tours begin at visitor center for audio-visual presentation; self-drive auto tours lead through park for views of earthworks, batteries, mortars, monuments, Crater area where Civil War's mightiest explosion occurred. Living history, evening presentations in summer. At Hopewell, 8 miles east, *City Point Unit* of the *Battlefield* (541–2206) preserves Appomattox Manor and grounds, with restored cabin where General Grant maintained headquarters during siege. Both Battlefield sites open daily, 8 A.M.–dark, except major holidays.

MUSEUMS AND GALLERIES. *Siege Museum,* 15 W. Bank St. (733–7690), in the fine Greek Revival 1842 Exchange Building, graphically displays dioramas and exhibits detailing the siege of Petersburg in dramatic detail. Superbly edited film, *The Echoes Still Remain,* narrated by native son Joseph Cotten, dramatizes effects of the war on the civilians who stayed behind. Open Mon.–Sat. 9–5, Sun. 12:30–5, closed holidays. Fee.

U.S. Army Quartermaster Museum, Fort Lee, 3 miles northeast on VA 36 (734–1854 or 4203), exhibits military artifacts, uniforms, equipment, weapons, flags dating from the Revolutionary War to the present. Open 8–5 Mon.–Fri., 11–5, Sat.–Sun., closed major holidays. Free.

USSSA Hall of Fame Museum, 3935 S. Crater Rd. (732–4099). The United States Slo-Pitch Softball Association Hall of Fame Museum honors those persons who have made outstanding contributions to the game of amateur softball. Numerous exhibits, displays, photographs, and films take visitors on a softball memory lane. Open Mon.–Fri. 9–4, Sat. 11–4, Sun. 1–4. Closed holidays. Fee.

SPECIAL INTEREST. *Flowerdew Hundred,* 10 miles southeast of Hopewell, VA 10, 1617 Flowerdew Hundred Rd. (541–8897), contains, extensive archaeological digs at site of a 1618 English settlement. Museum has audio-visual show, artifact displays; grounds include picnic sites, working eighteenth-century windmill grinding cornmeal for sale. Open Tues.–Sun. 10–5 Apr.–Nov.

Smith's Fort Plantation, about 30 miles southeast of Hopewell via VA 10, then north on VA 31 (834–2229), was built by Captain John Smith to defend Jamestown across the James River. Chief Powhatan gave the land to John Rolfe and Pocahontas as a wedding present. Their son sold it to Thomas Warren who built the brick *Rolfe-Warren House* there in 1652. House and grounds open Wed.–Sat. 10–5, Sun. 1–5, from the third week in Apr. to Sept. 30.

Chippokes Plantation State Park, about 35 miles southeast of Hopewell via VA 10 and side road 634, has been in continuous operation as a working farm since 1634. Visitor center programs describe the history of Jamestown and the James River and development of Virginia agriculture from 1619 to the present. Also in the Park are an 1854 manor house, eighteenth-century brick kitchen, 6-acre garden, picnic area, snack bar; hiking, bicycling, self-guiding nature trails, scenic auto tour. Visitor center open first Sat. in Apr.–last Sun. in Oct. Additional charge for use of swimming pool, beach on the river. Call 294–3625.

LIVELY ARTS. *The Petersburg Symphony* offers fall, winter, and spring concerts at Petersburg High School Auditorium; *The Swift Creek Mill Playhouse,* I-95 N., Exit 4, Colonial Heights, on U.S. 1 (748–5203), gives dinner shows in one of the nation's oldest grist mills. Reservations, information: P.O. Box 41, Colonial Heights, VA 23834; (804) 748–5203; and *Virginia State University music faculty* present four fall recitals at *Centre Hill,* Sun., 3 P.M. Free. Information: (804) 733–2400.

TOURING INFORMATION. Pick up free self-guiding brochures and buy museum admission tickets at Farmers Bank Visitors Center, 19 Bollingbrook St.; (804) 733–2400. Or write Petersburg Information Services, P.O. Box 2107, Petersburg, VA 23804; (804) 733–2400.

RICHMOND

by
EDGAR and PATRICIA CHEATHAM

Richmond retains delightful Old World charm as it steps to the beat of contemporary vitality. No major U.S. city has a longer recorded history than Virginia's handsome capital, now undergoing an exciting urban renaissance.

Captain John Smith landed in Richmond in 1607 and erected a cross. Richmond is located on the fall line of the James River and Smith's boat could not travel any farther because of the rocks. An early trading post, Shockhoe, was built, then in the 1730s William Byrd designed a city plan. Revolutionary patriots flocked to the 1775 Virginia Convention in St. John's Church, where Patrick Henry delivered his famed "liberty or death" speech.

After Virginia succeeded, Richmond became the Confederate capital. When the Civil War ended, much of the city lay in ruin.

Today, bordering the James River, historic warehouses and grain exchanges in Shockhoe Slip thrive as trendy restaurants, shops, and galleries. Rubber-wheel trolleys connect downtown to the retail district. In another urban revitalization, the Rouse Company has developed Sixth Street Marketplace where a glass-enclosed promenade fronts shops, restaurants, and landscaped plazas. Adjacent is the handsome new Richmond Centre, capable of handling

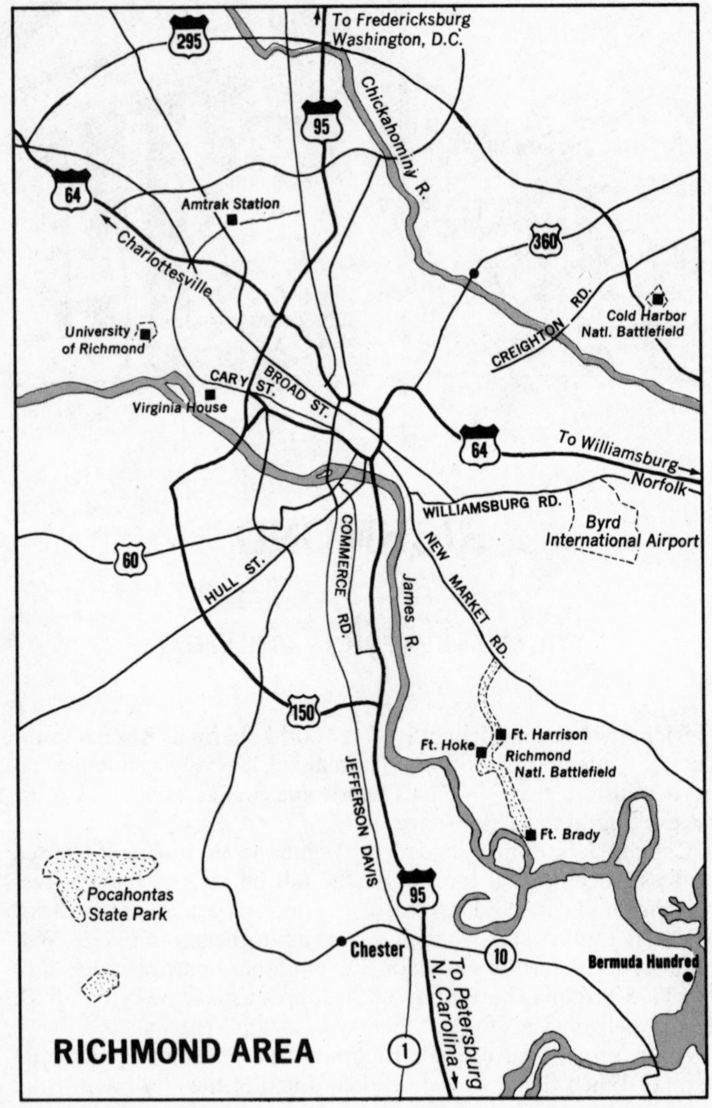

To Fredericksburg
Washington, D.C.
295
95
Chickahominy R.
64
Amtrak Station
Charlottesville
360
Creighton Rd.
Cold Harbor
Natl. Battlefield
University
of Richmond
Cary St.
Broad St.
Virginia House
64
To Williamsburg
Norfolk
Williamsburg Rd.
Byrd
International Airport
60
Hull St.
Commerce Rd.
James R.
New Market Rd.
150
Ft. Harrison
Ft. Hoke
Richmond
Natl. Battlefield
Jefferson Davis
Ft. Brady
95
Pocahontas
State Park
Chester
10
To Petersburg
N. Carolina
Bermuda Hundred
1
RICHMOND AREA

88 percent of the nation's conventions and exhibitions. Main Street Station, built in 1901, has reopened as a shopping mall and seafood restaurant. A nonprofit group has begun a riverfront project with nature and canal walks, boat rides, and other improvements.

PRACTICAL INFORMATION FOR RICHMOND

Note: The area code for Richmond is 804.

PLACES TO STAY

HOTELS AND MOTELS. Accommodations in Richmond run the gamut from properties of national and international systems to independent houses with prices suitable for varying budgetary requirements. General categories are based on nightly double-occupancy room rates. *Deluxe:* $100 and up; *Expensive:* $75–$100; *Moderate:* $40–$75; *Inexpensive:* below $40. Rates are subject to change without notice.

Commonwealth Park Hotel. *Deluxe.* Bank and 9th sts., 343–7300. 49 units, in an 11-story hotel. All-suites. Color TV, refrigerators, sauna, whirlpool, valet parking, lounge, coffee shop, dining room. AE, CB, DC, MC, V.

Hyatt Richmond. *Deluxe.* 6 miles west on U.S. 250 at junction with I-64, exit 38B; 285–8666. Color TV; in-room movies, 2 pools, sauna, tennis, lounge, entertainment, coffee shop, gourmet restaurant. 386 rooms. AE, CB, DC, MC, V.

Jefferson Sheraton Hotel. *Deluxe.* Franklin and Adams Sts. downtown; 788–8000. Color TV, Rotunda lobby, shops, boutiques, ice cream parlor, sidewalk cafe, lounge with entertainment, restaurant, gourmet dining room; ornately appointed late 19th-century hotel faithfully restored to original grandeur. 276 rooms, 26 suites. AE, CB, DC, MC, V.

Omni Richmond. *Deluxe.* 100 S. 12th St.; 344–7000. The city's newest luxury hotel has 363 rooms and suites, 19 equipped for the disabled. Indoor-outdoor pool, state-of-the-art health club, sundeck. Dining in dramatic Gallego, upbeat White Water Cafe. Sophisticated lobby bar, lounge with nightly entertainment. Valet parking. In the James Center, one of the Southeast's largest multi-use structures. AE, CB, DC, MC, V.

Richmond Marriott. *Deluxe.* 500 E. Broad St. downtown; 643–3400. 403 rooms in a 17-story hotel. 34 rooms on luxury level, with private lounge and minibars. Color TV, pool, health facilities, room service, lounge, restaurant. AE, CB, DC, MC, V.

Carrington Row Inn. *Deluxe to Moderate.* 4 rooms, 2 with private baths. 2309 E. Broad St.; 343–7005. Accommodations in one of a trio of row houses built in 1818 in the city's Historic Church Hill District, complimentary continental breakfast. 1 block from St. John's Episcopal Church. AE, MC, V.

Catlin–Abbott House. *Deluxe to Moderate.* 5 rooms, 3 with private baths. 2304 E. Broad St.; 780–3746. Bed-and-breakfast inn built in 1845 in Historic Church Hill District, complimentary traditional Richmond breakfast served in elegant dining room or in guest rooms, 1 block from St. John's Episcopal Church. AE, MC, V.

Best Western Kings Quarters. *Moderate to Expensive.* In Doswell, 20 miles north of Richmond, at junction I-95 and VA 30 near Kings Dominion theme park; 876–3321. Color TV, pool, playground, putting green, tennis, coin laundry, game room, gift shop, lounge, restaurant, free shuttle to Kings Dominion. 248 rooms. AE, CB, DC, MC, V.

Holiday Inn Downtown. *Moderate to Expensive.* 301 W. Franklin St. in business district, use exit 13 off I-95 S., exit 10 from I-95 N.; 644–9871. Color TV, in-room movies, heated pool, lounge, restaurant. 216 rooms. AE, CB, DC, MC, V.

Best Western Airport Inn. *Moderate.* 5700 Williamsburg Rd.; 222–2780. 123 rooms in a 2-story motor inn. Restaurant, bar, pool, room service, and airport transportation. Major credit cards.

John Marshall Hotel. *Moderate.* N. 5th and E. Franklin Sts.; 644–4661. 355 rooms. Color TV, in-room movies, barber and beauty shops, valet parking, lounge with entertainment, coffee shop, dining room. 418 rooms. AE, CB, DC, MC, V.

Quality Inn Commonwealth. *Moderate.* 515 W. Franklin St., 5 blocks from I-95 N., Belvedere-U.S. 1 and U.S. 301 N. exit; 643–2831. 182 rooms. Color TV, in-room movies, pool, coin laundry, lounge, restaurant. AE, CB, DC, MC, V.

Ramada Inn South. *Moderate.* At I-95 exit 6A on 2126 Willis Rd.; 271–1281. 98 rooms. Color TV, pool, lounge with entertainment, restaurant. AE, CB, DC, MC, V.

For information about additional bed-and-breakfast establishments in Richmond and vicinity, contact Lyn M. Benson, Bensonhouse of Richmond, P.O. Box 15131, VA 23227; 321–6277 or 648–7560 between 1–5 P.M.

PLACES TO EAT

RESTAURANTS. Richmond's renaissance has sparked growth of an extravagant new array of dining rooms. From southern specialties to Continental fare and ethnic cuisine, you'll find it here, along with a good variety of family-style dining. Those listed accept at least two major credit cards (MC, V). Area code: 804. Estimated costs are per person, excluding wine, cocktails, tips. *Deluxe,* $25 or more; *Expensive,* $15–$25; *Moderate,* $7–$15, *Inexpensive,* under $7.

Hugo's. *Expensive.* Hyatt Richmond, 6624 W. Broad St.; 285–1234. American regional cuisine, fresh fish, pasta specialties in elegant setting. Entertainment in Lightfoot's Lounge. Jackets, reservations requested. Dinner nightly, Sunday brunch. AE, CB, DC, MC, V.

Lemaire's. *Expensive.* Jefferson Sheraton Hotel, Franklin & Adams sts.; 788–8000. Named for Thomas Jefferson's French *maitre d'hôtel,* who introduced cooking with wine to the new nation, specialty restaurant features regional cuisine in 7 elegantly appointed rooms. AE, CB, DC, MC, V.

Chardonnay. *Moderate to Expensive.* The Richmond Marriott, 500 E. Broad; 643–3400. Continental cuisine in elegant surroundings. Dinner Mon.–Sat. AE, CB, DC, MC, V.

La Petite France. *Moderate to Expensive.* 2912 Maywill St.; 353–8729. Award-winning French cuisine in elegant setting. Chef owned. Jacket required. Children's menu. Lunch, dinner. Closed Sun., Mon. Reservations requested. AE, CB, DC, MC, V.

Sam Miller's Warehouse. *Moderate to Expensive.* 1210 East Cary St.; 643–1301. Another Dawn O'Brian choice, featuring oysters every which way. Open daily, with reservations requested. Also prime beef and a bar. Comfortable for the younger crowd, but not a turn-off for oldsters. AE, MC, V.

The Tobacco Company Restaurant. *Moderate to Expensive.* 1201 E. Cary St., Shockhoe Slip; 782–9555. Airy, multi-level, decorated with greenery, antiques, a Richmond favorite. Lunch Mon.–Fri., dinner nightly. Bar. Entertainment. AE, MC, V.

Poor Richard's. *Moderate.* 103 E. Cary St.; 643–1292. Seafood and Creole dishes. Garden dining. Entertainment Fri., Sat. Closed Sun. AE, MC, V.

Chesterfield Tea Room. *Inexpensive to Moderate.* 900 W. Franklin St.; 359–0474. Traditional Virginia fare, freshly baked breads, desserts, in city's oldest continually operating restaurant. MC, V.

Nielsen's 3N. *Inexpensive to Moderate.* 4800 Thalbro St.; 355–2266. Fresh Chesapeake Bay seafood, spoon bread are specialties. Quiet, warm surroundings, local favorite. Lunch Mon.–Fri., dinner Mon.–Sat. AE, CB, DC, MC, V.

THINGS TO SEE AND DO

HISTORIC SITES. Agecroft Hall, 4305 Sulgrave Rd., is an imported sixteenth-century Tudor manor house, reconstructed in 1928, furnished with original artifacts; formal period gardens. Open Tues.–Fri. 10–4, Sat.–Sun. 2–5. Call 353–4241. Fee.

Virginia State Capitol (1785), Capitol Square, was designed by Thomas Jefferson in style of classical temple. Inside is famed Houdon statue of George Washington. Open Mon.–Sun. 9–5 Apr.–Oct., Mon.–Sat. 9–5, Sun. 1–5 Dec.–Mar. Tours. Call 786–4344. Free. Behind is *Governor's Mansion,* nation's oldest, open by appointment only, except July–Aug.; 786–4576.

The Fan, bordered by Monument Ave., Main, Laurel sts., & Boulevard, is fan-shaped city within the city, with vintage structures renovated into homes, shops, restaurants, galleries. *Monument Avenue,* its northern border lined with trees, handsome houses, and statues, is considered one of nation's most beautiful thoroughfares.

John Marshall House, 818 E. Marshall St., is restored home of U.S. Chief Justice John Marshall. Open Tues.–Sat., 10–5; Sun. 1–5. Call 648–7998. Fee.

Maymont House, Hampton & Penn sts., a neo-Romanesque mansion of Major James Dooley, has, lavish furnishings, art work. Open daily 10–7. Call 358–7166. Free; fee for carriage rides.

Scotchtown, via U.S. 1, 15 miles north to Ashland, then 11 miles northwest on VA 54, was Patrick Henry's Revolutionary War home; beautifully restored house and grounds are National Historic Landmark. Open Apr.–Oct., Mon.–Sat. 10–4:30, Sun. 1:30–4:30. Call 227–3500. Fee.

Maggie L. Walker National Historic Site. 110-A E. Leigh St., is recently restored home of daughter of ex-slave, who became first woman president of an American bank. Open Wed.–Sat., 9–5. Call 780–1380. Free.

Wilton House, South Wilton Rd., is 1750 Georgian brick plantation home of William Randolph III, which was General Lafayette's headquarters during Revolutionary War. Open Tues.–Sat. 10–4:30, Sun. 2:30–4:30, closed Sun. in July; open Aug. appointment only. Call 282–5936. Fee.

BATTLEFIELDS. Richmond National Battlefield Park, headquartered at 3215 E. Broad St. (226–1981), preserves grounds that were setting of South's 1861–65 defense of Richmond. Chimborazo Visitor Center offers exhibits, audio-visual program, maps of 97-mile tour through Hanover, Henrico, Chesterfield sites. Fort Harrison Visitor Center also has brochures, exhibits, foot trails. Open daily 9–5. Free.

MUSEUMS. Museum of the Confederacy, 12th and Clay Sts., houses world's largest collection of Confederate memorabilia, including Robert E. Lee's sword and uniform. Open Mon.–Sat. 10–5, Sun. 1–5, closed major holidays. Call 649–1861. Fee. Next door is **White House of the Confederacy,** where Jefferson Davis lived.

Edgar Allan Poe Museum, 1914-16 E. Main St., in 1737 Old Stone House, city's oldest, opens on enclosed gardens; complex includes the Raven Room, Enchanted Garden. Open Tues.–Sat. 10–4, Sun.–Mon., 1:30–4. Call 648–5523. Fee.

Science Museum of Virginia, 2500 W. Broad St., in old Broad Street Station, features demonstrations, hands-on exhibits, several daily ride-through-space shows in UNIVERSE Planetarium/Space Theater. Open Mon.–Sat., 10–5, Sun. 11–5. Call 257–1013. Fee.

Valentine Museum, 1015 E. Clay St., in restored 19th-century Heritage Square, preserves city history in photographs, arts, memorabilia, antique clothing, toys. Open Mon.–Sat. 10–5, Sun. 1–5. Call 649–0711. Fee.

Virginia Museum of Fine Arts, Grove Ave. & N. Blvd., with new wing doubling exhibition space, is one of South's largest. Houses Oriental, European, American, Art Nouveau collections; large sculpture garden; famed collection of Russian imperial jewels features Fabergé Easter eggs. Open Tues.–Wed., Fri.–Sat. 11–5; Thurs. 11–10 P.M.; Sun. 1–5. Donation. Call 257–0844.

CHILDREN'S MUSEUMS. *Richmond Children's Museum.* 740 N. Sixth St.; 640–KIDO. Hands-on experiences for the 2-to-12 set. *Meadow Farm Museum.* Crump Memorial Park; 649–0566. A living history farm, museum, and park. Closed mid-Dec.–Feb.

LIVELY ARTS. Barksdale Dinner Theatre & Hanover Tavern, U.S.301, 22 miles north on I-95, across from historic Hanover Courthouse, offers performances in 250-year-old tavern where Patrick Henry tended bar. Nightly, Wed.–Sat.; dinner, 6:45, theater, 8:30. Reservations: 798–6547.

Richmond Ballet, Richmond Symphony, Virginia Opera Association performances, along with touring shows, appear at The Carpenter Center for Performing Arts, 6th & Grace Sts.; 782–3900.

Richmond Choral Society concerts, *Richmond Symphony Pops* performances, are at the Mosque, fanciful 1928 Shrine temple, Main and Laurel sts.; 780–4213.

Virginia Museum Theatre, Grove Ave. & N. Blvd., one of South's leading resident troupes, stages classic, contemporary works; 257–0844.

THEME PARKS. *Kings Dominion,* 22 miles north of Richmond on I-95, is one of nation's most popular family entertainment complexes. Five theme areas have over 100 rides, shows, live entertainment, lion country safari; park is home to the Smurfs, Yogi, and their pals. The park's newest attraction is the Avalanche Bobsled Ride, the first of its kind in the United States. Open daily June–Aug., weekends, spring and fall. Doswell, VA 23047, 876–5000.

SPORTS. **Boating, fishing, swimming, hiking, riding, picnicking** at 1,783-acre Pocahontas State Park, in large state forest, southwest on U.S. 360, southeast on VA 655.

Racquetball, tennis at Briarwood Wellness and Fitness Center (794–8454); Chesterfield Indoor Tennis Club (271–4500); Courtside at Brandermill (744–4263); Courtside West (740–4263); Courts Royal Nautilus (355–4311); Raintree Swim and Racquet Club (740–0026); Robious Racquet Club (272–1220); Westwood Racquet Club (282–3829).

White water rafting at James River Park—entrances at 22nd, 43rd Sts., Riverside Dr.—a spectacular wilderness in the heart of the city. Contact James River Experiences, 2971 Hathaway Rd., Box 34525, Richmond, VA 23234; 323–0062.

SPECTATOR SPORTS. *College basketball* at Randolph-Macon College, U. of Richmond, Virginia Commonwealth U., Virginia Union U.; *professional basketball, professional wrestling* at Richmond Coliseum.

TOURS AND TOURING INFORMATION. **By bus:** Gray Line Richmond City Bus Tour highlights historic cultural sites, daily except Sat., Apr.–Sept., with pick-up at hotels, Metro Richmond Visitors Center, Exit 14 off I-95/64, 1700 Robin Hood Rd.

By foot: pick up free brochure at Visitor Center to survey Richmond history, beginning at State Capitol.

By riverboat: Various theme cruises are available through Richmond-on-the-James. For details, call 780–0107.

With tour guide: Metro Richmond Convention and Visitors Bureau can arrange for trained guides who give special interest or standard tours; 782–2777.

Free sightseeing information: Metropolitan Richmond Convention and Visitors Bureau, 300 E. Main St., Richmond, VA 23219; 782–2777; Commonwealth of Virginia Vacation Information Center, the Bell Tower, 101 N. 9th St., Richmond, VA 23219; 786–4484.

NORTHERN NECK

by
RODNEY N. SMITH

Surrounded by natural waterways and laced with creeks and inlets, Virginia's Northern Neck is a boating and fishing paradise. Wherever you go on the Neck, you'll never be far from a marina or a boat landing. You can sail the Bay and the rivers, spend a day cruising in a powerboat, paddle a canoe on quiet ponds or creeks, or engage one of the friendly and experienced charter tour boat captains for a day of salt-water excitement. Northern Neck explorers shouldn't miss the daily guided cruises to historic Tangier and Smith islands.

At the end of the day, there is nothing better than a Northern Neck seafood feast. Visitors will find fresh fish, crabs, and oysters served everywhere on the Neck, along with vegetables from local gardens and hush puppies. It is all part of the "Chesapeake Bay lifestyle."

Peace and quiet are the Northern Neck's most precious assets, but there is also plenty to see and do. Visitors can loosen up with golf or tennis or unwind on secluded campsites or peaceful nature trails. Water skiing, swimming, and wind-surfing are all at their doorsteps.

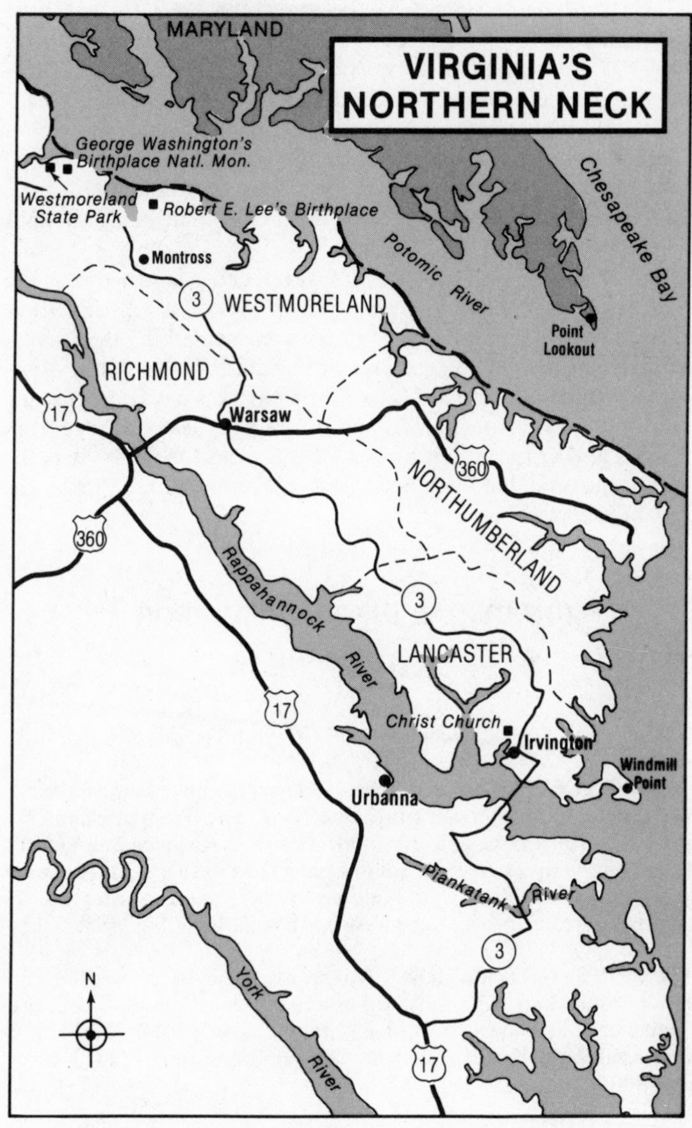
MARYLAND
VIRGINIA'S
NORTHERN NECK
George Washington's
Birthplace Natl. Mon.
Westmoreland
State Park
Robert E. Lee's Birthplace
Montross
Potomic
River
Chesapeake Bay
Point
Lookout
3
WESTMORELAND
RICHMOND
17
Warsaw
360
NORTHUMBERLAND
360
Rappahannock
River
3
LANCASTER
17
Christ Church
Irvington
Windmill
Point
Urbanna
Piankatank
River
3
York
River
17
N

The Neck is also rich with the early history of the Republic. At the upper end of the Neck, visitors can find the birthplace of George Washington and the ancestral home of the rich and powerful Lee family of Virginia. At the lower end are historic Christ Church and the tomb of Robert "King" Carter of Carter's Grove outside Williamsburg. In between are working plantations, Colonial churches, and quaint villages dating back 300 years. Just reading historic markers can take a full day in the Neck.

And if visitors are captivated by the past, there is no need to break the spell at the end of the day. Fine resorts, historic inns, and pleasant motels offer gracious hospitality that many thought had died.

History, relaxation, fishing and boating, and gracious dining are all a part of the Northern Neck, but they do not tell the whole story. There is something more to the area; something that makes visitors want to come back again and again. It is the charm of everyday country life and the lure of town market days and bustling country fairs. It is local crafts and music. It is seafood fresh from the boat and crisp garden produce fresh from the fields. It is the people who smile and say hello, and who want to help make the most of each visitor's stay.

PRACTICAL INFORMATION FOR NORTHERN NECK

Note: The area code for the Northern Neck is 804.

HOW TO GET THERE. Northern Neck is made up of four rural counties: Lancaster, Richmond, Northumberland, and Westmoreland. The area can be reached via U.S. 360, northwest from Richmond, or U.S. 17, north from Newport News or south from Fredericksburg. Rte. 3 crosses the Rappahannock River from Middlesex County into Lancaster near the Bay, then threads its way northwest up the middle of the Neck.

TOURING INFORMATION. For details about the above Northern Neck locations and attractions, call or write: Colonial Beach Chamber of Commerce, 2 Boundary St., Colonial Beach, 22443, (804) 224–7531; or Northern Neck Travel Council, Drawer H, Callao, 22345, (804) 529–7400.

PLACES TO STAY

HOTELS AND MOTELS. Virginia's Northern Neck, lying south of the Potomac River, is "country"—quiet towns, quiet farmlands, quiet river and Bay-front coves. Like neighboring Maryland and counties on the north bank of the river, the Neck's small towns and villages boast few notable accommodations. However, Williamsburg and Norfolk are but a few hours drive to the south, via. U.S. 17, and Richmond is even closer to the southwest (U.S. 360).

The Tides Inn. *Deluxe.* Located ¼ mile south of Irvington on Rte. 200, King Carter Dr.; 438–5000 or (800) 446–9981. 113 rooms in an inn that belies our opening statement. Golf lodge rooms. Private beach, paddle-boats, sailboats, canoes, and yacht cruises. Private patios and balconies. The inn is situated on 25 landscaped acres on a hill and is surrounded on three sides by water. Bar and a notable New Orleans restaurant, which has a plantation ambience. MC, V for both inn and restaurant.

The Tides Lodge. *Deluxe.* Rte. 200, just south of Irvington; 438–6000 or (800) 446–5660. 60 rooms, with golf course, tennis, yacht cruises, and heated pool. Luxury in a rural setting. Major credit cards.

The Inn at Montrose. *Moderate.* Courthouse Sq., Montrose; 493–9097. 6 rooms in a charming, old colonial inn. Fine dining. Open all year. Most major credit cards.

Whispering Pines. *Moderate.* Located 2 miles east of Irvington on Rte. 200; 435–1101. 29 rooms with golf privileges and picnic tables on wooded grounds. Restaurant near. AE, MC, V.

Windmill Point Marine Resort. *Moderate.* Located 9½ miles southeast of Irvington (Rte. 695); 435–1166. 62 rooms with private patios and balconies, marina with slips, and golf privileges. Bar, restaurant, and pool. Most major credit cards.

PLACES TO EAT

RESTAURANTS. Although our selection of restaurants in the Northern Neck area is not extensive, we are open to suggestions. Seafood, especially crab, is stressed here—and who could ask for anything more? Prices in general reflect the area's rural atmosphere; this is back-country Bayside, not Norfolk or Richmond or Virginia Beach.

Cap'n B's. *Expensive.* Tides Inn, ¼ mi. south of Irvington, Rte. 200; 438–5000. Luncheon only at Cap'n B's, but the Inn's main dining room is open for three meals daily. Excellent menu. Reservations suggested. AE, MC, V.

Northern Neck Seafood. *Inexpensive.* Located on U.S. 360, Red Hill, Warsaw; 333–3225. Open all year, this carry-out (only) offers steamed crabs, softshelled crabs, or—in fact—crabs just about any way you want them. Eight in the morning till 8 at night. Beer. Shell credit card only.

Pearson's Seafood. *Inexpensive.* 610 Colonial Ave., Colonial Beach; 224–7511. Live, steamed, and softshelled crabs. Open April to November. Carry-out only. Open to 6 P.M. No credit cards.

Pete Allen Oyster Company and Seafood. *Inexpensive.* Rte. 1, Montrose; 493–8711. Although this is a carry-out only, it's worth the effort; here is crab cookery at its best. Pete Allen's crab cakes are a delight. Open year round, longer hours during the crab season. No credit cards.

THINGS TO SEE AND DO

Lancaster County

Lancaster County, which was formed in 1651, is a blend of salt-water vitality and venerable Colonial history. Site of numerous outstanding marinas, quiet coves and anchorages, and beautiful scenery along the Rappahannock and Chesapeake shores, Lancaster County is "Chesapeake Bay living" at its best.

Windmill Point. Located on the southeastern tip of Northern Neck, Windmill Point offers a spectacular view of the Rappahannock where the river joins the Bay. Nearby, between White-Stone and Kilmarnock, is Christ Church, which has been described as "the most perfect example of Colonial church architecture now remaining in Virginia." It was completed in 1732 as a gift from Robert "King" Carter of nearby Corotoman. The Merry Point Ferry, one of the few remaining river ferries in Virginia, offers a delightful free crossing of scenic Corotoman River.

Lancaster Courthouse. The county seat since 1742, the town of Lancaster offers a trip into the past of early Tidewater Virginia. Around Court House Green are the original clerk's office (1797), Colonial jail, and Courthouse (1863). *Mary Ball Washington Museum and Library* is located in Lancaster House, also on the Court House Green. *Epping Forest,* built about 1690, was the birthplace of Mary Ball, the mother of George Washington.

Northumberland County

Northumberland is known as the "mother county" of the Northern Neck because several Virginia counties were carved from its original land. First settled in 1635 and officially formed in 1648, the county is bordered by the wide Potomac and sparkling Chesapeake Bay, blending recreational opportunities with the quiet, historic atmosphere for which the Neck is famous.

Reedville. Located near the northern tip of the Neck, Reedville is one of the busiest fishing ports in Virginia. The village provides a living image of the past with its magnificent Victorian mansions and seafaring atmosphere. Accessible by regularly scheduled boat cruises from Reedville, Smith and Tangier islands are quaint and historic. Their residents depend completely upon the Chesapeake for their livelihood. For cruise information, contact Evans Smith Island and Chesapeake Bay Cruise, (804) 453–3430; Smith Island Cruise, (804) 453–3430, or Tangier & Chesapeake Cruises, (804) 333–4656.

Chesapeake Bay and the Potomac River provide excellent fishing and crabbing as well as 438 miles of shoreline (including inland waterways). Public boat ramps are available throughout the county. Other attractions include charter fishing, marinas, and campgrounds. The fresh seafood available at local oyster and crab houses enhances any visit.

Sunnybrook Ferry. The ferry at Sunnybank offers free crossing for vehicles over the beautiful Little Wicomico River, and, *Heathville,* Northumberland's picturesque county seat, provides historic attractions including the *County Courthouse, Ball Memorial Library and Museum,* and *St. Stephens Church.*

Richmond County

Richmond County was formed in 1692 and named for the reigning favorite at the Court of William and Mary. The county stretches along the beautiful and unspoiled Rappahannock River. *Warsaw,* the county seat since 1730, was originally called Richmond County Courthouse. The village was renamed in 1831 in sympathy with the Polish struggle for liberty. Warsaw is the site of the *Courthouse* and *Clerk's Office,* built in 1816. The town is a commercial center, with a variety of shops and is the home of the North Campus of *Rappahannock Community College.*

North Farnham Church. Built in the form of a Latin cross, North Farnham Church is a beautiful example of Colonial architecture. *Naylors,* located beside an attractive Rappahannock River beach, was the seat of Richmond County's government from 1692 to 1730. The Rappahannock River offers beaches, crabbing, fishing, and watersports, plus lovely, peaceful countryside stretching back from the river's edge.

Oak Grove. Ingleside Plantation Vineyards and Winery, VA 638; 224–8687. Historic attractions and winery tours.

Warsaw. Rappahannock River Cruises from Tappahannock to Ingleside Winery and Wheatland. Phone 333–4656.

Westmoreland County

Westmoreland County, named for a British shire, was founded in 1653 by the Colonial government in Jamestown. The birthplace or home of more statesmen of national stature than any other county in the country, Westmoreland produced such leaders as George Washington, James Monroe, and Robert E. Lee.

Washington's Birthplace National Monument. Located in Wakefield, this is the site of our first president's birth. Wakefield provides a wealth of insight into life on an 18th-century plantation. Of special interest are the Visitor's Center, a memorial house of eighteenth-century design, a Colonial working farm, and the family burial plot. For details, call (804) 224–1732.

Stratford Hall. Perhaps the most majestic of the Colonial plantations in Virginia, Stratford Hall was the ancestral home of the Lee family and the birthplace of two signers of the Declaration of Independence and Robert E. Lee. Built in the 1720s, the restored mansion is furnished with exquisite period pieces. The 1,600-acre plantation includes gardens, stables, a working gristmill, and cliffs overlooking the Potomac. Phone 493–8038.

The Historic Courthouse Area in Montross features the old courthouse (circa 1707) standing on the site of the original courthouse (circa 1667) and the *Westmoreland Museum.*

Colonial Beach. Colonial Beach on the Potomac has been a popular river resort for more than a century. The town sponsors the *Potomac River Festival* and an outdoor art festival.

Westmoreland State Park. The park, also on the Potomac, offers cabins, camping, picnic areas, hiking, a public boat ramp, and swimming at the beach or in a new Olympic-size swimming pool.

NORTHERN VIRGINIA

by
RODNEY N. SMITH

Northern Virginia has been endowed with special historical, social, and cultural history since our earliest Colonial times. It is an almost perfectly balanced region, a blend of fashionable shops with cobblestoned streets; of fox hunts with opera and ballet; of rushing waterfalls over the Potomac with exciting nightlife. But above all, this is a place of history.

Famous men have walked this land. George Washington and George Mason, father of the Bill of Rights, were born and lived here. Robert E. Lee's boyhood home is here, as are several antebellum plantations like Woodlawn and Kenmore, once owned by the Washington family. And, of course, there is Washington's own eighteenth-century home, Mount Vernon.

From skyscraper to plantation is not a very great distance in Northern Virginia; in fact, a city like Alexandria has both. In Old Town Alexandria, however, eighteenth-century townhouses dominate the cobblestoned streets. Some of these historic homes are now delightful shops and restaurants with an ambience still of their Colonial past. The heritage lingers throughout the city, at Ramsay House, Gadsby's Tavern, and the Old Presbyterian Meeting House and Christ Church where both Washington and Lee worshipped on occasion.

Not all the heroes of Northern Virginia are even known by name. Each year millions of Americans visit Arlington National Cemetery and the Tombs of the Unknown Soldiers. Nearby is the famous monument where marines lift their flag in memorial to Iwo Jima. And Civil War battlefields at Chancellorsville, Spotsylvania-Fredericksburg, Manassas, and the Wilderness stand in solemn tribute to the valiant men who passed this way.

A few miles away, and 150 years later, supersonic jets land at Dulles International Airport, passing over the rich green countryside of Northern Virginia. It is a rapidly growing region but its essential character, its vitality, and its sense of the past have not changed. These are the qualities that make Northern Virginia the most distinctive and diversified part of the state.

Alexandria

Alexandria is a city born of Scottish merchants where, in the 1740s, clipper ships brought the booming tobacco trade to the Potomac shores. It is a city where George Washington came to worship, to dine, and to meet with fellow patriots as the nation fought for freedom. Today, it is a city where more than 100,000 residents and a million visitors from around the world come on foot, by bicycle, plane, train, tour bus, or horse-and-carriage to live, work, and play among more than 1,000 living landmarks.

Nestled a bike ride away from Washington, D.C., and George Washington's Mt. Vernon, Alexandria is a city where tradition is alive. It lives in historic homes, churches, and taverns, and in more than 100 of the Washington area's finest restaurants, serving everything from French, Greek, and Vietnamese to Scottish, Italian, and Colonial-American fare.

The city's rich heritage and colorful past live in more than 175 specialty shops and art galleries, many in restored eighteenth- and nineteenth-century buildings; in nearly 200 artists who ply their crafts at the restored 1918 Torpedo Factory Art Center on the revitalized waterfront; and in the parade of tartan-clad Scots who skirl, pipe, fiddle, fife, and dance through the streets during the city's many heritage celebrations. It is all part of the lively tradition that awaits visitors in Alexandria, a city where history lives today.

Specialty shops abound with American crafts and antiques, books, brass, baskets, candles, dollhouses, international fashions, fossils, and more. Colorful ethnic shops filled with unique handcrafted and imported goods make shopping in Alexandria an enjoyable way to spend a day.

Visitors may also want to go swimming, surfing, or just splashing around in Northern Virginia's only wave pool. They can set sail from one of several marinas, or take a picnic lunch and hike or bike their way through the parkland that lines the Potomac water-

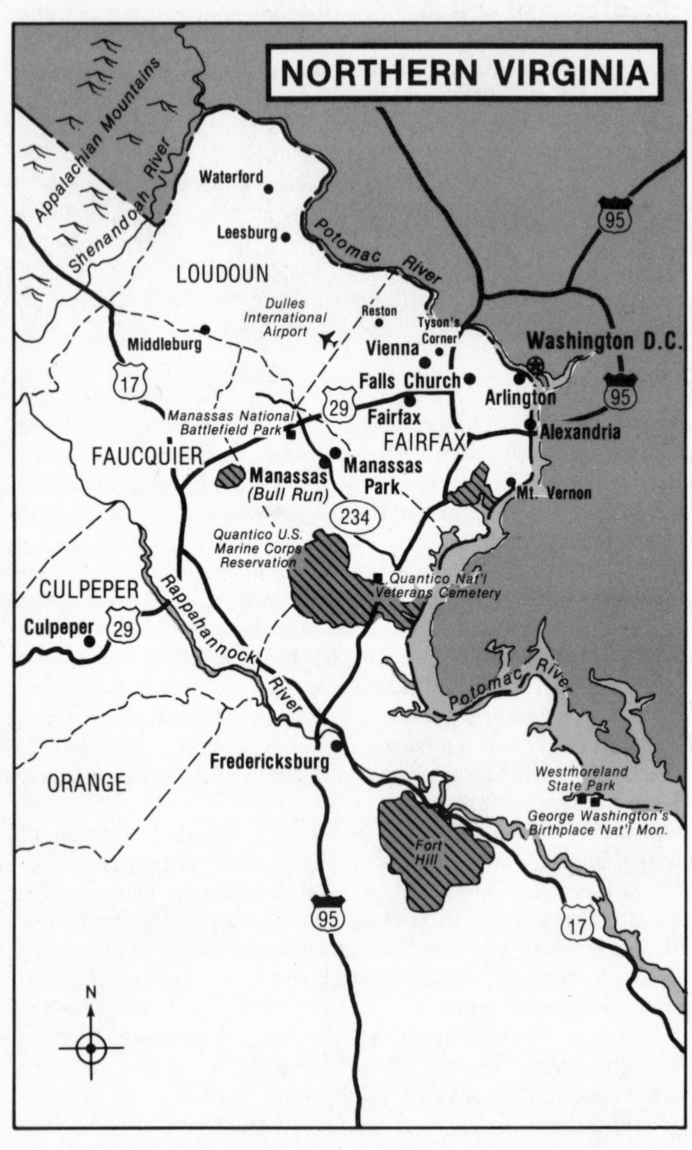
NORTHERN VIRGINIA
Appalachian Mountains
Shenandoah River
Waterford
Leesburg
Potomac River
LOUDOUN
Dulles International Airport
Reston
Tyson's Corner
Middleburg
Vienna
Washington D.C.
17
Falls Church
Arlington
95
29
Manassas National Battlefield Park
Fairfax
Alexandria
FAUCQUIER
FAIRFAX
Manassas (Bull Run)
Manassas Park
Mt. Vernon
234
Quantico U.S. Marine Corps Reservation
Quantico Nat'l Veterans Cemetery
CULPEPER
Culpeper
29
Rappahannock River
Potomac River
Fredericksburg
ORANGE
Westmoreland State Park
George Washington's Birthplace Nat'l Mon.
Fort Hill
95
17
N

front and follows the lazy trail of the former Washington and Old Dominion Railroad bed out into the hills of hunt country. It is all theirs to enjoy in Alexandria.

Arlington

When Capt. John Smith sailed up the Potomac in 1608 to explore what is now Arlington County, he saw lush banks dotted with Algonquin grass-mat longhouses. Already, Indians had been living in the area for more than 9,000 years. By 1669 an English ship captain, with land grant in hand, had laid claim to a 6,000-acre tract and sold it off to Scotsman John Alexander for 672 pounds of tobacco.

From then on the area flourished, agriculture and tobacco attracting new wealth and settlers. One of the most historic spots in the County is *Arlington House,* which commands a spectacular view of the area. George Washington Parke Custis, grandson of Martha Washington, built the home in 1817 and named it after the Custis estate in Virginia's Northampton County. In 1831 it became the home of Mary Anne Randolph Custis and her new husband, Lt. Robert E. Lee of the U.S. Army Corps of Engineers. Lee moved from the estate when the Civil War started and he took command of Northern's Virginia's Army and Navy. Today the home stands proudly in the heart of Arlington National Cemetery.

Since the Civil War Arlington's southern heritage has blended with the forces of its challenging and historic location. As the capital has soared in size and distinction, so has Arlington. Today its sleek hotels, impressive offices and shopping areas, and international cuisine all mark Arlington as Washington's most kindred suburb.

Five bridges connect Arlington to downtown Washington. Its rooftop restaurants offer the area's most dazzling views of the Washington skyline. The Jefferson and Lincoln Memorials, Washington Monument, White House, Georgetown, Kennedy Center, and Smithsonian are as easy to get to as they appear; all are located within 10 minutes of every hotel in Arlington. Visitors can turn north, west, or south from Arlington and even more history is within easy reach. Within Arlington itself are National Airport, the Pentagon, the Iwo Jima Memorial, and the business centers of Rosslyn and Crystal City—its popular Crystal Underground filled with delightful shops and restaurants.

Culpeper

Volunteers from Culpeper, Faucquier, and Orange counties marched on Williamsburg in 1777 in response to Governor Patrick Henry's call to arms. Their flag bore a coiled rattlesnake with the legends, "Don't Tread on Me" and "Liberty or Death."

In the winter of 1862, churches, homes, and vacant buildings in Culpeper were turned into hospitals for the wounded from the battles of Cedar Mountain, Kelly Ford, and Brandy Station. Later, the Union Army had its headquarters there.

Culpeper is now a light industry and trading center for a prosperous dairy and cattle-raising area.

Fairfax

Fairfax has been called the Silicon Valley of the East. It includes the growing cities of Falls Church and the City of Fairfax with its antebellum courthouse and modern highrise government buildings. There is a village of Vienna; Tyson's Corner, one of the fastest growing areas in the country with a modern shopping mall; and Reston, a modern Green-Belt city. Finally, there is Dulles Airport around which most of the county's future growth is planned and which is increasingly becoming a hub airport for major carriers.

Falls Church

Falls Church is a pleasant cosmopolitan suburb of Washington, just over the Arlington County line, graced with many interesting old houses, and one of the wealthiest communities in the United States. This was a crossover point between the Union and the Confederacy through which pioneers, armies, adventurers, and merchants passed.

Fredericksburg

If visitors have not been to Fredericksburg, they probably know very little about this historic town 50 miles south of Washington on I-95. But George Washington knew it well, and so did three-quarters of a million Union and Confederate troops during the Civil War.

Washington knew this place from a boyhood spent playing in its streets, exploring its bustling waterfront, and growing up across the river at Ferry Farm. Years later he would come to visit his mother Mary at the home he bought for her on Charles Street.

Others who figured prominently in the nation's early history have come as well: Capt. John Smith in 1608, touring England's New World Colonial empire; Thomas Jefferson and other patriots who shaped the ideals of the American Revolution; James Monroe, practicing law on the way to becoming our fifth president and again after leaving the chief executive's office.

Fredericksburg's role in history, however, does not end with the beginning of the country. From 1862 to 1864, the town witnessed more battles between North and South than any other town. In four major battles fought here, 17,000 died and more than 80,000 were wounded.

Fredericksburg has survived although the scars of war and time are still visible. Today, many of the more than 350 original eighteenth- and nineteenth-century buildings in Fredericksburg's 40-

block *National Historic District* are open to visitors, including Mary Washington's home, James Monroe's law office, the Rising Sun Tavern, and the magnificent 1752 plantation house, Kenmore, home of Washington's sister. Visitors can also dine in eighteenth-century fashion or enjoy some of the best cuisines of the modern world. This small town offers something to satisfy even the heartiest appetites.

Manassas (Bull Run)

The Manassas (Bull Run) *National Battlefield Park* is just 26 miles west of Washington at the junction of U.S. 29 and 234. This 3,000-acre park was the scene of two major Civil War battles. More than 24,000 men were killed or wounded here in struggles for the control of a strategically important railroad junction.

The first major land battle of the war was fought here on July 21, 1861, between ill-trained volunteer troops from the Union and from the Confederacy. The battle finally resolved itself into a struggle for Henry Hill, where "Stonewall" Jackson earned his nickname. With the outcome in doubt, Confederate reinforcements arrived by railroad from the Shenandoah Valley and turned the battle into a rout.

Thirteen months later, in the Second Battle of Manassas, Robert E. Lee outmaneuvered and defeated Union General John Pope and cleared the way for the Confederate invasion of Maryland.

Hunt Country

Loudoun County is the home of Middleburg, the unofficial capital of the "hunt country." Throughout the county visitors can enjoy point-to-point or steeplechase races, and perhaps even catch a glimpse of the fox hunts for which it is so famous.

Loudoun County is a perfect place to escape for a day in the country. If visitors want fine dining, country cuisine, craft fairs, antiques, or that special treasure, its towns and villages offer the very best.

Less than an hour from Washington, Loudoun County is another world. The historic towns and country estates reflect the grace and charm of hunt country living. Visitors can tour antebellum mansions, historic towns, or a Quaker village.

Country roads reveal one scenic oasis after another. Rolling past fields and creeks, visitors can discover quaint towns, historic churches, and breathtaking beauty to fill a day. If they are tempted to linger, the county's country inns will welcome them.

Nestled in the foothills of the Appalachian Mountains, Loudoun County is located only 30 miles from Washington metropolitan area. It is steeped in a long historical tradition, dating back to the early eighteenth century. Living examples of its tradition can be found daily in the historic communities of Leesburg, Waterford, and Lincoln as well as Middleburg. Oatlands and Morven Park, two exquisite homes that are open to the public, exemplify an era of country elegance that is typical of Loudoun's past. Fine examples of Loudoun's great history can be found in the museums and events that are offered to visitors throughout the year.

PRACTICAL INFORMATION FOR NORTHERN VIRGINIA

Note: The area code for Northern Virginia is 703.

TOURING INFORMATION. For advance touring information to Northern Virginia, contact: Alexandria Tourist Council, Ramsay House, 221 King St., Alexandria, VA 22314; (703) 838–4200; Arlington County Visitors Center, 735 S. 18th St., Arlington, VA 22202; (703) 521–0772; Fairfax County Office of Tourism & Visitors Service, 8300 Boone Blvd., Tyson's Corner, Vienna, VA 22180, (703) 790–0600; Fredericksburg Dept of Tourism, 706 Caroline St., Fredericksburg, VA 22401, (703) 373–1776; Loudoun County Office of Tourism, 108–D South St., SE, Leesburg, VA 22075, (703) 777–0519; Prince William County Tourism Services, 4349 Ridgewood Center Dr., Prince William, VA 22192, (703) 335–6680; or Rappahannock-Rapidan Planning District Commission, 121 W. Locust St., Culpeper, VA 22701, (703) 825–6140.

PLACES TO STAY

HOTELS, MOTELS AND INNS. There is no shortage of good, safe accommodations in Northern Virginia, from the Potomac westward to the mountains or southward to Fredericksburg. Because they are close to Washington, D.C., Alexandria, Arlington, Fairfax, and Tyson's Corner may be suburban in character, but price ranges often reflect their proximity to the Capitol. The following is a selection of accommodations throughout the region. Prices in general follow the guidelines set down in our *Planning Your Trip* section.

Alexandria

Morrison House. *Deluxe.* 116 S. Alfred St.; 548–4477. 47 rooms in a European-style inn. Excellent restaurant and bar. 24-hour room service. Facilities for the disabled. Major credit cards.

Radisson Mark Plaza & Conference Ctr. *Deluxe.* 5000 Seminary Rd.; 845–1010 or (800) 228–9822. 500 well-appointed rooms in 30 stories on 80 wooded acres. 5 restaurants and bars. Swimming and tennis. Views of the Capitol Plaza Club, with 35 rooms, on three high floors. AE, CB, DC, MC, V.

Guest Quarters Hotel. *Expensive to Deluxe.* 100 S. Reynolds St.; 370–9600. 212 rooms, some with balconies. Health club privileges. Restaurant and bar. Major credit cards.

Best Western Old Colony Inn. *Expensive to Deluxe.* 625 First St.; 548–6300 or 800–528–1234. 223 rooms. Meeting facilities. Pool, restaurant, and bar. Major credit cards.

Old Town Holiday Inn. *Expensive to Deluxe.* 480 King St. (Rte. 7); 549–6080. 227 rooms in the heart of Old Town with health club privileges. Some balconies, indoor pool, restaurant, and bar. AE, CB, DC, MC, V.

Holiday Inn. *Expensive.* 2460 Eisenhower Dr., near the Expressway; 960–3400 or (800) 465–8000. A convenient location, with 203 rooms, restaurant, and pool. Major credit cards.

Howard Johnson's. *Expensive.* 5821 Richmond Hwy.; 768–3300. Exercise room. 24-hour restaurant and bar. Major credit cards.

Ramada Inn Old Town. *Moderate to Expensive.* 901 N. Fairfax St.; 683–6000. 258 rooms with views of the Potomac and downtown Washington. Pool, restaurant, and bar. Major credit cards.

Ramada Seminary Plaza. *Moderate to Expensive.* I–395 and Seminary Rd.; 751–4510. 193 rooms. Indoor pool, restaurant, room service, and bar. AE, CB, DC, MC, V.

Imperial Inn. *Moderate.* 6461 Edsall Rd.; 354–4400. 204 rooms. Restaurant, room service, and bar. Pool. Major credit cards.

Travelers. *Moderate.* 5916 Richmond Hwy.; 329–1310. 29 rooms. Golf and ice-skating privileges. Restaurant nearby. AE, MC, V.

Arlington

Embassy Suites—Crystal City. *Deluxe.* 1300 Jefferson Davis Hwy., near airport; 979–9799. 267 suites in an 11-story hotel. Heated pool, restaurants, bar, and meeting rooms. Free full breakfast. Health-club privileges. Major credit cards.

Hyatt Arlington. *Deluxe.* 1325 Wilson Blvd.; 525–1234. 303 rooms with free garage in beautiful Rosslyn across the bridge from Georgetown. Restaurant, bar, convention facilities. Major credit cards.

Hyatt Regency Crystal City. *Deluxe.* 2799 Jefferson Davis Hwy., near National Airport; 486–1234. 688 units with concierge and health club and some with private patios and balconies across from Washington National Airport. Includes The Regency Club on the Luxury Level, 42 units with wet bars, deluxe toiletry amenities, private lounge and honor bar. Hotel restaurant and bar. Major credit cards.

Marriott—Crystal City. *Deluxe.* 1999 Jefferson Davis Hwy.; 521–5500. 340 rooms with concierge, shopping arcade and health club. Major credit cards.

Marriott Crystal Gateway. *Deluxe.* 1700 Jefferson Davis Hwy., 5 miles south on U.S. 1; 920–3230. 700 rooms with concierge. Modern hotel with luxurious furnishings. Restaurants, room service, and bar. Also, the super-luxury Regency Club. Major credit cards.

Holiday Inn—Key Bridge. *Expensive to Deluxe.* 1850 N. Ft. Myer Dr.; 522–0400. 177 rooms with free parking. Pool, cafe. Major credit cards.

Howard Johnson's—National Airport. *Expensive to Deluxe.* 2650 Jefferson Davis Hwy.; 684–7200. 276 rooms, some with balconies. Senior citizen discount. Major credit cards.

Holiday Inn—National Airport. *Expensive.* 1489 Jefferson Davis Hwy.; 521–1600. 306 rooms with free garage. Pool, meeting rooms. Near Metro. Major credit cards.

National Clarion. *Expensive.* 300 Army-Navy Dr.; 892–4100. 633 rooms, opposite Pentagon, with exercise room and free parking. Rooftop bar. Major credit cards.

Stouffer's Concourse Hotel. *Expensive.* 2399 Jefferson Davis Hwy.; 979–6800. 388 rooms with concierge, and health club. Bar entertainment and dancing. Major credit cards.

Best Western Rosslyn Westpark. *Moderate to Expensive.* 1900 N. Ft. Myer Dr.; 527–4814. 307 rooms. Free covered parking. Health club, game room, restaurant, dining room, and bar. Major credit cards.

Quality Inn Arlington Hotel. *Moderate to Expensive.* 1190 N. Court House Rd.; 524–4000. 384 rooms, some with balconies and refrigerators. Includes The Club Royale on the Luxury Level, 21 suites with kitchens, deluxe breakfast, and toiletry amenities, private lounge and honor bar. The hotel has a restaurant and bar. Major credit cards.

Cherry Blossom Motor Inn. *Moderate.* 3030 Columbia Pike; 521–5570. 76 rooms with free morning coffee and doughnuts. Restaurant for lunch and dinner. Major credit cards.

Imperial Inn—Rosslyn. *Moderate.* 2201 Arlington Blvd.; 525–0300. Pool, cafe, and game room. Major credit cards.

Culpeper

Graves' Mountain Lodge. *Deluxe.* Guest ranch in Syria, 20 miles west on VA 670; 923–4231. 38 rooms and 7 cottages, 2 with kitchens. Pool, playground, tennis, golf privileges, recreation room. Dining room, meeting rooms. Closed Dec.–Mar. MC, V.

Holiday Inn. *Moderate.* 2½ miles south on U.S. 29; 825–1253. Pool, playground, cafe, bar. Room service. Major credit cards.

Econo Lodge. *Inexpensive.* Junction of U.S. 15 and 29; 825–5097, 48 rooms. Senior citizen rates. Restaurant nearby. Major credit cards.

Fairfax

Ramada Renaissance—Washington Dulles. *Deluxe.* 71 Park Center Rd., Herndon, on VA 28, Sully and McLearen Rds.; 478–2900. 300 rooms. Full hotel facilities, with a luxury-level Renaissance Club with 65 rooms. Meeting rooms and free airport transportation. All major credit cards.

Courtyard by Mariott—Fair Oaks. *Expensive.* 11220 Lee Jackson Hwy.; 273–6161. 146 rooms in a 3-story motel. Restaurant, bar, pool, and meeting rooms. Balconies and patios. Major credit cards.

Holiday Inn Fairfax City. *Moderate.* 3535 Chain Bridge Rd.; 591–5500. 127 rooms. Includes kennels. Pool, restaurant, bar. Major credit cards.

Falls Church

Ramada Hotel Tyson's. *Expensive.* 7801 Leesburg Pike; 893–1340 or (800) 228–2828. 209 rooms. Restaurant and pool. Suburban location, 8 miles from National Airport. AE, CB, DC, MC, V.

Best Western Falls Church Inn. *Moderate.* 6633 Arlington Blvd; 532–9000. 106 rooms. Restaurant, bar, meeting rooms. Major credit cards.

Quality Inn Executive. *Moderate.* 6111 Arlington Blvd; 534–9100. 109 rooms. Pool, game room. Restaurant and bar. Major credit cards.

Fredericksburg

Sheraton Fredericksburg Resort & Conference Center. *Expensive.* 2801 Plank Rd.; 786–8321. 196 rooms with tennis court and 18-hole golf course. Pool, playground. Restaurants and bar with entertainment, meeting rooms. Tennis and golf. Major credit cards.

Best Western Johnny Appleseed Inn. *Moderate.* Rte. 12, I–95, Falmouth-Warrenton exit; 373–0000. 88 rooms. Johnny Appleseed Restaurant & Lounge. Pool. Major credit cards.

Best Western Thunderbird. *Moderate.* 3000 Plank Rd. at I–95, Culpeper exit; 786–7404. 76 rooms. Restaurant. Major credit cards.

Days Inn—North. *Moderate.* I–95 and US 17 N; 373–5340. 120 rooms. Near the Expressway. Restaurant and pool. Major credit cards.

Fredericksburg Colonial Inn. *Moderate.* 1707 Princess Anne St., less than an hour south of Washington on the Rappahannock; 371–5666. 36 rooms, furnished with Civil War antiques. Meeting facilities. Refrigerators in each room. MC, V.

Holiday Inn—North. *Moderate.* U.S. 17 and I–95; 371–5550. 150 rooms. Pool. Cafe, bar, dancing. Senior citizen discount. Major credit cards.

Holiday Inn—South. *Moderate.* On U.S. 1 at I–95; 898–1102. 200 rooms. Restaurant and bar. Pool, hot tub, sauna. AE, CB, DC, MC, V.

Howard Johnson's. *Moderate.* 5327 Jefferson Davis Hwy.; 898–1800. 137 rooms with private patios or balconies. Pool, restaurant, and bar. Major credit cards.

Ramada Inn on-the-Mall. *Moderate.* 3 miles west of Rte. 3, at junction I–95; 786–8361. 130 rooms. Golf privileges. Pool. Restaurant, bar, and room service. Major credit cards.

Scottish Inn. *Inexpensive.* 5309 Jefferson Davis Hwy.; U.S. 1 and I–95; 898–1000 or (800) 251–1962. 100 rooms, with a restaurant and lounge. Major credit cards.

Leesburg

Colonial Inn. *Expensive to Deluxe.* 19 S. King St.; 777–5000. 10 rooms with Early American decor. Excellent restaurant, with service bar. Free Continental breakfast. Major credit cards.

Westpark Hotel & Golf Club. *Moderate to Expensive.* 1100 Club House Dr.; 777–1910 or (800) 222–7666. 131 rooms. Lighted tennis and golf privileges. Restaurant and bar. Major credit cards.

Manassas

Holiday Inn. *Moderate.* 10800 Vandor La.; 361–0131. 160 rooms, typical Holiday Inn accommodations. Meeting rooms. Restaurant. Major credit cards.

Ramada Inn. *Moderate.* 7104 Sudley Rd.; 631–0221. 128 rooms. Meeting facilities. Major credit cards.

Olde Towne Inn. *Moderate.* 9403 Main St.; 368–9191. 56 rooms, with coffeehouse and pool. Major credit cards.

Middleburg

Red Fox Tavern. *Deluxe.* 2 East Washington St., Rte. 50, Middleburg; 687–6301. 6 rooms in Red Fox and 8 rooms in the **Stray Fox,** plus 5 in the **McConnell House,** nearby on Liberty St. rooms, some with private patios and balconies. Built in 1728, this is the oldest building in America continuously operated as an inn. Restaurant and bar. Antique furnishing. Mosby's Tavern. AE, MC, V.

Tyson's Corner

Sheraton Premiere. *Deluxe.* 8661 Leesburg Pike; 448–1234 455 rooms in a 24-story hotel. Restaurants, bars, pool, and concierge. Golf and tennis privileges. Health club. Major credit cards.

Holiday Inn—Tyson's Corner. *Expensive to Deluxe.* 1960 Chain Bridge Rd.; 893–2100. 321 rooms, some with balconies. Restaurant and bar. AE, CB, DC, MC, V.

Marriott—Tyson's Corner. *Expensive to Deluxe.* 8028 Leesburg Pike; 734–3200. 393 rooms with concierge, health club, and some breathtaking views of Washington and the rolling countryside. Restaurant, room service, and bar. Typical of Marriott's efforts to please. Major credit cards.

Ramada Inn—Tyson's Corner. *Expensive.* 7801 Leesburg Pike; Falls Church; 893–1340. 404 rooms. Health club privileges. Restaurant, room service, and bar. Major credit cards.

Tyson's Westpark (Best Western). *Expensive.* 8401 W. Park Dr., near Exit 10W off I–495; 734–2800. 301 rooms with concierge. Restaurant and bar. Major credit cards.

PLACES TO EAT

RESTAURANTS. As is true with accommodations in Northern Virginia, the visitor has an ample selection of good and safe places to eat—those restaurants that satisfy our needs for good food, good service, and "good prices" for the food and service they offer. The following is merely a *selection* of restaurants in the area.

Alexandria

The Dandy. *Expensive to Deluxe.* A somewhat past-her-prime riverboat, moored at the foot of Prince St., Potomac River; 683–6076. Two-hour luncheon cruises several times a week and three-hour dinner cruises nightly. Major credit cards.

Chez Andre. *Expensive.* 10 E. Glebe Rd.; 836–1404. French menu, specializing in salmon hollandaise and coquille St. Jacques, with French decor. Serving bar and a fine wine cellar. Reservations. Major credit cards.

King's Landing. *Expensive.* 121 S. Union St., Potomac waterfront; 836–7010. Seafood reigns supreme here. Try the King's Landing seafood in cream sauce. Reservations requested. AE, CB, DC, MC, V.

La Bergerie. *Expensive.* 218 N. Lee St., Old Town; 683–1007. Exceptional Basque and French dishes, including a sophisticated bean and cabbage soup from the Pyrenees. One of Old Town's most attractive restaurants, formerly a warehouse. Jacket and tie required. Closed Sunday. Major credit cards.

Le Chardon d'Or. *Expensive.* 116 S. Alfred St., Morrison House; 838–8008. Breakfast, lunch, and dinner, and a pleasant Sunday brunch in an elegant dining room. Seasonal and local dishes, with a new menu daily. Jackets. Table d'hôte dinner in the *Deluxe* range. Major credit cards.

Portner's. *Expensive.* 109 South St. Asaph St.; 683–1776. A beautifully appointed pub, with excellent light-fare menu. Sunday brunch. AE, DC, MC, V.

Seaport Inn. *Expensive.* 6 King St.; 549–2341. Seafood in an 18th-century building overlooking the Potomac. Bar. Closed Thanksgiving and Christmas. Major credit cards.

The Wayfarer. *Expensive.* 110 S. Pitt St.; 863–2749. Veal chops, kidney pie, trifle, and British ales and beers in attractive British colonial rooms. Major credit cards.

Bamiyan. *Moderate to Expensive.* 300 King St.; 548–9006. This Afghan restaurant's menu combines Middle Eastern and Indian cooking. Try the *aushak* (leek- or scallion-fried ravioli with meat sauce, mint, and yogurt), sautéed pumpkin or eggplant, kebabs, and baklava or "elephant ears" for dessert. MC, V.

Gadsby's Tavern. *Moderate to Expensive.* 138 N. Royal St.; 548–1288. Built in 1792, this Georgian inn is where General Washington last reviewed his troops and then probably sat down for a hearty meal. International, American, and French menu, specializing in Washington's favorite duck recipe and Sally Lunn bread. Gadsby's is a must for most visitors. AE, MC, V.

Terrazza Ristorante. *Moderate to Expensive.* 710 King St.; 683–6900. Classic Italian fare in a charming setting in the heart of historic Old Town. Major credit cards.

219. *Moderate to Expensive.* 219 King St.; 549–1141. French-Creole-Cajun menu in an interesting turn-of-the-century residence. Victorian furnishings. Wine list. Sunday brunch. Reservations requested. AE, MC, V.

Bilbo Baggins. *Moderate.* 208 Queen St.; 683–0300. A Tolkien character, but hardly a Hobbit menu. Fish, pasta, and beef, with oak tables, plank floors, and a center-floor brick oven. Good wine list, and wonderful desserts. Dinner reservations suggested. AE, MC, V.

Ernie's Original Crab House. *Moderate.* 1623 Fern St.; 836–1623. Ernie's features a $12 all-you-can-eat dinner special, with crab the original house specialty. MC, V.

Scotland Yard. *Moderate.* 728 King St.; 683–1742. Traditional Scottish dishes in a pleasant, cozy atmosphere. Dinner only. MC, V.

Hard Times Cafe. *Inexpensive.* 1404 King St.; 683–5340. Chili—Texas or Cincinnati styles—with corn bread and Country-Western jukebox music. Beer, wine, and no reservations. Usually jammed to the rustic rafters. MC, V.

Annandale

Duck Chang's. *Inexpensive.* 4427 John Marr Dr.; 941–9400. Regulars crowd this tiny suburban restaurant for its tasty Peking duck. One duck serves two, and no advance notice is necessary. Sunday brunch. AE, MC, V.

Arlington

The View Restaurant. *Expensive to Deluxe.* 1401 Lee Hwy., 14th floor Key Bridge Marriott; 524–6400. Aptly named, this elegant dining room overlooks the Potomac River and Washington's breathtaking buildings and monuments on the far bank. Especially spectacular at night. Lobster bisque, veal, and poached salmon are house specialties. Major credit cards.

Top o' the Town. *Expensive.* Prospect House, 14th and Oak sts.; 525–9200. Noted for its spectacular view of the nation's capital, but also dinner dancing and Sunday brunch. AE, MC, V.

Veronique's. *Expensive.* 1700 Jefferson Davis Hwy., Marriott Crystal Gateway; 892–8793. French cuisine in a garden setting. Fresh seafood in season. Service bar. Dinner only on Sundays. Jackets required, but available there. Major credit cards.

Capriccio. *Moderate to Expensive.* 1999 Jefferson Davis Hwy., Marriott Crystal City Hotel on U.S. 1; 521–5500. Capriccio features an Italian menu and ambience. Major credit cards.

Woo Lae Dak. *Moderate to Expensive.* 1500 S. Joyce St., River House complex; 521–3706. Korean dishes prepared at your table. Korean decor. Bar. Reserve weekends. AE, MC, V.

Ristorante Michelangelo. *Moderate.* 2900 Columbia Pike at Walter Reed Dr.; 920–2900. Northern Italian cooking, featuring seafood and veal. Open daily, except major holidays. AE, DC, MC, V.

Alpine. *Inexpensive to Expensive.* 4770 Lee Hwy.; 528–7600. Italian veal, pastas, and seafood for the family, with outdoor dining in season. Service bar. Lunch and dinner. Closed major holidays. Major credit cards.

Kabul Caravan. *Moderate.* 1725 Wilson Blvd.; 522–8394. An attractive Afghan restaurant, a short drive from Georgetown via Key Bridge. Excellent kebabs, Afghan breads and puddings. MC, V.

Matuba. *Moderate.* 2915 Columbus Pike; 521–2811. Sushi and sashimi are featured, but Matuba also serves hot dishes. CB, DC, MC, V.

Bangkok Gourmet. *Inexpensive to Moderate.* 523 S. 23rd St.; 521–1305. Thai food, spicy and memorable. Flavorful soups, spicy beef, and red Thai curry with rice. Try a Thai beer to cool things down. AE, MC, V.

Crystal Dinery. *Inexpensive to Moderate.* 18th St. and Jefferson Davis Hwy., Crystal City; 920–3930. 10 international and deli outlets under one roof, featuring exotic dishes from exotic lands. Open daily, lunch through dinner, Mon.–Sat. Some credit cards.

Tom Sarris' Orleans House. *Inexpensive to Moderate.* 1213 Wilson Blvd.; 524–2929. Prime beef and an excellent salad bar. New Orleans ambience. Major credit cards.

Fairfax

The Alibi. *Moderate to Deluxe.* 10418 Main St., junction of Rtes. 236 and 123; 591–6319. An imaginative French menu, well served in a Provincial French decor. Bar. Closed Sun. Jackets necessary. Reservations requested. AE, DC, MC, V.

J.R.'s Steak House. *Moderate to Expensive.* 9401 Lee Hwy.; 591–8447. Steak, lobster, and fresh seafood. Bar and salad bar. Closed Mon. and major holidays. AE, MC, V.

P.J. Skidoo's. *Inexpensive to Moderate.* 9908 Lee Hwy.; 591–4516. Chicken, fish, and beef in a Gay Nineties saloon. Full bar, music, but children welcome. Closed major holidays. AE, MC, V.

Falls Church

La Guinguette. *Expensive to Deluxe.* 8111 Lee Hwy.; 560–3220. French menu. Bar. Sunday brunch. Major credit cards.

Mountain Jacks. *Moderate to Expensive.* 127 E. Broad St.; 532–6500. Seafood and beef, with a bar, entertainment. Lunch and dinner daily except Christmas. Major credit cards.

V.I.P. Ocean Seafood. *Inexpensive to Expensive.* 7161 Lee Hwy.; 237–1161. A bewildering Chinese menu with a full-service bar. Seafood, including lobster, is a house specialty. Major credit cards.

Country Squire. *Inexpensive to Moderate.* Leesburg Pike and Patrick Henry Dr.; 534–4200. Seafood and steak. Major credit cards.

Sir Walter Raleigh Inn. *Inexpensive to Moderate.* 8120 Gatehouse Rd.; 560–6768. Seafood, steak, and salad bar. Lunch and dinner daily, except Thanksgiving and Christmas. Major credit cards.

Fredericksburg

Old Towne Steak and Seafood. *Expensive.* 1612 Caroline St., Old Town; 371–8020. "Surf and turf" in a Colonial atmosphere. Closed Mon. Reservations suggested. AE, MC, V.

Chimney's. *Moderate to Expensive.* 623 Caroline St., Old Town; 371–9229. Regional and classic cuisine in a charming old Georgian structure, registered as a Virginia landmark. AE, CB, DC, MC, V.

Diamond Head. *Moderate to Expensive.* Exit 44, I–95, north to 5097 Rte. 1; 898–1333. Seafood and steak with a Polynesian accent. Open daily, lunch and dinner. AE, MC, V.

Kenmore Inn. *Moderate to Expensive.* 1200 Princess Anne St.; 371–7622. This private home, dating back to the 1700s, is one of Dawn O'Brien's favorite Virginia historic restaurants. Reservations recommended. MC, V.

La Petite Auberge. *Moderate to Expensive.* 311 William St.; 371–2727. Another marvelous old Virginia restaurant, historic but with food to match its appealing ambience. Try the backfin crab Norfolk. Luncheon and dinner. Reservations a must. Major credit cards.

Dauphine. *Moderate to Expensive.* Sheraton Fredericksburg Resort, 2801 Plank Rd.; 786–8321. Loin lamb chops a special treat. Jackets requested. Major credit cards.

Old Mudd Tavern. *Moderate.* 12 miles south of Fredericksburg on I–95 in Thornburg; 582–5250. 18th- and 19th-century ambience. Fresh vegetables, steaks, and fresh baked goods. Major credit cards.

Great Falls

L'Auberge Chez Frannois. *Expensive.* 332 Springvale Rd.; 759–3800. A superb French country inn that may be difficult to find, but well worth the effort. Advance reservations are a must. The ambience is charming and the food a delight. Two seatings nightly, three on Sunday. Jacket required. Good wine cellar. AE, MC, V.

Serbian Crown. *Moderate to Deluxe.* 1141 Walker Rd., north of town on Rte. 7, then Rte. 743; 759–4150. They seem to be hiding their restaurants around Great Falls, but delighted diners manage to find them. This one has a French-Serbian menu, with gypsy music some nights and outdoor dining in season. Enclosed terrace. Jacket. Major credit cards.

Leesburg

Colonial Inn. *Moderate to Expensive.* 19 S. King St. at the Inn; 777–5000. A Continental menu in a pleasant atmosphere. Lunch and dinner daily and a Sunday brunch. Bar. Major credit cards.

Laurel Brigade Inn. *Moderate to Expensive.* 20 W. Market St.; 777–1010. Chicken pot pie or curried chicken in an old inn with a lovely garden. The Apple Brown Betty is recommended. Reservations also recommended. No credit cards.

Tuscarora Mill. *Moderate to Expensive.* 203 Harrison St. SE; 771–9300. Fine American cuisine, featuring seafood and meat dishes, in a charming old mill. Open daily, lunch and dinner, Sunday brunch. AE, MC, V.

McLean

Evans Farm Inn. *Moderate to Expensive.* 1696 Chain Bridge Rd.; 356–8000. Fresh seafood and Virginia ham, Colonial style, served outdoors in season. Try the Chicken Barbara. Service bar. Children welcome. Lunch and dinner daily. Also a country store and animals on a 40-acre farm. Major credit cards.

Kazan. *Moderate to Expensive.* 6813 Redmond Dr.; 734–1960. Wonderful Turkish food, including sliced beef in yogurt, tomato, and dill sauce—*yogurtlu* kebab. This restaurant is popular with locals. AE, DC, MC, V.

La Mirabelle. *Moderate to Expensive.* 6645 Old Dominion Dr., McLean Square shopping center; 893–8484. Pleasantly French, with a bar and good wine list. Lunch and dinner, with jackets required in the evening. Closed Sun. and major holidays. Major credit cards.

Middleburg

Red Fox Tavern. *Moderate to Expensive.* 2 E. Washington St.; 687–6301. Charming historic country inn, with an imaginative country menu. Breakfast, lunch, and dinner served daily. Reservations suggested. AE, MC, V.

Rosslyn

Tivoli. *Expensive.* 1700 N. Moore St., Rosslyn Center; 524–8900. Interesting Continental dishes well served in a beautifully decorated third-floor dining room atop Rosslyn Metro station. Sunday brunch. AE, DC, MC, V.

China Garden. *Moderate.* 1901 N. Moore St., across Key Bridge from Georgetown; 525–5317. First-rate Cantonese menu, including *dim sum* on weekends in a spacious dining room. Good views of the Potomac. AE, CB, MC, V.

Tyson's Corner

Company Inkwell. *Expensive.* 8330 Old Courthouse Rd. in Tycon II building; 356–0300. In spite of its name, the menu is French, with seafood and veal house specialties. Like many better Northern Virginia restaurants, jackets are required. Piano bar. Closed Sun. Major credit cards.

American Cafe. *Moderate to Expensive.* 8601 Westwood Center Dr.; 848–9476. Mesquite-grilled fare in a chain restaurant that welcomes children. Bar and dancing. Sunday brunch, 11 A.M.–3 P.M. AE, MC, V.

Da Domenico's. *Moderate to Expensive.* 1992 Chain Bridge Rd., near Exit 11B, I–495; 790–9000. Lunch and dinner, with a fine Northern Italian menu. Bar. Closed Sun. Major credit cards.

Le Mistral. *Moderate to Expensive.* Near Exit 11B, I–495, Tyson's Corner Center. Decidedly French, featuring seafood and veal. Bar. Sunday brunch. Closed Christmas and New Year's Day. Major credit cards.

Vienna

Pierre et Madeleine. *Deluxe.* 246 E. Maple Ave.; 938–4379. Pleasantly French, but try the fresh Maine lobster with the chef's special sauce. Bar and wine list. Lunch weekdays but dinner only Sat. and Sun. Reservations suggested. Major credit cards.

Clyde's. *Moderate to Expensive.* 8332 Leesburg Pike, near Exit 10W, I–495; 734–1901. Seafood and steak in pleasant surroundings. Jackets. Sunday brunch. Major credit cards.

Le Canard. *Moderate to Expensive.* 132 Branch Rd. at Rte. 123; 281–0070. An excellent French menu, with veal and seafood house specialties. Piano bar most nights. Lunch and dinner weekdays. Closed Sun. Reservations suggested. Major credit cards.

Hunan Lion. *Moderate.* 2070 Chain Bridge Rd. on Rte. 123; 734–9828. Full and excellent Chinese menu. Bar. Open daily, lunch and dinner. Closed Christmas and New Year's Day. Major credit cards.

Warrenton

Sixty-Seven Waterloo. *Moderate to Expensive.* 67 Waterloo; 347–1200. Pleasant dining and an excellent and imaginative menu in a restored antebellum mansion. Try the crabmeat with hazelnuts or the veal Française. Lunch and dinner. Reservations suggested. AE, MC, V.

Warsaw

Lowery's Roma. *Moderate.* 500 W. Richmond Rd.; 333–9333. Italian cuisine, featuring steaks and seafood. Mixed beverages. Open daily, breakfast through dinner. MC, V.

Washington

Inn at Little Washington. *Deluxe.* Off U.S. 211 (and 522), Middle and Main Sts.; 675–3800. An outstanding Hunt Country restaurant in a fine old country inn. Continental menu and an excellent wine cellar. The Coeur à la crème with raspberry sauce and crab and spinach timbale are house specialties. Dinner only, jacket and tie. Closed Mon. and Tues. Reservations required. MC, V.

THINGS TO SEE AND DO

Alexandria

HISTORIC SITES. Walking tours of the historic sights start at the Alexandria Tourist Council in *Ramsay House* (circa 1724), 221 King St. It is the oldest house in Alexandria and during its lifetime has been used as a tavern, a grocery store, and a cigar factory. Visitors can take in a 13-minute movie about Alexandria, pick up a self-guided walking tour brochure, and buy "block tickets" for four of the city's historic properties. Other visitor information is also available. For more details, contact Alexandria Tourist Council, King and Fairfax Sts.; 549–0205.

The stately *Carlyle House,* just up the street at 121 North Fairfax, is a country-manor style Scottish stone mansion. It was the site of a 1755 meeting between General Edward Braddock and five British Colonial governors to plan the early campaigns of the French and Indian War.

Old churches abound in Northern Virginia. *Christ Church* at 118 North Washington St. was built in 1773. Washington and Lee were both pew holders. The interior features a fine Palladian window, interior balcony, and a wrought-brass and crystal chandelier brought from England at Washington's expense. It is a fine example of an English, Georgian country-style church. The nearby *Old Presbyterian Meeting House* at 321 South Fairfax St. was built in 1774, and the Tomb of the Unknown Soldier of the Revolution is in the courtyard. This was an important meeting place for Scottish patriots during the Revolution.

Stabler–Leadbeater Apothecary Shop at 105 S. Fairfax St. was built in 1792 and is the oldest apothecary shop in the state and the second oldest in the country. It houses a fine collection of more than 900 apothecary bottles. The original building is now a museum of early pharmacy and an antique shop. Open Tues.–Thur., 10–3; Fri. and Sat., 10–5. Call 838–4399 for information.

The boyhood home of Robert E. Lee is also open to the public at 607 Oronoco Street. It features Federal-style architecture and antique furnishings and paintings. Other sights include the *Lee-Feddall House,* (the home of General Henry Light Horse Harry), Lee's home, the *Lafayette House* and the *Lyceum,* together with many restored but private homes and stores.

George Washington Masonic National Memorial stands over the city on Shooter's Hill at the west end of King St. It is patterned after the ancient lighthouse at Alexandria, Egypt. The 333-foot high building has an observation platform, organ, and relics of Washington's term as master of the Alexandria-Washington Lodge of Masons. Phone 683–2007.

The Torpedo Factory Arts Center at 105 North Union St. on the River in Old Town is a renovated munitions plant. It houses an Artists' Center with over 200 professional artists of various media. It includes studios, cooperative galleries, and a school, and most of the pieces of art are for sale at reasonable prices.

Arlington

Originally part of the District of Columbia laid out for the capital in 1791, this land across the Potomac River was returned to Virginia in 1846. Arlington is the urban center of northern Virginia. The Arlington Visitor Service is located at 735 S. 18th St., Arlington. Phone 521–0772.

ARLINGTON NATIONAL CEMETERY. Arlington is the most famous of our national cemeteries. It was established in 1864. Almost 200,000 men and women who have served their country are buried here, including two presidents: John F. Kennedy and William Howard Taft. "Tourmobiles" take visitors around the cemetery grounds.

On November 11, 1921, the unidentified remains of an American soldier of World War I were entombed in the Tomb of the Unknown Soldier. A memorial was erected in 1932. On Memorial Day in 1958, an unknown soldier who died in World War II and another who died in the Korean War were added. On Memorial Day 1984, an unknown soldier from the Vietnam War was interred here. Sentries guard the site 24 hours a day, with formal changing of the guard every hour.

Arlington House, now a national memorial to Robert E. Lee, stands on a nearby hill overlooking the solemn graves of John and Robert Kennedy. It was built between 1802 and 1818 by George Washington Parke Custis, Martha Washington's grandson and the foster son of George Washington. In 1831 his daughter, Mary Randolph Custis, married Lt. Robert E. Lee and it was here that they raised their family.

The site was confiscated in 1864 and a 200-acre section was set aside for the national cemetery. G.W. Custis Lee, the general's son, later regained title to the property through a Supreme Court decision and sold it to the U.S. Government in 1883 for $150,000.

Restoration of the house to its 1861 condition was begun in 1925. This is a beautiful Greek Revival home furnished with authentic period pieces, some from the Lee family. From the grand portico with its six massive Doric columns, there is a panoramic view of Washington, D.C.

Nearby, the Iwo Jima Statue or Marine Corps War Memorial on Arlington Boulevard depicts the raising of the flag on Mt. Suribachi on February 23, 1945. It is the largest sculpture ever cast in bronze. The Marine Corps conducts formal marches with martial music every Tuesday night in season. Concerts are also played on a nearby 49-bell carillon that was a gift from the people of the Netherlands. Phone (202) 697–2131.

THE PENTAGON. The Pentagon Building, bounded by Jefferson Davis Hwy., I-95, and Washington Blvd., is the largest office building in the world with almost 4 million square feet. It offers an 80-minute tour of the home of the Defense Department. It is a major stop on the Metro and the northern terminus of the Virginia mass transit system. The Pentagon houses a large underground shopping center, built for military personnel but open to the public, accessed from the Metro. Tours Mon.–Fri. Phone (202) 695–1776.

Culpeper

MUSEUM. Visitors to Culpeper will want to take in the *Culpeper Cavalry Museum,* 133 W. Davis St. The museum houses a comprehensive collection of weaponry, cavalry equipment, artifacts, and memorabilia from the Civil War. Some highlights are examples of Fayetteville and Mississippi rifles, stirrups and spurs, and a complete collection of Confederate weapons.

Fairfax

HISTORIC SITES. Fairfax is the home of impressive antebellum *Sully Plantation* (ca 1794), which can be found 10 miles west of town on VA Rte. 28. It is the restored home of Richard Bland Lee, brother of "Lighthorse" Harry Lee. It includes some original furnishings, an outdoor kitchen-washhouse, and smokehouse on the grounds. Guided tours are offered.

George Mason University, 4400 University Dr., is a fast growing branch of the University of Virginia system. Its Fenwich Library maintains the largest collection of material relating to the Federal Theater Project of the 1930s. Its 15,000 students will soon be the beneficiaries of Virginia's new High Tech Center.

PARKS. Fairfax County maintains an impressive network of parks. They include: *Burke Lake,* 6 miles south of Fairfax on Rte. 123 in Fairfax Station, is 888 acres of parkland for fishing, boating, and picnicking. There is a playground with a miniature train; *Lake Fairfax* on Rte. 606 near Leesburg Pike in Reston offers swimming, boat rentals, fishing and camping with picnicking, and miniature golf; *Washington and Old Dominion Regional Park* offers the longest bike trail in Virginia and one of the narrowest parks in the U.S. Its 25-foot width stretches from the shores of the Potomac to Leesburg; *Bull Run Regional Park,* Exit at Centerville off I-66 W. Swimming, boating, and camping.

Falls Church

HISTORIC SITES. *The Falls Church* (ca 1769), 115 Fairfax St., is the oldest standing church in the Washington area. The original wooden building was built in 1732 and had to be replaced when it was discovered the wooden foundation was rotting. George Washington was one of 12 vestrymen at each of the Episcopalian churches in Truro parish, as this large area was then known. It served as a recruiting station during the Revolution and then was abandoned until 1830. It was used as a hospital and stable during the Civil War. Falls Church was restored in 1959 and is open to the public daily. Call 532–7600 for information.

The Fountain of Faith in *National Memorial Park* is a memorial dedicated to four chaplains (two Protestant, one Jewish, and one Catholic) who were on the U.S.S. *Dorchester* when it was torpedoed off Greenland in 1942. They lost their lives when they gave their life jackets to four soldiers.

Fredericksburg

HISTORIC SITES. Visitors should start a tour of this historic Civil War area at the Fredericksburg Visitor Center at the junction of Lafayette Blvd. and Sunken Rd. It includes a museum with slide program, diorama, and exhibits. It borders the *Fredericksburg National Cemetery* where more than 15,000 Union and 13,000 unknown soldiers are buried. There is also a Visitor Center in Chancellorsville where there is a slide program and museum with exhibits and dioramas. The battlefields area, which is open daily except Christmas and Jan. 1, is part of the *Fredericksburg and Spotsylvania National Military Park.* Phone 373–4461 for information.

The *Stonewall Jackson Memorial Shrine,* 12 miles south of Fredericksburg on I-95 in Guinea, is perhaps the most historic site in the area. It includes the plantation office where, on May 10, 1863, Confederate General Stonewall Jackson, ill with pneumonia after his shattered left arm had been amputated, died.

Other sights include *Chatham Manor,* a Georgian manor house owned by a wealthy Virginia planter, converted to a federal headquarters during two of the battles for Fredericksburg. The home was eventually used as a hospital where Clara Barton and Walt Whitman nursed the wounded. Finally, there is the *Old Salem Church* (ca 1844), 1 mile west of Fredericksburg on I-95. It sits on the site of the May 3–4, 1863, battle of Fredericksburg, and was used as a field hospital and refugee center.

Hunt Country

Set in the heart of a scenic area of rolling hills and picturesque rural towns, where thoroughbred horse farms, point-to-point racing, and steeplechases are popular, Leesburg is being restored to its Colonial appearance.

Visitors should start a hunt country tour at the *Loudoun Museum and Visitor Center,* 16 West Loudoun Street, Leesburg, in a century-old restored building that contains exhibits and memorabilia of the area and an audio-visual presentation. It offers brochures and information about Loudoun County, home of hunt country. Call 777–0519 (Office of Tourism), or 777–7427 (Museum).

HISTORIC SITES. The most famous spot in Virginia's hunt country is *Oatlands* (ca 1804), six miles south of Leesburg on U.S. 15. Oatlands features a Classical Revival mansion built by George Carter, grandson of Williamsburg's Robert "King" Carter, and once the center of a 5,000-acre plantation. It was practically remodeled in 1827 when the impressive portico was added. Most of the building materials came from the estate. The mansion is filled with American, English, and French antiques. The formal garden has one of the finest boxwood collections in the United States. The farm fields provide the space for the equestrian events that are its most popular attraction. Call 777–3174.

Morven Park on Old Waterford Road, a mile north of Leesburg, features a mansion with 16 rooms open to the public, boxwood gardens, nature trails, and the Winmill Carriage Museum with over 100 horse-pulled vehicles. *The International Equestrian Institute* is also located on the 1,200-acre estate. It was originally the home of Thomas Swann, an early Maryland governor, and was enlarged by Westmoreland Davis, governor of Virginia from 1918 to 1922. Call 777–2414.

The American Horse Museum is four miles west of Leesburg on VA 662 in Paeonian Springs. Established in 1971, the museum presents the role of the work horse and its importance in the development of the country. The museum includes thousands of articles related to work horses and two live Clydesdales. No admission charge. Phone 338–6290.

Waterford is three miles northeast of town on Rte. 7 and two miles on VA Rte. 66. It is a restored eighteenth-century Quaker village with an Annual Homes Tour with crafts demonstrations, exhibits, and traditional music. Call 882–3018.

Balls Bluff on U.S. 15 features the smallest national cemetery in the United States and marks the site of the fourth armed engagement of the Civil War. On October 21, 1861, four Union regiments suffered catastrophic losses while fighting the Confederates here. The Union commander was killed and half his troops were killed, wounded, or captured. One Union soldier wounded here, Oliver Wendell Holmes, went on to be the chief justice of the U.S. Supreme Court.

VINEYARDS. Special new attractions of the area are its vineyards and wineries, many of which offer tours. Two in particular stand out: *Piedmond Vineyards* via I-66 to Plains and *Meredyth Vineyards* on VA 628 via U.S. 50 in Middleburg. Both open their arms to visitors and offer good and improving samples of wines of all kinds, The Leesburg Visitor Center, 108 South St. S.E. (777–0519) or the Virginia Division of Tourism (804–786–4484) can provide additional information about vineyard tours. See also "Virginia Vineyards" in the *Planning Your Trip* section.

Manassas

HISTORIC SITES. Visitors should start a tour of the Manassas (Bull Run) National Battlefield Park at the Visitor Center on Henry Hill just north of I-66 off Rte. 234. The hill offers a view of much of the Civil War battlefield area. The Center has self-guided tours that start there and follow markers throughout the battlefield. Phone 754–7107.

The *Battlefield Museum* is in the same building. The museum's exhibits present stories of the Bull Run battles and audio-visual presentations of background information.

The *Stone Bridge* is where federal artillery opened the battle of First Manassas. It afforded an avenue of escape for the Union troops in both battles. Also of note are the *Unfinished Railroad,* a graded railroad bed that was never completed, but became a defensive line for Confederate forces. It was here that Stonewall Jackson's men were positioned during the Second Battle of Manassas.

Other attractions include the *Chinn House Ruins,* which served as a field hospital in both engagements and marked the left of the Confederate line at the first battle. It was also the scene of Longstreet's counterattack in the second battle; the *Stone House,* which was originally a tavern but served as a field hospital in both battles; and *Dogan House,* which was an original structure at Groveton, a village that gave its name to the second day's battle of Second Manassas.

Mount Vernon

Mount Vernon is one of the best loved and most visited national shrines in America, attracting a million or more visitors each year. A stately home, though far from spacious, George Washington's beloved Mount Vernon is the one place you can really feel the presence and the personality of the man.

Mount Vernon is about 10 miles south of Alexandria on George Washington Pkwy.

Tours of the sprawling grounds are self-guided. Inside the house, small groups are ushered from room to room, each of which is staffed by a guide who describes the furnishings and answers questions. It's best to visit it on a weekday, when crowds aren't quite so heavy. Mount Vernon is open every day of the year, 9 A.M.–5 P.M. from Mar. 1–Oct. 31, 9 A.M.–4 P.M. the rest of the year; 780–2000.

There's a wonderful view of the Potomac over wide, sweeping lawns, and the grounds are a delight. The towering trees include some planted by Washington himself, and members of the Mount Vernon Ladies Association continue to plant trees from the cuttings or seeds of the original. Visitors can buy a tiny boxwood or other plant nurtured at Mount Vernon.

Washington's conscientious journal of his daily routine as a farmer has enabled the staff to keep a kitchen garden with vegetables, herbs, and espaliered fruit trees as he cultivated them. This was his home from 1754 until his death here in 1799, except for his absences for army and presidential duties. The house and museum contain the bed in which he died, clothing, and other articles belonging to both himself and Martha Custis Washington, the widow whom he married. Visitors are fascinated by his substantial case of traveling wine bottles and what is reputed to be the key to the Bastille presented him by the Marquis de Lafayette.

If you don't care to drive to Mount Vernon, there are regularly scheduled tours from Washington, D.C., via Gray Line and other operators. An especially pleasant trip is down the Potomac River. Washington Boat Lines, Inc. offers sailings aboard the paddlewheeler, *The First Lady,* twice daily, 9 A.M. and 2 P.M., late Mar.–July 4; and once daily, 11:30 A.M. July 5–mid Oct., from Pier 4, Sixth and Water Streets, S.W.; (202) 554–8000. There also is a Mount Vernon Bike Trail along the river, paralleling the

George Washington Memorial Parkway, some 16 miles between Arlington Memorial Bridge and Mount Vernon.

Also in the Mount Vernon area are two mansions worth a visit: *Woodlawn Plantation,* a gift of George Washington to his ward, Eleanor Parke Custis, and his nephew, Maj. Lawrence Lewis, and Gunston Hall, completed in 1758, the home of George Mason, author of the Virginia Declaration of Rights.

The Woodlawn mansion was designed by Dr. William Thornton, first architect of the U.S. Capitol. Also on the grounds is the *Pope-Leighey House,* designed by Frank Lloyd Wright in the 1940s and moved to the grounds in 1965. Woodlawn is open daily except on Thanksgiving, Christmas, and New Year's Day, 9:30 A.M.–4:30 P.M.; the Pope-Leighey House only on weekends, March through October. Nearby is the George Washington *Grist Mill,* accessible year-round, via VA 235 connecting Mount Vernon to U.S. 1.

Driving to Gunston Hall, you can look in at *Pohick Church.* Built in 1774, both George Washington and George Mason were vestrymen of the church. It is open 8 A.M.–4 P.M. daily; 550–9449. Gunston Hall is known particularly for its gardens and boxwood, some of it now 12 feet high. One well-traveled British visitor, Lord Balfour, said Gunston's boxwood was even superior to that of the Vatican, which had been considered the world's finest. Perhaps because it's so close to the *Mason Neck National Wildlife Refuge,* Gunston is a mecca for birdlife. Those eagles, which occasionally hover over Mount Vernon and are also seen here, nest in the refuge, where they are closely protected. Gunston Hall is open daily except Christmas, 9:30 A.M.–5 P.M.

There are self-guided tours of Woodlawn Plantation and guided tours of the Gunston Hall mansion. Gunston Hall, 550–9220; Woodlawn, 557–7880.

SHENANDOAH VALLEY

by
ELEANOR LOUTTIT

"Oh Shenandoah, I long to see you . . . " Here in one of America's most beautiful valleys one can truly empathize with the song writer who felt the lure of the river in western Virginia. The Shenandoah Valley, carved by the Shenandoah River and the James River, lies between the Blue Ridge Mountains on the east and the Allegheny Mountains on the west. These mountains, thrust up by great grinding paroxysms of the continent millennia ago, were already smoothed and gentled into a cradle for the rivers when the first men arrived in the valley about 12,000 years ago. Here was game for the taking, grain for the picking, and water that tumbled over the rocks or rippled into clear pools endlessly. The early travelers in this hospitable valley roamed generation after generation as they came to their tribal identity, the Shawnee. They spoke of their home range among the mountains, along the rivers, and in the glades as "Shenandoah, daughter of the stars."

The Shawnee lived in their wigwam villages along the riverbanks, moving with the game and gathering the abundance of the forests. They preferred to stay away from large tribal units and left little evidence of their habitations. Apparently, theirs was a peaceful existence at least until 1716 when the then lieutenant-governor of the Virginia Colony, Alexander Spotswood, led the first band of white men through Swift Run Gap to explore the great valley of the west. Spotswood had, since taking office in 1710, tried to regulate the fur trade with the Indians and, after his explorations, encouraged white settlers to move into the western regions. From then until the mid-1700s many families, mainly Scotch-Irish and English Quakers and mostly from Pennsylvania, trekked the rude wagon road into the mountains.

In 1750 Daniel Boone entered, traversed, and left the valley on his way to find the Cumberland Gap. In doing so, he opened the gate to westward expansion beyond the Appalachians into the riches of the Mississippi outlands.

Indian Wars

The Shawnee, meanwhile, were increasing their resistance to the influx of white men into their lands and for 40 years they fought so hard that they became known as the most hostile tribe on the western frontier. Finally, in 1774, under the leadership of their chief, Cornstalk, the Shawnee were defeated at Point Pleasant in what is now West Virginia. The Indian threat to the Shenandoah Valley was gone and settlement continued peacefully even through the upheaval of the Revolutionary War.

The valley itself seems to have been a mountain range removed from the War of Independence although there are interesting highlights. George Washington owned farm lands near Winchester, rented them out to tenants, and required each tenant to plant four acres of apple trees, thus starting today's production of five million bushels of apples a year in that area. Washington surveyed much of the valley before he became prominent and later endowed the small college, which would become Washington and Lee University at Lexington. In 1781 the Virginia Assembly fled to Staunton's Trinity Church to escape the British forces near the capital, Williamsburg. Thomas Jefferson once actually bought the Natural Bridge!

During the post-Revolutionary years as Americans pressed westward, the people of the Shenandoah Valley farmed and developed a rugged temperament that matched the terrain. Their harvests were so rich that, in the ensuing War Between the States, the valley would become the granary of the Confederacy.

The Civil War Years

It was the Civil War years, 1860 to 1865, which brought the valley national prominence, honor, grief, and devastation.

"There is Jackson standing like a stone wall . . . ," said General Bernard Bee at the first Battle of Bull Run (Manassas, 1861). At least he and his forces stood long enough to earn him this famous sobriquet. The next year he was no longer standing; he was moving so swiftly up the Shenandoah Valley with his 17,000 troops that

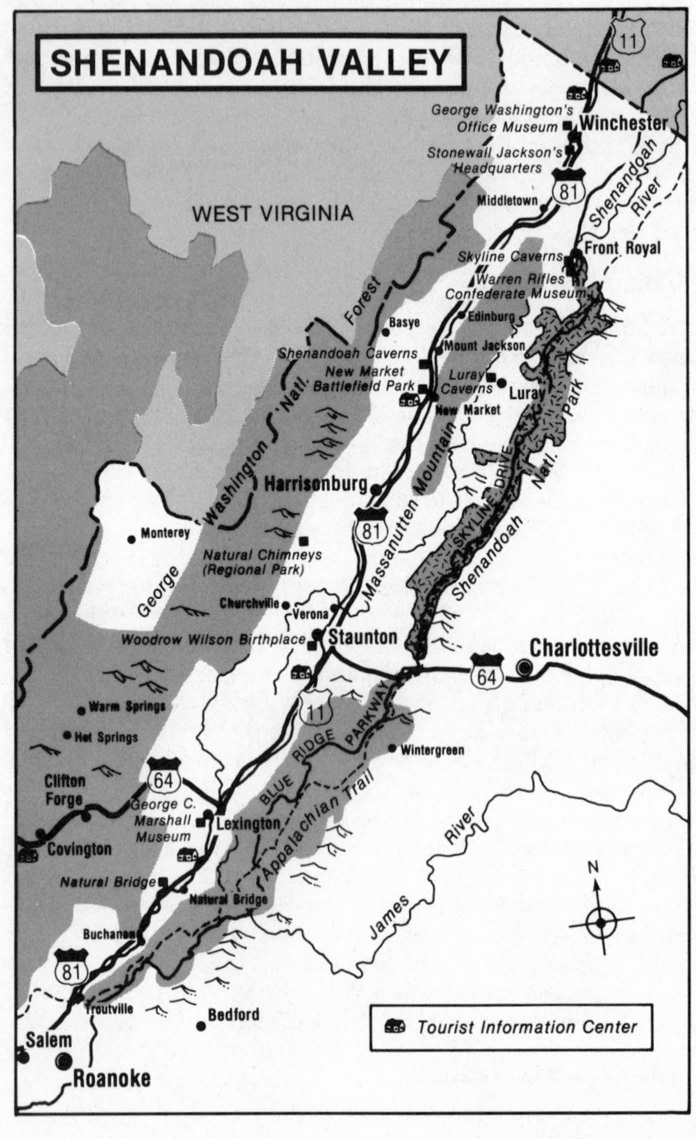
SHENANDOAH VALLEY
WEST VIRGINIA
George Washington's Office Museum
Winchester
Stonewall Jackson's Headquarters
Middletown
Shenandoah River
Front Royal
Skyline Caverns
Warren Rifles Confederate Museum
Edinburg
Basye
Mount Jackson
Shenandoah Caverns
New Market Battlefield Park
Luray Caverns
Luray
New Market
George Washington Natl. Forest
Massanutten Mountain
Skyline Drive
Shenandoah Natl. Park
Harrisonburg
Monterey
Natural Chimneys (Regional Park)
Churchville
Verona
Staunton
Woodrow Wilson Birthplace
Charlottesville
Warm Springs
Hot Springs
Wintergreen
Blue Ridge Parkway
Clifton Forge
George C. Marshall Museum
Lexington
Covington
Appalachian Trail
James River
Natural Bridge
Natural Bridge
Buchanan
Troutville
Bedford
Salem
Roanoke
N
Tourist Information Center
11
81
64

they too earned a nickname "the foot cavalry." They met and defeated 60,000 Union troops who thought Jackson was going to attack Washington. Jackson's real aim, however, was to force the Union to withhold powerful reinforcements that McClellan, who was threatening Richmond, had counted on. Jackson soon had to retreat but his glory and fame became secure in military history.

Throughout the four years of the war, Confederate forces appeared in the valley because of the Valley Pike, now U.S. Highway 11. Jubal Early was sent up the valley in 1864 by Lee to raid Washington in hopes that Grant would send troops to guard the capital. North and South armies met at Cedar Creek on October 19. Grant had not sent troops to Washington but instead had sent General Philip Sheridan to command all the Union forces in the Shenandoah Valley. His orders were to follow Early to the death, to drive the enemy from the valley, and to destroy the region's economic resources. Sheridan didn't completely accomplish the first two tasks, but the third he did with singular efficiency. At the end of the war, the Shenandoah Valley, particularly the northern third, was devastated.

After Appomattox

After the surrender of the Confederacy in 1865 the people of the Shenandoah picked up what pieces were left and treated the wounds that scarred the valley. With the return of peace came the return of abundance. Slowly, but once more, the valley became a veritable market basket.

Robert E. Lee, the sad-eyed, heavy-hearted general of the Confederacy, spent the years after defeat serving as president of Washington College in Lexington. It was the nation's sixth oldest college and had been endowed by and named for George Washington in 1798. Under Lee's guidance it became a university of national stature. When Lee died in 1870 it was again renamed, Washington and Lee University, to honor him as well.

While war was tearing the South to shreds, two little boys were growing up in the Shenandoah Valley. One, the son of a Presbyterian minister; the other, a slave until the Emancipation.

"One Negro boy (Booker)—valued at $400" lived on the Burroughs plantation south of Roanoke. Freed in 1865, he and his family moved to West Virginia and, from there, Booker Taliaferro Washington went on to study, to teach, and to found Tuskegee Institute, a major educational establishment for blacks in Alabama.

The son of the Presbyterian minister in Staunton grew up to be the twenty-eighth president of the United States. His name was Woodrow Wilson and his war was bigger but no more bloody. This time the blue mountains and the green valley would not be the contested lands; they would be contributors of men and material. By having nurtured Wilson in the years of his youth, they may have helped him to formulate his plan for world peace, the League of Nations.

In 1901 a cadet at the Virginia Military Institute in Lexington graduated and went on to become World War II chief-of-staff, secretary of defense, secretary of state, designer of a world recovery program, and Nobel Peace Prize winner. George C. Marshall, general of the Army of the United States, was the only professional soldier ever to be so honored.

The Shenandoah Today

Today the Shenandoah Valley of Virginia is a splendid patchwork quilt of majestic mountains, rich farms, spectacular scenery, rushing waters, and a satisfying feast for a visitor's menu.

Predating all the visible and memorable history of the Shenandoah Valley are the relics of a time before time began. Four hundred million years ago the limestone foundations of the young mountains that had been thrust up by a restless continental mass began to dissolve. Each drop of water that made its way down to these foundations melted a grain of limestone and eons of drops later incredible underground caverns waited for men to find them. If, at any time in the twelve thousand years of occupation by the Indian and his forebearers, the caves were discovered, nobody made it high-priority news. The Indian tells us nothing about caves in his lovely valley. In 1878 two white men, Andrew Campbell and Benton Stephens, lowered themselves on a rope into a big black hole and, when they lighted the candles, knew they had made a spectacular find. All that had gone on in the dark void for millions of years is now a very current part of the Shenandoah Valley's story.

Exploring the Shenandoah Valley

The Shenandoah Valley is a fairly secluded region of Virginia. It is possible "to get there from here" but you almost have to do it by car. The region is served throughout its length by three major motor routes, Interstate 81, U.S. Highway 11, and the Skyline Drive-Blue Ridge Parkway. Because most visitors enter the valley from the north, our exploration will be north to south using all three routes as reference points. They are, after all, just a few miles from each other and, at times, U.S. 11 and I-81 are interchangeable. The route you choose will depend on how fast you want to go.

Route 81, a U.S. Interstate, sticks to the lower elevations, is wide and speedy, and scenery is of secondary importance but quite satisfying to those who only want to look at it. Route U.S. 11 is the old Valley Pike, hacked out by Indians, men in coonskin caps, families in wagons, Confederate soldiers, farm carts, and honeymooners in pre-war Chevys. It visits uncountable small towns, every major town, and is never very far from an interesting little side trip. While it parallels I-81 closely, it is narrow, more responsive to changes in terrain, and thus slower.

The Skyline Drive-Blue Ridge Parkway is the scenic route. It's actually one road with two names. The first 105 miles as it bisects the Shenandoah National Park is the Skyline Drive; the next 215 miles through the George Washington National Forest, the Blue Ridge Parkway. When it was built it was a new concept—not an express highway but a road intended for leisurely travel. It does not go to or through any towns and its top speed limit is 45 miles per hour. Its entire length is two-lane and winding; it has no commercial traffic (but 30 miles behind a big camping van can detract from the pleasure); lodging is limited, as is food availability; many sections can be closed at some times of the year due to fog, ice, or snow. But overlooks, picnic spots, campsites, nature trails, things to see and to do, points of interest, all are well-marked and accessible. If unspoiled mountain country and breathtaking scenery are your things, take the parkway.

Winchester

Winchester, the gate city to the Shenandoah Valley and the oldest Colonial city west of the Blue Ridge Mountains, has been a hub of activity for the valley since its founding in 1732. It has always been an intersection for travel in all directions and the place to be when there was something important to do in western Virginia. Washington, at 16, set off for Winchester to begin his career as a surveyor. At 23 he was back again erecting Fort Loudon, working from a building at the corner of Cork and Braddock Streets. Today the building is a museum of French and Indian War, Revolutionary War, and Washington relics.

During the Civil War Winchester, the hub, literally spun with the wheel. It changed hands 72 times (once 13 times in one day). Jackson was headquartered there for six months at 415 North Braddock Street. Sheridan, two years later, close by at Braddock and Piccadilly streets.

Today Winchester is the home of the largest apple cold-storage plant in the world and one of the largest apple-processing plants. Nearly four million bushels of apples are harvested annually in Frederick County, and Winchester's Apple Blossom Festival the first week in May pays tribute to all that applesauce.

Front Royal

Even for those who have been warned away from negotiating the Skyline Drive, a trip to Front Royal is recommended. Routes U.S. 11 and I-81 intersect I-64 a few miles below Winchester to lead to Front Royal, which is the north entrance to the Skyline

Drive and the Shenandoah National Park. Originally a frontier pack-horse stop, it was called Hell Town until some city fathers heard the command to "Front the Royal Oak!" given by British officers to raw mountain recruits and, somewhat obscurely, made it Front Royal. So goes the story.

Today Front Royal bustles with thousands of motorists who are there to see the local attractions or to drive on down the mountain crests. A day's stop at Front Royal can include a visit to Dinosaur Land for the only authentic reproductions in the East of the great beasts of prehistory; a slide show presentation of 12,000 years of Indian living at Thunderbird Museum, an operating archaeological site; a stroll through the Civil War memorabilia of such as Belle Boyd and Mosby's Rangers at the Warren Rifles Confederate Museum on Chester Street; or a look at the only anthodites in the world at Skyline Caverns. An anthodite, you will discover, is a calcite formation that grows one inch every 7,000 years and that, in defiance of gravity, up!

New Market

At the junction of I-81, U.S. 11, and VA 211 is New Market, a town that thrives on a legend. Here, on May 15, 1864, 247 teenaged cadets from the Virginia Military Institute at Lexington suddenly became full-fledged Confederate soldiers in a clash of arms that the southerners won. The quaint main street of the town reflects the era with several restored homes of the period. In the 160 acres of park surrounding Bushong House, the battle is reenacted annually on the Sunday preceding May 15. The park itself, a $2 million nonprofit enterprise, is a comprehensive museum of the entire war with exhibits done in chronological order, always a help to those of us who had trouble with dates in history class.

Just north of New Market are the Shenandoah Caverns and east, between the Interstate and the Skyline Drive on VA 211, are the Luray Caverns, largest in the eastern United States.

Staunton

Staunton is pronounced STAN-ton, and this writer suspects it's another of those English-derived Pell Mell, Pall Mall things. Its real claim to fame, however, is that Woodrow Wilson, the twenty-eighth president of these United States, was born and grew up there. His home is now a museum.

Northwest of Staunton is the Natural Chimneys Regional Park where an above-ground version of the erosion that formed the spectacular caverns of Virginia carved out seven 120-feet-high rock formations of many hues. Here, on the third Saturday in August, America's oldest continuous sporting event, a jousting tournament (!), is held.

Warm Springs—Hot Springs

Healing Springs, Blowing Springs, Millboro Springs, etc.—there are a lot of places to "take the waters" in the Shenandoah Valley. Most of them are within an hour's drive from Lexington or Staunton. In fact, the whole area is located within Bath County, named for the famous town of sulphur springs in England. The waters here at Warm Springs and Hot Springs have been favorably compared to the most celebrated natural springs of Europe. The waters bubble from the earth at 95°F, are supposed to be restorative, and are at the center of almost anything a visitor could want to do. The area has been a resort since 1761, a long time to practice hosting with style.

Lexington

" . . . is known for attractive homes, trim farms, fine old mansions, and two of the leading educational institutions in the Commonwealth, Washington and Lee University and Virginia Military Institute."

So goes one of the town's press releases. Are these the things that led George Washington to endow the college in 1798, Stonewall Jackson to buy the only home he ever owned on Washington Street, Robert E. Lee to accept the presidency of the university until his death in 1870, Cyrus McCormick to stay at home here and invent the mechanized reaper? Or was it something else that made George C. Marshall choose VMI for his cadetship, James Gibbs come up with the idea for a pedal-driven sewing machine, or Sam Houston light out for Texas?

The best way to look for answers is to take the walking tour of Lexington, one of the few towns in the Shenandoah to lend itself easily to walking, which begins at the Visitors' Information Center at 107 East Washington Street.

Natural Bridge

A few miles south of Lexington is one of the Seven Natural Wonders of the World. Maybe the list is longer than seven but this is one of them. Natural Bridge is an arch of stone left after the relentless water carved the gorge it spans. The arch is 215 feet high, 90 feet long, and 150 feet wide. It's big, it's awesome, and when you stand beneath it and look up, you can well imagine why the Shawnee worshipped there. Thomas Jefferson saw it in 1774 and promptly bought it! For 20 shillings! The deal included 157 acres around the bridge and Jefferson hired a caretaker, built a guest cabin, and took friends to view the magnificent sight. A decade later, the names in his guest book were those of the fathers of a whole new country.

Roanoke

At the foot of lovely Shenandoah Valley in a bowl cupped between the Blue Ridge and Allegheny Mountains is the commercial and cultural center of western Virginia, Roanoke; Star City of the South. It is the largest community along the Parkway and has been, since Indian days, a crossroads for urban and mountain cultures. Even before its days as a railroad junction, when in 1832 it was christened Roanoke, it was a meeting place for all, including animals who came to its salt licks. (It was called Big Lick then.) Today, the visitor can wander its Center-in-the-Square to find a museum of fine arts, enjoy a bluegrass festival, tinker with hands-on exhibits at a natural and physical science hall, or buy fresh produce from a farmer whose fields are minutes away.

Mill Mountain, the only mountain in the United States within city limits, rises 1,000 feet above the city center, offering, besides all the hiking, scenic views, and foliage of the usual mountain, a neat little zoo and the largest man-made star in the world electrically lighted! The Star City of the South.

A traveler to Roanoke can enjoy the amenities of city life; the four-star dining room at one to the last grand hotels or a Broadway road show. A traveler can also use the city as a headquarters and within a few minutes driving time descend into the Dixie Caverns, fish in Smith Mountain Lake, hike the trails of the Peaks of the Otter, or visit the birthplace of Booker T. Washington.

PRACTICAL INFORMATION FOR THE SHENANDOAH VALLEY

Note: The area code for the Shenandoah Valley is 703.

PLACES TO STAY

HOTELS, MOTELS, AND RESORTS. There are excellent accommodations at most of the major stopping points throughout the length and breadth of the Shenandoah Valley. The following selection, as a general rule, is merely a guide—places to stay that may enhance your enjoyment of the valley. Not the cheapest, nor the most expensive, they are a *selection* only, places you may consider as you tour up or down the valley. Also, in general, we list average prices at the double rate, mainly through a personal feeling that most journeys are more enjoyable if they are shared. If you are traveling alone, either on business or by preference, your single rate will probably be slightly less than the average tariff reported. Prices may vary, of course, depending on the room and the season. If you're in doubt, ask before you commit yourself.

Basye

Bryce Resort. *Expensive to Deluxe.* 11 miles west of I–81 on Rte. 263, Box 3; 22810; 856–2121. 65 condominiums and town houses some with kitchens, at a resort in the mountains. Restaurant and bar. Entertainment and dancing weekends. Swimming, golf, tennis, riding, skiing, and fishing. AE, MC, V.

Best Western Mt. Jackson. *Moderate.* Exit 69 off I–81. 100 rooms, with restaurant and bar. Pool, tennis, and game room. Major credit cards.

Buchanan

Wattstull. *Moderate.* 1.8 miles south of Natural Bridge, U.S.11, Exit 48 off I–81 and 2 miles from Blue Ridge Pkwy. via Rte. 43. 26 units. Restaurant. Pool, with view of Shenandoah Valley. MC, V.

Covington

Holiday Inn. *Moderate.* U.S. 60, Exit 5 off I–64; at I–64; 962–4951 or (800) 238–8000. 79 rooms. Restaurant, room service, and pool. AE, MC, V.

Comfort Inn. *Inexpensive to Moderate.* Exit 5 off I–64, Mallow Rd.; 962–2141. 55 rooms, with Continental breakfast. AE, MC, V.

Pinehurst Motel. *Inexpensive.* Exit 5 off I–64, 2 miles east on U.S.60. 30 rooms, with restaurant nearby. AE, MC, V.

Front Royal

Pioneer Motel. *Moderate.* 541 S. Royal Ave., U.S. 340 intersection with Rte. 55, a block from the north entrance to Skyline Drive; 635–4784. 28 rooms, with a pool. Major credit cards.

Quality Inn—Front Royal. *Moderate.* U.S. 522 Bypass at end of Main; 635–3161. 3 stories, 107 rooms. The motel has a pool and an all-day restaurant with a bar. Meeting rooms and room service. AE, DC, MC, V.

Front Royal. *Inexpensive to Moderate.* 1400 Shenandoah; 635–4114. 47 rooms, with a pool and playground. AE, MC, V.

Twin Rivers. *Inexpensive.* 1801 Shenandoah Ave.; Front Royal Exit off I–66; 635–4101. Small (20 rooms), but with a pool and playground. AE, MC, V.

Harrisonburg

Econo Lodge. *Moderate.* Exit 64, I–81, then east on U.S. 33E. A 2-story motel with 89 rooms. Restaurant next door. AE, MC, V.

Holiday Inn. *Moderate.* Exit 62, I–81, 1 Pleasant Valley Rd., U.S. 11; 434–9981. Typical of this reliable chain, the Holiday Inn has a restaurant, bar, and room service. 130 rooms. AE, CB, DC, MC, V.

Howard Johnson's. *Moderate.* East of I–81 by a long block, Exit 63; 434–6771. A 2-story motel, including a 24-hour restaurant, with 134 rooms. Balconies, patios, and a pool. AE, CB, DC, MC, V.

Sheraton Harrisonburg Inn. *Moderate.* 1400 E. Market St.; 433–2521 or (800) 325–3535. 140 rooms in a 5-story motor hotel, with a restaurant, lounge, and indoor-outdoor pools. AE, CB, DC, MC, V.

Village Inn. *Inexpensive to Moderate.* U.S. 11, a short drive south between Exits 62 and 63, I–81. 434–7355. Small (36 rooms), but well maintained, with a pleasant restaurant. MC, V.

Hot Springs

The Cascades Inn. *Deluxe.* 3 miles south of Hot Springs on U.S. 220; 839–. A resort hotel/motel, with cottages. 50 rooms. Open April through late Oct. Use of The Homestead's facilities, but with a restaurant and bar of its own. Golf, tennis, and swimming in lovely Cascades Gorge setting. Some private patios. AE, MC, V.

The Homestead. *Deluxe.* U.S. 220; Hot Springs; 24445; 839–5500, (800) 336–5771, or in Virginia (800) 542–5734. 600 rooms in a world-famous resort hotel. Golf, tennis, swimming, riding, skeet or trap shooting, fishing, skiing, and ice skating on 15,000 beautiful acres. Excellent dining and bar. Convention facilities, including a 5,600-foot air strip. Hot Springs is 70 miles from Roanoke. AE, MC, V.

The Vine Cottage Inn. *Moderate.* Box 918; 24445; U.S. 220; 839–2422. 17 rooms in a 3-story inn. Rooms individually and uniquely decorated, creating a relaxing atmosphere. Restaurant nearby. Ski and golf plans. Open year-round for winter and summer sports. Closed Christmas Eve, Christmas. MC, V.

Lexington

Best Western Keydet General. *Moderate.* Rte. 60, west 1 mile; 463–2143 or (800) 528–1234. 56 ground-floor rooms. Restaurant on premises. AE, CB, DC, MC, V.

Holiday Inn. *Moderate.* U.S. 11, ½ mile north of I–81, Exit 52; 463–7351. 72 rooms in a 2-story Holiday Inn with a restaurant, bar, and room service. Entertainment and dancing. AE, CB, DC, MC, V.

Howard Johnson's Motor Lodge. *Moderate.* I–81 and I–64, Exit 53, U.S. 11. 100 rooms, with some deluxe suites. 24-hour restaurant, with beer and wine. AE, CB, DC, MC, V.

Econo Lodge. *Inexpensive to Moderate.* U.S. 11 and I–81; 463–7371 or (800) 446–6900. 48 rooms. Free Continental breakfast. Restaurant nearby. AE, CB, DC, MC, V.

Luray

Luray Inn and Conference Center. *Moderate to Expensive.* Junction U.S.211 Bypass and VA 656; 743–4521. 101 rooms, convenient to Skyline Drive and Luray Caverns. Pool and restaurant. Closed Nov.–mid-Apr. Major credit cards.

Big Meadows Lodge. *Moderate.* 103 rooms in Shenandoah National Park; P.O. Box 727; 22835; 743–5108. Full-service restaurant and taproom. AE, MC, V.

Jordan Hollow Farm Inn. *Moderate.* Rte. 2, Stanley; 22851; 778–2209 or 778–2285. Rte. 340 south from Luray, left on Rte. 624 and right on 626. Open all year, a 20-room, 45-acre horse farm in the Blue Ridge Mountains. Farmfresh food, beer, and wine. MC, V.

The Mimslyn Motor Inn. *Moderate.* 401 W. Main St.; 22835; 743–5105. Located downtown, with 49 rooms. Restaurant. AE, DC, MC, V.

Skyland Lodge. *Moderate.* 158 rooms in Shenandoah National Park; Box 727; 22835; 743–5108. Facilities and rates same as Big Meadows Lodge. AE, MC, V.

Luray Caverns Motel East. *Inexpensive to Moderate.* U.S.211 Bypass, opposite entrance to Luray Caverns. 743–6551. A resort motel, with 44 rooms. AE, MC, V.

Intown Motel. *Inexpensive to Moderate.* 410 W. Main St.; 743–6511. 40 rooms. Restaurant open, lunch through dinner. Bar. AE, DC, MC, V.

Monterey

Highland Inn. *Moderate.* Main St., Jct. U.S.220, 250; 468–2143. A 3-story white Victorian clapboard hotel, 40 miles west of Staunton. Formerly the Monterey Hotel, "The Pride of the Mountains," the inn was built in 1904. 20 rooms, each with antiques. Local folk talent frequent the tavern. MC, V.

Natural Bridge

Natural Bridge Hotel and Motor Inn. *Moderate.* Exits 49–50, I–81 at U.S. 11 and VA 130; 291–2121 or (800) 336–5727. 180 units between the hotel and the opposite inn. Indoor pool, tennis, cafes, bar, room service, and meeting rooms, with golf privileges. Some patios and balconies in this resort facility near Natural Bridge. AE, MC, V.

Wattstull. *Inexpensive to Moderate.* 8 miles south on U.S.11, Exit 48 off I–81. 26 rooms. Pool and restaurant. MC, V.

New Market

Quality Inn—Shenandoah Valley. *Moderate.* U.S. 211 at Exit 67, I–81; 740–3141. 101 rooms in a 2-story motel. Restaurant, room service, and bar. AE, CB, DC, MC, V.

The Shenvalee. *Moderate.* 9660 Fairway Dr., a mile off I–81 on U.S. 11; 740–3181. 42 rooms with a restaurant, lounge, and pool. AE, CB, DC, MC, V.

Battlefield. *Inexpensive.* Exit 67, I–81, then a mile north of U.S. 211 on U.S. 11. Small—14 rooms. Restaurant nearby. DC, MC, V.

Roanoke

Marriott (Roanoke Airport). *Expensive to Deluxe.* 2801 Hershberger Rd. N.W.; 563–9300. 320 rooms. Two restaurants—Lily's for casual dining and Remington's. Indoor/outdoor pools, lighted tennis courts, and golf course adjacent to hotel. Major credit cards.

The Roanoke Hotel. *Expensive.* Downtown at 19 N. Jefferson St.; 24026; 343–6992. Southern hospitality in a 7-story, 425-room hotel. Valet parking, indoor/outdoor pool, and the Regency Room, an excellent restaurant. The Roanoke has shopping and convention facilities, plus tennis and golf privileges and an Old English inn decor. AE, CB, DC, MC, V.

Sheraton Airport Inn. *Expensive.* 2727 Ferndale Dr. N.W.; 24017; 362–4500 or (800) 325–3535. 150 rooms, convenient to the airport, with restaurant, pool, and tennis. AE, MC, V.

Holiday Inn South. *Moderate.* 1927 Franklin Rd. S.W.; 343–0121 or (800) 238–8000. 127 rooms. Restaurant, room service, and bar. AE, MC, V.

Patrick Henry Hotel. *Moderate.* Downtown Roanoke at 617 S. Jefferson; Box 2241; 24009; 345–8811. 121 rooms. Dining room. AE, CB, DC, MC, V.

Holiday Inn—Civic Center. *Moderate.* Orange Ave. at Williamson Rd.; 342–8961. 125 rooms, with restaurant, bar, room service, and bellhops. Pool. AE, CB, DC, MC, V.

Holiday Inn—South. *Moderate.* 1927 Franklin Rd. SW; 343–0121. 125 rooms. Restaurant, bar, and pool. AE, CB, DC, MC, V.

Comfort Inn. *Inexpensive to Moderate.* Exit 44, I–81, Rte. 11S; 992–5600 or (800) 288–5150. A quality budget motel with a pool. Major credit cards.

Starlight Motor Court. *Inexpensive.* 4448 Melrose Ave. N.W., near Lakeside and VA Hospital; 366–3403. 30 rooms. Pool. AE, MC, V.

Traveltown Motel. *Inexpensive.* Exit 44 off I–81; U.S. and Rte. 220; Cloverdale; 992–1521 or (800) 322–8029. Restaurant and pool. AE, V.

Salem

Holiday Inn Salem. *Moderate.* 1671 Skyview Rd., Exit 40, I–81; 389–7061. 102 units with a marvelous view of Roanoke Valley. Pool, dining room, and mixed beverages. Major credit cards.

Quality Inn. *Moderate.* VA 419, Exit 41 off I–81; 563–9711. 120 rooms, with restaurant, pool, room service, and bar. Major credit cards.

Staunton

Holiday Inn—North. *Moderate.* I–81 and Woodrow Wilson; P.O. Box 2526; 24401; 248–5111 or (800) 238–8000. 100 rooms, with a pool, bar, and restaurant. Near the Expressway. AE, DC, MC, V.

Ingleside Red Carpet Inn. *Moderate.* U.S. 11, several miles north of I–81, Exit 57; Box 1018; 24401; 248–1201. 165 rooms, with a dining room, bar, tennis, and pools. Meeting rooms and golf course, with some patios overlooking the fairways and greens. AE, CB, DC, MC, V.

Quality Inn Downtown. *Moderate.* 268 N. Central at Lewis St., 3 miles west of I–81; 24401; 886–3401. 102 rooms in a 4-story, elevator motor inn. Pool, cafe, and bar. Meeting rooms. AE, CB, DC, MC, V.

Hessian House. *Inexpensive to Moderate.* Exit 55S, I–81, 10 miles south on U.S. 11; Box 364, Rte. 2; 24401; 337–1231. 32 rooms, some with balconies and patios, pool. Restaurant nearby. AE, MC, V.

Troutville

Howard Johnson's—Troutville. *Moderate.* U.S.11, Exit 44, I–81, then 10 miles north. 992–3000. 72 rooms in a 2-story motel, Bellhops and cafe, with swimming and wading pools. AE, CB, DC, MC, V.

Warm Springs

The Inn at Gristmill Square. *Expensive.* 2 blocks west of U.S. 220; Box 359; 24484; 839–2231. 14 rooms, including some 2-room suites. Pool and sauna and tennis, with golfing privileges. Excellent restaurant—The Waterwheel—at The Inn. Bar. AE, MC, V.

Winchester

Holiday Inn-East. *Moderate.* U.S. 50 E., just north of Exit 80 E, I–81; 667–3300. 124 rooms in a 2-story motor inn with a restaurant, bar, and room service. Meeting rooms and golf privileges. AE, CB, DC, MC, V.

Howard Johnson's. *Moderate.* 1509 Martinsburg Pike; 667–3802. 2 stories, 84 rooms, with a 24-hour restaurant and a bar. AE, CB, DC, MC, V.

Quality Inn East. *Moderate.* 603 Millwood Ave.; 667–2250. 102 rooms, with restaurant, pool, and bar. Tennis, golf privileges. Major credit cards.

Quality Inn Boxwood South. *Moderate.* 2649 Valley Ave.; 662–2521. 72 rooms. Restaurant nearby. Pool and playground. Major credit cards.

Travelodge of Winchester. *Inexpensive to Moderate.* 1825 Dominion Ave.; 22601; Exit 80E, I–81, intersection Rtes. 50E and 522S; 665–0685 or (800) 255–3050. 100 rooms. Major credit cards.

Apple Blossom Lodge. *Moderate.* 2951 Valley Ave.; 667–1200. 66 rooms. Restaurant, lunch through dinner. Bar and pool. Major credit cards.

Best Western Lee-Jackson Motor Inn. *Inexpensive.* 711 Millwood Ave.; 662–4154. 138-room motor inn. Restaurant, bar, and pool. AE, CB, DC, MC, V.

Bond's. *Inexpensive.* 2930 Valley Ave.; 667–8881. 16 rooms with a restaurant nearby. AE, MC, V.

Econo Lodge. *Inexpensive.* 1020 Millwood Pike; 667–5000. 72 rooms. Restaurant nearby, open from breakfast through dinner. AE, MC, V.

PLACES TO EAT

RESTAURANTS. Like our accommodations section, the following selection of restaurants is just that—a *selection;* it is not meant to be all-inclusive. Restaurants come and go (even the best) and we have tried wherever possible to include only those that have been here for awhile, serving good food, and may be expected to continue to satisfy travelers this year and the next and the next. With some notable exceptions, most of the restaurants in this section are located in or close to the main stopping points in the Shenandoah Valley area. If you, the traveler, find an exceptional restaurant that we've overlooked, Fodor's Travel Guides would be delighted to consider it for future editions. (The editors give special thanks to Dawn O'Brien for pointing out a number of historic Shenandoah restaurants in her excellent book, *Virginia's Historic Restaurants.)*

Basye

Sky Chalet Country Inn. *Expensive.* 10 miles from Mt. Jackson, off Rte. 263 west of Basye; 856–2147. Remote and beautiful, with good food and pure mountain air. Dinner from 5 P.M. through 8 or 9 P.M. Resist, if you can, the Inn's flowerpot bread. Reservations recommended Sat. and Sun. in season. AE, MC, V.

Bedford

Peaks of Otter Lodge Restaurant. *Moderate.* Blue Ridge Pkwy.; 586–1081. Located at Mile Post 86 on the Parkway. Open daily, breakfast through dinner. Mountain trout, seafood, and ribs. Cocktails. MC, V.

Churchville

Buckhorn Inn. *Expensive.* 6 miles west of Churchville on Rte. 250; 337–6900. A 2-story inn with a veranda view of the mountains. Once a stagecoach stop, the Buckhorn served as a hospital during the Civil War. Fried chicken and oysters and peanut butter pie, served with good domestic wines. Lunch and dinner. Closed Mon. No reservations. MC, V.

Edinburg

Edinburg Mill Restaurant. *Expensive.* Rte. 11, just south of town; 984–8555. it was once a mill, supplying flour to Confederate soldiers; Sheridan's raiders twice tried to burn it down. Fortunately for today's diners, they failed. The mill produced flour for 130 years and was converted into a tasteful restaurant in 1978. Cocktails or wine. Open daily, breakfast through dinner. Reservations a necessity. AE, MC, V.

Front Royal

My Father's Moustache. *Inexpensive to Moderate.* 108 South Royal, in the Victorian Manor House; 635–3496. Well rated by locals and travelers. Dinners, including Maine lobster, from 5:30 till 10, with a bar that stays open till 2 A.M. This establishment is closed Mon. and Tues. and on some holidays. 1920s atmosphere. AE, MC, V.

Constant Spring Dining Room. *Inexpensive.* 413 S. Royal Ave., Intersection of Rtes. 55 and 340, ½ mile north of Skyline Drive; 635–7010. Breakfast, lunch, and dinner—served family style. Wine. MC, V.

Harrisonburg

Calhoun's. *Moderate to Expensive.* Exit 64W, I–81, 1½ miles west on Rte. 33 (E. Market St.); 434–4464. A year-round restaurant, featuring chicken tarragon and charbroiled steaks. Cocktails, beer, and wine. MC, V.

Olympic Room. *Moderate to Expensive.* I–81 and U.S. 33, 1400 E. Market St.; 22801; 433–2521. An award-winning restaurant in the Sheraton Harrisonburg Inn. Breakfast through dinner, with Sunday brunch and the Scruples lounge and cafe. Major credit cards.

Lloyd's. *Moderate.* 2455 S. Main St.; 22801; 434–9843. Serving lunch and dinner. Lloyd's is located about a mile north of Exit 62, I–81. Barbecued ribs, fried chicken, and a bar. AE, MC, V.

Train Station. *Inexpensive to Moderate.* 1 block east of Exit 63 on I–81, Port Republic Rd.; 434–0505. Breakfast, lunch, and dinner in an old-timey RR station atmosphere. Bar. MC, V.

Victor's. *Inexpensive to Moderate.* 1 Pleasant Valley Rd., Exit 62, I–81, then south on U.S. 11; 434–0823. Victor's, like the Village Inn, specializes in southern cooking. Breakfast, lunch, and dinner. AE, CB, DC, MC, V.

Hillsville

Shenandoah Restaurant. *Moderate.* West Stuart Dr., Hickory Hills Shopping Center; 728–3251. Specializes in seafood and prime beef. Beer and wine. Live entertainment Fri. and Sat. nights. MC, V.

Hot Springs

Regency Room. *Expensive.* The Homestead, U.S. 220; 839–5500. Breakfast, lunch, and dinner, 7:30 A.M. to last seating at 8:30 P.M. Try the Homestead's roast turkey Marco Polo. Reservations suggested. AE, MC, V.

Sam Snead's Tavern. *Moderate to Expensive.* 1 Main St. (U.S. 220); 839–2828. Excellent dining in a sporty setting that was once a bank. Bar. Trout, chicken, and barbecued ribs. Baking on premises. Try the Tavern's chicken curry broccoli soup. Lunch and dinner. Bar. MC, V.

Lexington

Willson-Walker House. *Moderate.* 30 N. Main St.; 463–3020. Lunch and dinner, Tues. through Sat, in a 19th-century residence. Seafood and veal are house specialities. Wine list and service bar. Outdoor dining in season. MC, V.

Southern Inn. *Inexpensive.* 37 S. Main St. (U.S. 11); 463–3612. Greek, Italian, and American food. Beer and wine. AE, MC, V.

Luray

The Mimslyn. *Moderate to Expensive.* 401 W. Main St.; 743–5105. An excellent cuisine and award-winning wine list in a charming inn—southern hospitality at its best. Open daily, breakfast through dinner. AE, MC, V.

Parkhurst Inn Restaurant. *Moderate.* U.S. 211, 2 miles west of Luray Caverns; 743–6009. "A nice place to dine." Closed Mon., Tues. off season. AE, MC, V.

Caverns and Coach Restaurant. *Inexpensive.* U.S. 211 Bypass at Luray Caverns; 743–6551. Open year-round, 9 A.M. till 5 P.M. March till mid-Nov. and 10 A.M. till 2 P.M. rest of year. Fast food. AE, MC, V.

Middletown

Wayside Inn. *Expensive.* 7783 Main St.; 869–1797. In one word: "Exceptional." Another word—considering this eighteenth-century inn's roast turkey with peanut dressing—might be "delicious." Breakfast, lunch, and dinner daily, except Sun. when meals are served from noon until 8:30 P.M. Reservations recommended. AE, DC, MC, V.

Mount Jackson

Best Western Mount Jackson Restaurant. *Inexpensive to Moderate.* Exit 69 off I–81; 477–2911. Dining room and lounge near Shenandoah Caverns. Open daily, lunch and dinner. Major credit cards.

Natural Bridge

Natural Bridge Restaurants. *Inexpensive to Expensive.* U.S. 11 and VA 130; 291–2121. Dining from snacks to cafeteria to an elegant Colonial dining room. Open daily, breakfast through dinner. AE, MC, V.

New Market

Southern Kitchen. *Inexpensive to Moderate.* S. Main St.; 740–3514. Specializes in good country cooking, from barbecued short ribs to Virginia ham. Beer and wine. MC, V.

Johnny Appleseed Restaurant. *Inexpensive to Moderate.* Quality Inn, Exit 67, I–81; 740–3141. Open daily, breakfast through dinner. Family dining at a reasonable price. AE, DC, MC, V.

Roanoke

Fesquet's. *Expensive.* Upper level, Crossroads Mall; 362–8803. Some say this is "Roanoke's finest French restaurant"—and they may be right. Reservations requested. Dinner only. Closed Sun. Major credit cards.

The Library. *Expensive.* 3117 Franklin Rd. SW (Picadilly Sq.); 985–0811. An excellent restaurant, with reservations a must. Dinner only. Major credit cards.

La Maison. *Expensive.* 5732 Airport Rd.; 366–2444. Cocktails in the fireplace lounge and elegant dining in a Colonial mansion. Lunch and dinner. Closed Sun. Major credit cards.

Regency Room (Roanoke Hotel). *Expensive.* N. Jefferson St.; 343–6992. Popular with hotel guests and locals, the Regency's standards are consistently high. Steak Diane and peanut soup are specialties. Cocktails with dinner, or in nearby Whistlestop Lounge. Open daily—breakfast, lunch, and dinner. Jacket and tie for dinner. Outdoor dining in season. Reservations recommended. Major credit cards.

Charcoal Steak House. *Moderate to Expensive.* 5225 Williamson Rd. NW (Hershberger or Peters Creek Exits off I–581); 366–3710. Closed Mon. Excellent ribs of beef or seafood, with cocktail lounge. Live entertainment. Major credit cards.

Coach & Four Restaurant. *Moderate to Expensive.* 5206 Williamson Rd. NW, Hershberger Exit off I–581; 362–4220. A popular—and boisterous—lounge, with two pleasant dining rooms. Cocktails. Prime ribs, steaks, seafood, and veal in a friendly atmosphere. Closed Mon. AE, MC, V.

Luigi's. *Moderate.* 3301 Brambleton Ave. SW; 989–6277. Italian cooking, family style. Veal, chicken, seafood, and pasta cooked to order. Open daily. AE, MC, V.

Sunnybrook Inn. *Moderate.* 7342 Plantation Rd. NW; 1 mile off I–81, Exit 43; 366–4555. Casual home-cooked meals—breakfast, lunch, and dinner in old Sunnybrook Farm. Open daily. MC, V.

Ye Olde English Inn. *Moderate.* 6063 Brambleton Ave., US 221 south of Cave Spring area; 774–2670. Prime ribs in a Tudor-style inn. MC, V.

Billy's Ritz. *Inexpensive to Moderate.* 102 Salem Ave. SE; 342–3937. Steaks, chops, and "other stuff" at the Roanoke City Market. Open daily. AE, MC, V.

Salem

J. Hannon's. *Inexpensive to Expensive.* Exit 41 off I–81 at VA 419, Quality Inn; 563–9711. Breakfast, lunch, and dinner daily. Bar. Major credit cards.

Staunton

McCormack's Pub & Restaurant. *Moderate.* 41 N. Augusta St.; 885–3111. Beef!—and that almost says it all; fillet of beef McCormack or roast beef and brie on a croissant. Note the walnut-paneled lobby. Lunch, dinner, and Sun. brunch. Reservations recommended. AE, MC, V.

The Wharf Deli & Pub. *Moderate.* 123 S. Augusta St.; 886–2329. "Wharf," in this case, means warehouse. Built in 1880 as a grocery store, food is served from 11:30 A.M. until 8 P.M., Mon. through Thurs., and until 9:30 P.M. Fri. and Sat. The Pub stays open later. Try the Wharf's deli chicken salad—and the German chocolate pie, if you dare. MC, V.

Edelweiss. *Inexpensive to Moderate.* U.S. 340 and U.S. 11, Greenville Exit 55 off I–81; 337–1203. Lunch and dinner, with a German flavor. Open Tues. through Sun. Beer and wine. Reservations suggested. MC, V.

Warm Springs

The Waterwheel. *Moderate.* 2 blocks west of U.S. 220 at the Inn at Gristmill Sq.; 839–231. A charming restaurant in a lovely setting. The wheel dates back to 1771. Continental dining and bar in historic setting; Tues. through Sun. Allegheny mountain trout, local vegetables, and home-baked breads. Try the Amaretto souffle or the honey mustard glazed spare-ribs. Dinner only off season. AE, MC, V.

Winchester

The Elms. *Moderate.* 2011 Valley Ave.; 662–0535. A pleasant restaurant that features both seafood and steak. Lunch and dinner. Closed Sun. and major holidays. MC, V.

The Rebel. *Inexpensive to Moderate.* 603 Millwood Ave., Quality Inn; 662–2571. American cooking with a country flavor. Breakfast, lunch, and dinner. Bar. AE, DC, MC, V.

Woodstock

Spring House. *Inexpensive to Moderate.* 325 S. Main St.; 459–4755. Breakfast, lunch, and dinner in an early-American cabin. Bar after 3 P.M. Major credit cards.

THINGS TO SEE AND DO

TOURING INFORMATION. For advance information about the Shenandoah Valley, write or phone: Shenandoah Valley Travel Association, Box 1040, New Market, VA 22844; (703) 740–3132.

Clifton Forge

Route I–64 west of Lexington, exit U.S. 220 S.

Douthat State Park. Nearly 5,000 acres of mountain scenery for hiking and camping; 70-acre lake for swimming, fishing, boating; Apr.–Nov.; lodge, cabins; 862–7200.

Alleghany Highlands Arts and Crafts Center. Galleries and antiques. Tues.–Sat., 10:30–4:30 P.M. Phone 862–4447.

Covington

Route I–64, west of Clifton Forge, exit 220 N.

Moomah Lake. A 12 mile-long lake with rugged shoreline; boating, swimming, fishing, water-skiing, camping; 962–1138.

Humpback Bridge. A unique covered bridge; 1835; 3 miles west of U.S. 60/I–64.

Front Royal

U.S. 340, Skyline Drive, south of I-66.

Skyline Caverns. An underground showplace with cavern tours, free picnic grounds, miniature train ride; Memorial Day to Labor Day daily, weekends spring and fall; 635–4545.

Thunderbird Museum and Archaeological Park. A working archaeological site, museum, 3-mile nature trail; mid-Mar. to mid-Nov.; fee; 635–7337.

Sky Meadows State Park. 1,100 acres of sky-high hiking, walk-in camping, picnicking; parking fee; 592–3556.

Dinosaur Land. The only prehistoric park in the East; authentic reproductions; fee.

Warren Rifles Confederate Museum. Historic relics from 1861–1865. Open mid-Apr.–mid-Oct. Call 635–2692 for appointment.

Harrisonburg

U.S. 11/U.S. 33, west of I-81.

Natural Chimneys Regional Park. 7 rock towers; picnic and camp sites, bicycle and nature trails, pool, playground; open all year; Jousting Tournament, third Sat. in Aug.; parking fee.

Grand Caverns Regional Park. Underground chambers with spectacular formations; tours, swimming, tennis, miniature golf, picnicking, hiking, biking; Mar.–Nov.; fee; 249–5705.

Lake Shenandoah and *Silver Lake.* Bass fishing in the Shenandoah River.

Warren-Sipe Museum. 301 S. Main St.; 434–4762. Electric map displaying Stonewall Jackson's Valley Campaign. Local history.

Hot Springs–Warm Springs

U.S. 220/VA39.

Homestead Ski Resort. A 3,500-foot chair lift, a school, ski rental and patrol, food and drink, nursery; Nov. to Mar.; fee; 839–5079 or (800) 336–5771. Homestead Ski Resort also has ice skating on an Olympic-size rink; Nov. to Mar.; fee.

Warm Springs Bathhouses. Soak or shower in natural sulphur water.

Lexington

U.S. 60, west of I-81, south of I-64.

Stonewall Jackson House. The restored home of the famous general; guided tours; closed Jan. 1, Easter, Thanksgiving, Dec. 25; fee. 8 E. Washington St.; 463–2552.

Washington and Lee University. A lovely campus that includes Lee Chapel with Lee tomb and family collections; Reeves china collection, one of the largest in the United States. S. Jefferson and W. Washington St.; 463–9111.

Virginia Military Institute. Here are mementos of Jackson, Matthew Maury (inventor and explorer), George C. Marshall museum; dress parade Sept. to May, weather permitting; closed Jan. 1, Thanksgiving, Dec, 25; U.S. 11; 463–6232 (VMI) or 463–7103 (Marshall Museum).

Chessie Nature Trail. A 7-mile footpath with access points; begins at VMI; flora, fauna, history; ends at Buena Vista.

Lime Kiln Arts, 27 W. Washington St.; 463–7088. Outdoor professional theater, mid-July and Aug.

Virginia Horse Center. A multipurpose facility for all breeds and riders (including children on ponies). Workshops and demonstrations. Write Box 1052, Lexington 24450, or call 463–2194.

Lexington Visitor Center, Sloan House, 107 E. Washington St. (463–3777) can provide a wealth of information about this beautiful and historic area.

Luray

U.S. 211 and U.S. 340.

Luray Caverns. Huge underground chambers, one with an organ; guided tours year-round, hours change with seasons; grounds include car and carriage museum; fee; 743–6551.

Luray Singing Tower. An impressive 47-bell carillon played in daily recital Mar. – Oct.; free; adjoining caverns; 743–5062.

"Christmas in Luray." Special activities for the month of Dec., parade, caroling, other events of the season; 743–3915.

Natural Bridge

U.S. 11/VA 130.

Natural Bridge. A stone arch of truly impressive proportions; musical with lights evenings; daily, year-round; fee.

Caverns of Natural Bridge. Split-level caves, 300 feet underground; guided tours; closed winter; fee.

New Market

I-81, U.S. 11 at U.S. 221.

Shenandoah Caverns. There is an elevator to the subterranean rooms; picnic area; daily except Dec. 25; fee; 477–3115.

New Market Battlefield Park. The original embattled farm house has been restored; Hall of Valor; exhibits, film, scenic overlook and walking tour; daily except Dec. 25 and 3rd Sun. in Sept. when the reenactment of the 1864 battle takes place; fee; 740–3101. Exit 67 off I-81.

Tuttle and Spice General Store. 8 unusual early American shops and Indian exhibit; daily except Jan. 1, Thanksgiving, Dec. 25; 477–2601.

Shenandoah Vineyards. The valley's first winery; tours and tastings; free; 984–8699.

Roanoke

I-581 east off I-81 at U.S. 220.

Center-in-the-Square. A unique facility with a science museum, fine arts museum, historical society museum and planetarium, surrounded by interesting shops and a farmers' market; year-round except holidays; some fees; Roanoke Chamber of Commerce, 344–5188 or 342–6025 (Roanoke Valley Visitors Bureau).

Mill Mountain Zoo. A city park that encompasses a mountain; picnic areas, scenic views, miniature train; zoo open May – Oct.; fee; 343–3241.

Roanoke Transportation Museum. A large exhibit of vehicles, past and present; train exhibit is special; year-round except holidays; fee; 342–5670.

Dixie Caverns. 5-million-year old caves; shops, camping; year-round; fee.

Smith Mountain Lake. A lovely setting for year-round water recreation; resorts, marinas, camping; state park with picnicking, hiking, nature trails; *Birthplace of Booker T. Washington* nearby; exhibit, movies daily; closed holidays; free.

Staunton

U.S. 11, I-81, U.S. 250, I-64.

Woodrow Wilson Birthplace. The restored home with mementoes of the twenty-eighth president; gardens, exhibits, film; year-round, closed Sun. Dec. – Feb., major holidays; fee; 885–0897.

Museum of American Frontier Culture. I-64 and I-81; 332–7850. Working farms of the 18th and 19th centuries.

Winchester

I-81, U.S. 11, U.S. 522, U.S. 50.

Abram's Delight. A very old restored house, garden, log cabin; Apr. – Oct.; fee; 662–6519.

Jackson's Headquarters; Memorabilia of The Civil War years; Apr. – Oct.; fee; 667–3242.

Washington's Office. French-Indian War, Revolution, and Civil War relics; Apr. – Oct.; fee; 662–6550.

Shenandoah Apple Blossom Festival. The nationally televised festival takes place during the first week in May; parade, crafts, music, food; 662–4118. For information write to Chamber of Commerce of Winchester, 2 N. Cameron St., Winchester, VA 22601.

Shenandoah National Park–Skyline Drive

This lovely Blue Ridge area is just east of the Shenandoah Valley along the crests of the mountains that, five million years ago, were at the bottom of a sea. Today the Park averages 2,000 feet above sea level, is 80 miles long, and from 2 to 13 miles wide. The Skyline Drive runs the full length of the park and is the best way to explore its entirety. There are five main entrances and exits to the Drive so one can savor as much or as little as one wishes.

The Park is 95 percent wooded with over 100 species of trees and one stand of hemlock that is over 300 years old. It is a wildlife sanctuary with bear, deer, bobcat, fox, and about 200 varieties of birds. The entire park is a panorama of wild but peaceful vistas any time of the year but fall displays of color are spectacular and winter sometimes sees part or all of the area closed because of weather. Accommodations in the park are limited. Naturalist programs, hiking, riding, fishing, camping, and picnicking are featured at various special points of interest along Skyline Drive. For information, write to Superintendent, Shenandoah National Park, Luray, VA 22835, or call 999–2266.

Blue Ridge Parkway and Environs

Continuing the Skyline Drive along the spine of the Blue Ridge is the Blue Ridge Parkway. It meanders to the border of North Carolina and beyond. The mountains along this section of the highway are higher and the views tend to be more breath-taking. As in the Skyline Drive section, there are overlooks, picnicking areas, self-guided nature walks, and some camping. The *Peaks of the Otter Recreation* area near Roanoke is the most spectacular stop with its 360° panorama. The Parkway is open all year but driving can be hazardous from winter to early spring. The accommodations are open from about May 1 – Oct. 31. For information, write to Superintendent, Blue Ridge Parkway, 700 Northwest Bank Building, Asheville, NC 28801.

George Washington National Forest

This one-million-acre National Forest is spread throughout the mountains of northwestern Virginia in three separate segments. Between Front Royal and Harrisonburg it is a narrow strip of woodland named for its dominant mountain, *Massanutten.* A botanically remarkable area, it boasts a quaking bog that the Indians called "muskeg" and that is today one of those places you should see, if only from a distance, before it vanishes. A second section of the Forest runs along the Blue Ridge Parkway and the Appalachian Trail, but the largest area of the George Washington National Forest straddles the Virginia–West Virginia border for more than 100 miles. It is a particularly fine hiking area with rewards of wildflowers, rock outcrops, and the purest of streams.

SPECIAL INTERESTS

BIKING. A bicycle is a vehicle in Virginia and all traffic regulations apply. They are forbidden on interstate highways and controlled access roads. The favorite routes for longer trips are the Skyline Drive and the Blue Ridge Parkway. For information, write to State Bicycle Coordinator, Virginia Department of Highways, Richmond, VA 23219.

CANOEING. The Shenandoah River in the north of the valley and the James River in the south are both rivers ideally suited for canoe trips. Both have leisurely quiet water and white water. There are some campsites. For information, write to Front Royal Canoe Company, Box 473, Front Royal, VA 22630; Shenandoah River Outfitters, Rte 3, Luray, VA 22835; Downriver Canoe Company, Route 1 Box 256A, Bentonville, VA 22610; or James River Basin Canoe Livery, Route 4 Box 125, Lexington, VA 24450.

VINEYARDS. A newly acknowledged premium grape-growing region, Virginia is now taking root as a center of wine industry. Thomas Jefferson spent 30 years cultivating grapes and making wine at Monticello. After the Civil War wine was a growing industry in Virginia but, with the advent of Prohibition, it failed. Today the interest is revived and the wines are growing in acceptance. There are several vineyards in the Shenandoah Valley that welcome visitors and a nice little booklet about Virginia's wine-making is available from Wine Marketing Program, Virginia Department of Agriculture, P.O. Box 1163, Richmond, VA 23209. For specific information about the Shenandoah Valley vineyards, contact Shenandoah Valley Travel Association, P.O. Box 1288, New Market, VA 22844.

SKIING. The Old Dominion's mountains offer several moderate ski slopes: the Homestead at Hot Springs, Bryce Mountain near Bayse, Massanutten at Harrisonburg, and Wintergreen. For information contact the individual resorts.

CAMPING. For information, write for "Campgrounds in Virginia," a helpful booklet, which is available from The Virginia Travel Council, P.O. Box 15067, Richmond, VA 23227. The booklet has a complete list of commercial and public campgrounds.

THE HIGHLANDS

by
JAMES LOUTTIT

"Take nothing but pictures—leave nothing but footprints."

Daniel Boone took no pictures when he walked this wild and wonderful highland country in 1775 and, because he valued his scalp, he left no footprints.

But the advice is still good; this is a land to be cherished—and protected. Tucked away in Virginia's southwest corner, the Appalachian high plateau west of the Blue Ridge Mountains was once America's first frontier. If you're looking for off-the-beaten-path country, Virginia's Highlands are for you. America's pioneer legacy survives in the Highlands—the solid folkways of our past, the old crafts, the thump and twang of our ancestors' music.

There is a right way and a wrong way to explore Virginia's Highlands: Don't rush; this is a land to be enjoyed at your leisure—an easy drive over excellent highways, a hike along a steep mountain trail, or a pleasant stroll through a mountain village.

In 1609, the "Starveing Tyme," when a handful of English adventurers were clawing for survival on the mudflats of eastern Virginia, the Highlands beyond the western frontier were beyond comprehension.

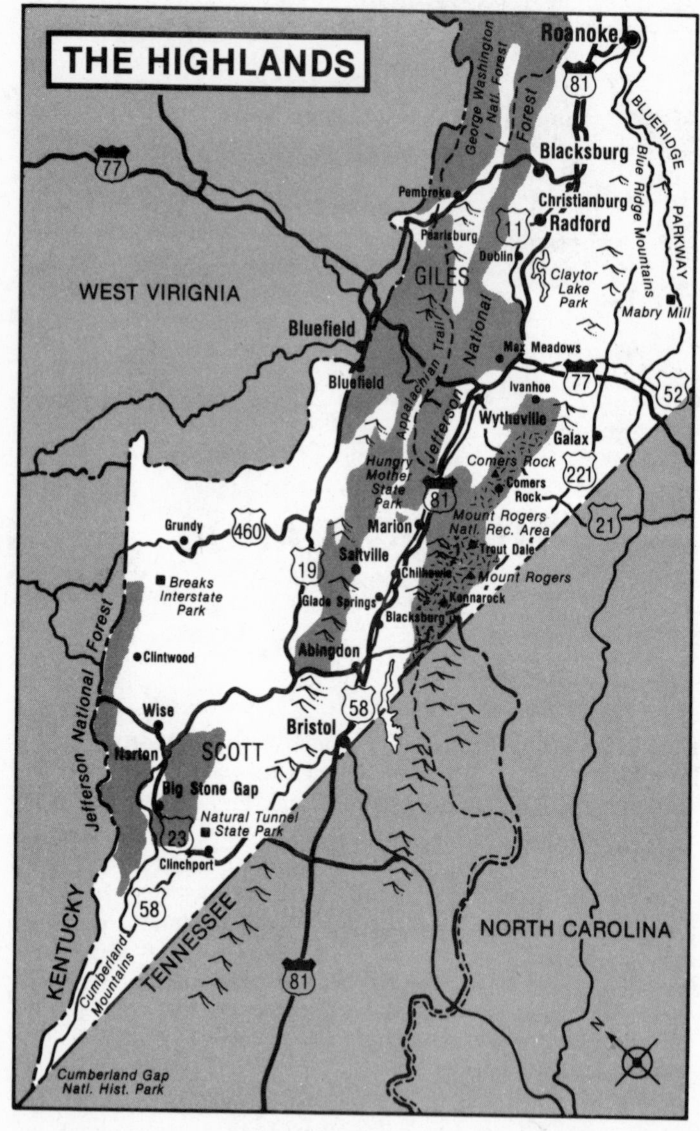
THE HIGHLANDS
Roanoke
Blacksburg
Christianburg
Radford
Pembroke
Pearisburg
Dublin
GILES
Claytor Lake Park
Mabry Mill
BLUERIDGE PARKWAY
Blue Ridge Mountains
George Washington Natl. Forest
Jefferson National Forest
Appalachian Trail
WEST VIRIGNIA
Bluefield
Bluefield
Max Meadows
Ivanhoe
Wytheville
Galax
Comers Rock
Comers Rock
Hungry Mother State Park
Mount Rogers Natl. Rec. Area
Marion
Trout Dale
Saltville
Chilhowie
Mount Rogers
Glade Springs
Konnarock
Blacksburg
Abingdon
Grundy
Breaks Interstate Park
Clintwood
Wise
Norton
SCOTT
Big Stone Gap
Natural Tunnel State Park
Clinchport
Bristol
Jefferson National Forest
KENTUCKY
Cumberland Mountains
TENNESSEE
NORTH CAROLINA
Cumberland Gap Natl. Hist. Park
N
77
81
11
52
221
21
460
19
58
23
81

In the third quarter of the 1700s, when frontiersman Boone and his axmen were blazing the Wilderness Road westward through these mountains and Cumberland Gap, Virginia's Colonial boundary was on the banks of the Mississippi and included plains and wilderness country that later became eight new states. Between 1775 and 1840, perhaps 200,000 westward-bound settlers followed Boone's footsteps through the Gap to the free and open lands beyond the mountains. Today's "frontier explorer" can reach the Gap via U.S. 58, 13 miles west of Ewing, Virginia, or U.S. 25 E., which comes up from Tazewell, Tennessee. Located in the extreme southwest tip of Virginia, Cumberland Gap was designated a national historical park in 1940.

Exploring the Highlands

Although Dan'l and Cumberland Gap may typify Virginia's high country, the Gap's remote location and distance from the Atlantic Coast makes it less accessible to eastern tourists than many other Highlands' natural and home-spun attractions.

Other than Roanoke, at the southern end of the Shenandoah, or Bluefield, across the border (and over a few mountains) in West Virginia, there are no major airports in the Highlands and chances are good that you'll enter—and explore—the Highlands by car. Happily, Virginia has an excellent highway system, vastly improved since those days when Boone followed an ancient buffalo trail through the woods.

Interstate 77 (northwest–southeast) and I-81 (northeast–southwest) bisect the Highlands, merging at Wytheville, but much of the high country will be explored along the Blue Ridge Parkway, U.S. 58, 23, 19, 11, 52, 21, 221, and 460, or a network of well-maintained state routes. Although the elevation in the Highlands often exceeds 3,000 feet and Mount Rogers (5,729 feet) is Virginia's highest point, there are few touring sites that can't be reached easily by car. (Here and there we may ask you to park your car and walk a few steps, but you needn't be a strapping 20-year-old back-packer to enjoy the best of the Highlands.)

Let's start at Wytheville, where I-77 and I-81 intersect. (If you elect to explore to the southwest from the comforts of Roanoke, see our Shenandoah Valley chapter for "Places to Eat and Stay.")

A strategically important town during the Civil War for its salt and lead mines, Wytheville has a fair share of natural and historical sites—*Shot Tower Historical Park,* south on U.S. 52; *Wytheville National Fish Hatchery,* 12 miles to the southwest via I-81, U.S. 52, and SR 629, and *Big Walker Lookout,* 12 miles north on U.S. 21 and 52, where you can look out at a breath-taking view from a chairlift and observation tower, or down into a snake pit, if snakes in a pit are your idea of a breath-taking view.

Natural attractions in the Highlands include the Blue Ridge, Allegheny, and Cumberland mountains, each with its own sparkling-clear streams and falls, quiet country roads and hiking trails, and mountain park recreation areas.

Jefferson National Forest

Jefferson National Forest dominates the Highlands, sprawling across southwestern Virginia from the Kentucky border, northeast to the James River (near Roanoke) where it merges with George Washington National Forest. Of Jefferson's 697,000 acres of scenic beauty, all but 27,000 acres are in Highland Country. This is the natural home of the bobcat, black bear, and the endangered bald eagle—rugged country that welcomes responsible campers, either at designated camping areas (with parking, toilets, and water) or primitive campsites throughout the general forest area. Maps and brochures are available at district ranger stations in Blacksburg, Wise, Natural Bridge Station, New Castle, Marion, and Wytheville. (If you're planning ahead, write to: Forest Supervisor, 210 Franklin Road SW, Roanoke, VA 24001.)

Mount Rogers

Mount Rogers National Recreation Area, south of Marion and southwest of Wytheville, both on I-81, is the focal point of the forest, the one area a visitor must see if time or constitution rules out wilder forest areas such as the Mountain Lake Wilderness Study Area, northeast of Pembroke on U.S. 460. State Route 16, out of Marion, and U.S. 21, south from Wytheville, bisect the Mount Rogers area, and U.S. 58 loops across a corner of the area in the southwest, skirting 5,520-foot White Top Mountain, and near the area's namesake, Mt. Rogers, which at 5,729 feet is the highest peak in Virginia. Route 603—between Konnarock, just off U.S. 58, and Troutdale on U.S. 21—rounds the northern shoulders of the two peaks. A third notable peak, Comers Rock (4,102 feet), stands near the eastern end of the area, where U.S. 21 tops out at 3,060 feet. A 50-mile horse trail, beginning at Ivanhoe on Route 94, crosses most of the recreation area, with horses for hire available on Virginia 603.

Also notable, if you have time, are Hungry Mother Park near Marion, Claytor Lake Park near Dublin (Exit 32 off I-81), or Natural Tunnel State Park off U.S. 23 near Cinchport. There are two breath-taking parks on the Kentucky border: Breaks Interstate Park, west of Grundy, where a five-mile-long, 1,600-foot-deep gorge has earned the name "Grand Canyon of the South," and Cumberland Gap National Historical Park, off U.S. 58 in the extreme western part of the state.

Blue Ridge Parkway

Other Highland attractions include a beautiful stretch of the Blue Ridge Parkway, Roanoke to the North Carolina border; picturesque Mabry Mill, off the Parkway, a dozen or so miles northeast of I-77; the Pocahontas Exhibition Mine at Bluefield, America's first commercial coal mine (1883); and the Southwest Virginia Museum at Big Stone Gap; the famous Barter Theatre in Abingdon near U.S. 58 and I-81; and the June Tolliver House, home of "The Trail of the Lonesome Pine," Route 613, Big Stone Gap.

But finally, there are the people—the inhabitants of Virginia's southwestern Highlands frontier. The mountains are there, rugged and natural, but it is the people of the Highlands who make the Highlands an unforgettable touring experience.

If its peaks are its castles, the hardy, independent people of the Highlands are its kings and queens. In them, the pioneer spirit survives in the hamlets, villages, and towns of southwestern Virginia—from Roanoke to Ewing, from Rich Creek to Fancy Gap. Meet them, listen to them—and appreciate the naturalness of their lives and their approach to life.

In order to appreciate fully the splendid isolation of the Highlands and the fierce independence of its inhabitants, you might ponder this: It is estimated that there are some 23,000 moonshine stills in the United States—most of them hidden away in the mountains of the Appalachian plateau. How many, one wonders, of *those* are in the Highlands of Virginia?

PRACTICAL INFORMATION FOR THE HIGHLANDS

Note: The area code for the Highlands is 703.

PLACES TO STAY

HOTELS, MOTELS, AND RESORTS. Not too surprising, many better—and more expensive—accommodations are often found in larger cities or towns, usually on a main artery or near the intersection of several major highways. Wytheville, which might be considered the crossroads of the Highlands, is just such a place; happily situated on U.S. Rte. 11 and 52, Wytheville is also blessed with the nearby intersection of the Highlands' two Interstates— I-81 and I-77. Wytheville has more than a fair share of excellent accommodations, and additional facilities are currently under construction. There are exceptions to the above rule of thumb, of course, for some mountain resorts and country places are where they are because the locale *is* remote. Rates for the following selection of accommodations might be classified as *Expensive* if over $75, *Moderate* if between $40 and $75, or *Inexpensive* if less than $40. Prices may vary with the season or the size and location of a room. If in doubt, ask—or perhaps request to see the room—before you check in.

Abingdon

Martha Washington Inn. *Moderate to Expensive.* 160 W. Main; 24210; 628–3161 or (800) 533–1014. Circa 1830–1832. Bar, notable restaurant, golf privileges, and meeting rooms. Antique decor. 65 rooms. AE, CB, DC, MC, V.

Alpine. *Moderate.* Exit 9 off I–81, a mile east on U.S.11; 628–3178. A small, but attractive motel on a knoll near the Empire. 19 rooms. MC, V.

Empire Motor Lodge. *Inexpensive to Moderate.* 628–7131. A spacious 2-story lodge, with balconies, restaurant, and meeting facilities. Exit 9, I–81, east on U.S. 11. 105 units. MC, V.

Big Stone Gap

Country Boy Motel. *Inexpensive.* 6 blocks south, U.S. 23/58A; 523–0374. 46 units in a 2-story motel. AE, MC, V.

Trail Motel. *Inexpensive.* 509 Gilley Ave., U.S.23/58; 523–1171. 40 rooms, restaurant nearby. AE, MC, V.

Blacksburg

Mountain Lake Resort. *Expensive.* 7 miles north of U.S. 460 on Rte. 700; 626–7121. 116 units in a 1-to-3 story hotel, with cottages and some patios. Private beach, golf, and tennis. Cafe and entertainment. American plan during season; closed Nov.–Apr. AE, CB, DC, MC, V.

Blacksburg Marriott. *Moderate.* 900 Prices Fork Rd.; 552–7001 or (800) 228–9290. 148 rooms on Rte. 412, off U.S. 460 Bypass. Indoor, outdoor, and wading pools. Restaurant and bar, with entertainment. Room, valet, pool, and bellhop service. Meeting facilities. Tennis and golf. AE, CB, DC, MC, V.

Holiday Inn. *Moderate.* 3503 S. Main; 951–1330 or (800) HOLIDAY. 97 rooms in a suburban 2-story motel on U.S. 460 Bypass. Room service, restaurant, and bar, with entertainment. Swimming and wading pools. AE, CB, DC, MC, V.

Sheraton Red Lion Inn. *Moderate.* 900 NW Plantation Rd.; U.S. 460 Bypass at Prices Fork Rd.; 552–7770 or (800) 325–3535. 104 rooms on 13 wooded acres. Tennis courts, restaurant, and lounge. Golf privileges. Room service and poolside services. AE, CB, DC, MC, V.

Bristol

Best Western—Regency Center. *Moderate.* Bristol, TN; 968–9119. 100 rooms in 2-story motel, 1½ miles west on U.S. 11. Pool, restaurant, and lounge. AE, CB, DC, MC, V.

Holiday Inn—West. *Moderate.* Euclid Ave. and W. State St.; 669–7171. Restaurant, lounge, and pool. 124 units. AE, MC, V.

Howard Johnson's Motor Lodge. *Moderate.* 4766 Lee Hwy., 669–1151. 60-unit lodge, 6 miles north on U.S. 11, Exit 5, I–81. Pool and restaurant. AE, DC, CB, MC, V.

Comfort Inn. *Inexpensive.* 536 Volunteer Pkwy. Bristol, TN; 968–2171. 2-story, 63-unit motel, 3 miles southeast Exit 3, I–81. Pool, bar, and adjacent cafe. AE, CB, DC, MC, V.

Econo Lodge. *Inexpensive.* 912 Commonwealth Ave.; I–381; 466–2112. 2-story, 48-room motel, a mile south of Exit 2, I–81. Adjacent restaurant. AE, MC, V.

Chilhowie

Best Western Mount Rogers Inn. *Moderate.* SW Quad, Exit 13 off I–81. 646–8981 or (800) 528–1234. 42 units, with restaurant, pool, and meeting facilities. Major credit cards.

Duffield

Ramada Inn. *Moderate.* U.S.58/421W, intersection of U.S.23, 5 miles from Natural Tunnel State Park and 14 from Big Stone Gap; 431–4300 or (800) 2RAMADA. 102 units, with meeting facilities. Outdoor pool, restaurant, and lounge, with nightly entertainment. AE, CB, DC, MC, V.

Galax

Rose Lane Motel. *Inexpensive.* 312 W. Stuart Dr.; 236–5117. 51 rooms. Restaurant nearby. Rates higher late Aug. AE, MC, V.

Marion

Holiday Inn of Marion. *Moderate.* 1424 N. Main; 24354; 783–3193 or (800) 238–5510. 100 units, some with balconies. Cafe and beer and wine, pool, room service and bellhops, and meeting facilities. AE, CB, DC, MC, V.

Village Motel. *Moderate.* Exit 18 off I–81; 783–5811 or 783–9936. 20 rooms. Restaurant open for breakfast, lunch, and dinner. AE, MC, V.

Virginia House Motor Inn. *Moderate.* 1419 N. Main; Exit 17 off I–81; 783–5112. 40 units and pools. AE, CB, DC, MC, V.

Norton

Holiday Inn Norton. *Moderate.* 551 U.S.58E, edge of town; 679–7000. 121 rooms. Lonesome Pine restaurant. Lounge. Major credit cards.

Radford

Best Western Radford Inn. *Moderate.* 1501 Tyler Ave.; 639–3000 or (800) 528–1234. 104 rooms. Restaurant, bar, and pool. Room service, health club, meeting rooms, and bellhops. Major credit cards.

Dogwood Lodge. *Inexpensive.* 2 miles west of town on U.S.11; 639–9338. 13 rooms. Restaurant nearby. MC, V.

Executive. *Inexpensive.* U.S. 11W, I–81 Exits 34,35. 26 rooms, with restaurant nearby. MC, V.

Wise

The Inn at Wise Courthouse. *Moderate.* 1 block east of U.S. 23 (Bus.) on Main St.; 328–2241. 3 stories, 44 rooms. Restaurant and bar, with meeting rooms. AE,MC,V.

Wytheville

Holiday Inn. *Moderate.* Box 166; 24382; 228–5483 or (800) 465–4329. 199 rooms in u-shaped, 2-story suburban and motel, Route 11, near the intersection of I–77 and I–81, Wytheville exit. Room service, pool, fire-place restaurant. Cocktails, beer, and wine. Meeting facilities. AE, CB, DC, MC, V.

Interstate Motor Lodge. *Moderate.* 705 Chapman Rd., Exit 23 off I–81/I–77; across from Holiday Inn; 228–8618. 42 rooms with restaurant nearby. MC, V.

Ramada Inn Wytheville. *Moderate.* 955 Pepper Ferry's Rd., near intersection I–81/I–77, Exit 22; 228–6000 or 800–2RAMADA. 154 rooms. Full service restaurant. Bar. Heated pool. Major credit cards.

Howard Johnson's Motor Lodge. *Moderate.* P.O. Box 552; 24382; 228–3188 or (800) 654–9122. 100 units, with 24-hour restaurant, heated pool, meeting facilities, and tennis. Some units with Blue Ridge Mountain view. Located at U.S. 11, I–81, and I–77. Major credit cards.

Econo Lodge. *Inexpensive.* 1190 E. Main; 228–5517. 72-unit motel on Route 11, ¼ mile west of I–77 and I–81. Nearby restaurant. Major credit cards.

Wythe Motor Lodge. *Inexpensive.* Exit 23, I–81 and I–77; 228–5525. 34 rooms, each with 2 double beds. 24-hour restaurant nearby. AE, MC, V.

PLACES TO EAT

RESTAURANTS. Dining out is a subjective thing, often influenced as much by our mood and pocketbook as by the ambience of the place and the food we are served. We know we have neglected or overlooked many fine dining places in Virginia's Highlands, and we have not included those mainstays of survival-on-the-road, convenient, fast-food spots such as McDonald's, Hardee's, or Wendy's. The following, then, is merely our *selection*—places you may consider while you are exploring the Highlands. Keep in mind that many hotels and motels often have "the best dining room in town" (or they'll know what and where it is). Also, our prices do not include alcoholic beverages or taxes.

Abingdon

First Lady's Table. *Moderate to Expensive.* Martha Washington Inn, 150 W. Main St.; 628–3161. Southern hospitality and food at its best. Breakfast, lunch, and dinner, with a cocktail lounge and nightly entertainment. AE, DC, MC, V.

The Tavern. *Moderate.* 222 E. Main; 628–1118. An historic atmosphere in the heart of a pleasant, hilly mountain town. Tavern lunches and candlelight dinners, featuring homemade American fare. Est. 1779. Mon. through Sat. MC, V.

Western Steer of Abingdon. *Moderate.* Exit 9 off I–81 at U.S. 11. Prime steaks, plus 55-item salad bar, 12-item vegetable bar, and 12-item potato bar. Lunch and dinner. Closed Sun. MC, V.

Empire Restaurant. *Inexpensive to Moderate.* R.F.D. 4, at the intersection of 11 E. and I–81; 628–6131. Western beef and home-made pasta in a family atmosphere. No credit cards.

Peking. *Inexpensive to Moderate.* Train St. and Market Pl.; 466–4523. Chinese-American "country" cooking! Closed Sun. MC, V.

Blacksburg

Jacob's Lantern. *Moderate to Expensive.* Dining in a garden setting at the Blacksburg Marriott, 900 Prices Fork Rd.; 552–7001. Open for breakfast, lunch, and dinner. Bar, Sun. brunch, and seafood buffet Wed. Outdoor tables and background music. AE, CB, DC, MC, V.

Erny's. *Inexpensive to Moderate.* Prices Fork Rd. at Red Lion Inn. Seafood and beef in a British-pub atmosphere. Breakfast, lunch, and dinner. Major credit cards.

Bristol

Athens Steak House. *Moderate to Expensive.* 105 Goodson St.; 466–8271. Greek-American cuisine. Bar. Closed Sun. MC, V.

Vinyard. *Inexpensive to Expensive.* 603 Gate City Hwy.; 466–4244. Italian-American cuisine. Bar and wine list. Breakfast, lunch, and dinner. Veal and seafood are specialities. AE, DC, MC, V.

Marion

Tallent House. *Moderate to Expensive.* 230 E. Main; 783–2100. Steaks, seafood, and chicken; breakfast, lunch, and dinner. Closed Sun. MC, V.

Village Cafe. *Moderate.* 1424 N. Main; 783–3193. A pleasant dining room—breakfast, lunch, and dinner—in the Holiday Inn. Major credit cards.

House of Hunan. *Inexpensive to Moderate.* Rte. 16, Exit 16, I–81; 783–2186. New, Mandarin Chinese. Closed Mon. MC, V.

Wytheville

The Log House Restaurant. *Moderate.* 520 E. Main (U.S. 11); 228–5488. Choice steaks and seafood in an 18th-century atmosphere. Homemade bread and desserts. Daily, lunch and dinner, in season. MC, V.

The Manor House. *Moderate.* 410 W. Main (U.S. 11); 228–6419. Pleasant decor. Cocktails. Choice beef, chicken, and seafood. Reservations accepted. Sun. brunch, 11–3. MC, V.

Bonanza Family Restaurant. *Inexpensive to Moderate.* U.S. 11 and Marshall St.; 228–3198. Steak, chicken, and seafood. Open daily, lunch and dinner. MC, V.

Durham's Restaurant and Cafeteria. *Inexpensive to Moderate.* 150 N. 11th St., near Exit 21, I–81. 228–5241. Family fare. Breakfast, lunch, and dinner. MC, V.

THINGS TO SEE AND DO

TOURING INFORMATION. For advance touring information, contact: Virginia Highlands Travel Association, c/o Mt. Rogers Planning District Commission, 1021 Terrace Dr., Marion, VA 24354, (703) 783–5103, or Virginia's Southwest Blue Ridge Highlands, Inc., Box 656, Wytheville, VA 24382, (703) 228–6066.

Abingdon

Daniel Boone called it Wolf Hill, but this pleasant mountain town has been Abingdon since 1778. Abingdon was a jumping-off point for settlers traveling on to Kentucky or Tennessee.

Abingdon is the home of the *Barter Theatre of Virginia,* founded by Robert Porterfield in 1932. The theater was a haven for Broadway actors during the Depression, and a boon for locals who bartered local goods for tickets. Performances nightly, except Mon., Apr.–Oct. Call 628–3991 for times and prices.

Abingdon is also the largest burley tobacco market in Virginia. *The Burley Tobacco Festival and Farm Show,* the first weekend in Oct., is an annual Abingdon highlight. Location: one mile west of Abingdon on Rte. 11.

The Virginia Highlands Arts and Crafts Festival, featuring Highlands crafts, painting, antiques, music, drama, and tours, is held annually the first two weeks in Aug. Contact Washington County Chamber of Commerce, 304 Depot, 24210; 628–8141.

Mountain arts and crafts are featured at *Cave House,* 279 E. Main St., a cooperative owned by local craftspeople, and *Dixie Pottery,* 5 miles west on U.S. 11.

Big Stone Gap

Located in Wise County, Big Stone Gap is the site of the *Southwest Virginia Museum Historical State Park,* a four-story mansion housing a fine collection of pioneer and Indian artifacts. Open daily, 10 A.M.–6 P.M., Memorial Day through Labor Day, and 9–5, Tues.–Sun., the rest of the year. A modest admission fee is charged at the museum. *Natural Tunnel State Park,* an awesome natural tunnel through Purchase Ridge, lies 23 miles to the southeast via U.S. 23. The park is open Memorial Day through Labor Day. Phone 940–2674 for details.

Big Stone Gap attractions also include the *John Fox, Jr. House,* a Virginia Historical Landmark (1888). Fox immortalized mountain life with his *The Little Shepherd of Kingdom Come* and *The Trail of the Lonesome Pine* in the early 1900s. His home, 117 East Shawnee Ave., is open to the public for a nominal admission fee. Call 523–1235.

The June Tolliver Playhouse (outdoor) presents *The Trail of the Lonesome Pine* each Thurs.–Sat. in July and Aug.

The June Tolliver House, (1890) next to the Playhouse, is named for the heroine of Fox's novel. Open Tues.–Sat., 10–5, and Sun. from 2 till 6, May into Dec. Rte. 613, Jerome St. and Clinton Ave. Free. Call 523–1235.

Blacksburg

Home of *Virginia Polytechnic Institute and State University,* Blacksburg, at an altitude of 2,100 feet, was the birthplace of two Virginia governors—James Patton Preston and John Buchanan Floyd. *Smithfield,* a pre-Revolutionary War mansion (1773) is open to the public from Apr. 15 until the first of Nov. Contact Blacksburg Chamber of Commerce, 141 Jackson St. (552–4061) for information.

Bluefield

The *Pocahontas Exhibition Coal Mine,* Rte. 20, is open to the public daily from 10 A.M. till 5 P.M., May 1–Oct. 31. Pocahontas is the only exhibition mine in the world that can be toured by car. Also in the Bluefield area are the *Historic Crab Orchard Museum,* with Indian, pioneer, Revolutionary, and Civil War exhibits, and *Pipestem State Park and Pinnacle Rock,* a towering sandstone formation. Contact Wythe-Bland Chamber of Commerce, First and Main, Wytheville (228–3211) for information about the Bluefield-Wytheville area.

Bristol

The Virginia-Tennessee state line runs down the middle of Bristol's main street, giving this southwestern mountain town something of a split personality. Bristol is the site of the *Bristol Caverns* and the *Appalachia Music Days Festival,* which is held in Steele Creek Park the first week in May. The *Guild Gallery,* 501 State St. (669–0821) promotes regional and traditional handicrafts. Closed Sun.

Chilhowie

Known for good reason as the Apple Center of Southwest Virginia, Chilhowie celebrates its bumper crops each year with the *Apple Festival,* the third week in Sept., Mount Rogers Recreation Area, via Rtes. 762 and 600.

Clintwood

The small town of Clintwood (Rtes. 72 and 83 off U.S. 58) honors Appalachia's mountain people with the *Cumberland Museum,* which displays an excellent collection of tools, crafts, and "primitive things," from a log cabin to a moonshine still. Open weekends, Apr.–Sept., for a nominal fee. Call 926–6632.

Cumberland Gap National Historical Park

Tucked away in the extreme southwestern corner of Virginia (Route 58 west of Ewing to Rte. 25 E., which passes through the Gap over portions of Daniel Boone's Wilderness Road), the historical park includes *Pinnacle Overlook,* which is reached by a four-mile scenic drive. Near the Gap are an old charcoal iron furnace and Civil War fortifications. The 20,271-acre natural park encompasses portions of Virginia, Tennessee, and Kentucky. For advance planning, write to the Superintendent, Cumberland Gap National Historical Park, Box 840, Middlesboro, KY 40965.

Duffield

Natural Tunnel State Park, south of Big Stone Gap and near Duffield, is the site of an 850-foot, 10-story natural tunnel, carved by a stream through a limestone ridge. The tunnel is reached via U.S. 23 and 871. Facilities for outdoor activities, with a visitors' center; 940–2674. The park is open from Memorial Day through Labor Day.

Galax

Six miles north of the Blue Ridge Parkway via Rtes. 89 and 97, Galax attracts a fair share of Highlands explorers to its *Jeff Matthews Memorial Museum,* (236–7874), which has an interesting collection of Indian artifacts, farm tools, and Civil War relics, and to the *Rooftop of Virginia Craft Shop Project,* which features quality native crafts and operates a sales outlet at 206 N. Main. The annual *Old Fiddlers Convention* is held in Galax the second weekend in Aug.

Giles County

Noted for its rugged natural beauty, Giles County attracts tourists to its *Mountain Lake,* a true wilderness retreat in part of Jefferson National Forest, as well as the *Cascades* near Pembroke (U.S. 460), the *White Rocks Recreation Area,* the *New River Narrows,* and the *Palisades* near Egglestow. The Appalachian Trail runs the length of the county.

Grundy

The *Breaks Interstate Park* (17 miles west of Grundy via U.S. 460, then Rte. 609). This craggy, natural park is known as the "Grand Canyon of the South."

Jefferson National Forest

Sprawling over more than half a million acres of Virginia's Blue Ridge and Allegheny Mountains, this great public forest covers sections of the Highlands from Kentucky and Tennessee in the southwest to Lexington, where it meets George Washington National Forest in the north. Elevations in the forest range between a low of 660 feet to a high of 5,729 feet at the top of Mount Rogers, Virginia's highest peak. A long stretch of the Appalachian Trail winds through sections of the forest, but many excellent roads, including I–77, also bisect parts of the forest. *Mount Rogers National Recreation Area,* south of Marion on Route 16, is one of the more accessible forest areas, and *Grayson Highlands State Park,* a short drive out of Mouth of Wilson on U.S. 58, borders Mount Rogers. Old mountain crafts and a restored mountain cabin are on display in the park, which also includes some of Virginia's most beautiful Highlands scenery.

Marion

Hungry Mother State Park, Mount Rogers National Recreation Area, and *Grayson Highlands State Park* are easily accessible from Marion. Hungry Mother is three miles north of Marion, while Mount Rogers and Grayson are only 20 miles from town via Rte. 16 to Volney. The *Hungry Mother Arts & Crafts Festival* is held annually the third week in July. *Smyth County Historical Museum* features local artifacts in an 1838 schoolhouse. Sun., Memorial Day–Labor Day. Phone 783–2745.

Norton

Hardy visitors can see into four states from the 4,162-foot crest of *High Knob,* the highest peak in Wise County. *Powell Valley Overlook* on Rte. 610 is a photographer's delight. (It has been estimated that three billion tons of "black gold" lie beneath the surface of this Appalachian coal county.)

Saltville

Once the "Salt Capital of the Confederacy," Saltville (five minutes off I–81 via Rte. 107) has the *Saltville Museum Park,* plus a number of restored historic homes.

Scott County

Old time music in a rustic setting is revered—and preserved—at the Hiltons, a few miles east of Weber City on Rte. 58, where performances are held year-round every Sat. night.

Natural Tunnel State Park, a 900-foot natural cavern that is used as a railway pass, is in Scott County. William Jennings Bryan, with a flair for hyperbole, called this spectacular attraction "the eighth wonder of the world."

Wytheville

Beautifully situated as a jumping-off point for Highlands explorers, Wytheville has such home-grown attractions as *Big Walker Lookout* (13 miles north on U.S. 21), the *Rock House Museum* (a National Historic Landmark at Monroe and Tazewell sts; 228–4718), *Rural Retreat Lake and Park,* the *Wytheville State Fish Hatchery* (where 150,000 pounds of rainbow trout are produced annually), and *Shot Tower Historical Park,* which made shot for frontiersmen and settlers in the early 1800s. One of only three surviving shot towers in the country, the tower stands on a knoll where U.S. 52 intersects New River at the Popular Camp Exit, I-77. Free. Call 677–5492.

Index

Fodor's Travel Guides

U.S. Guides

Alaska
American Cities
The American South
Arizona
Atlantic City & the New Jersey Shore
Boston
California
Cape Cod
Carolinas & the Georgia Coast
Chesapeake
Chicago
Colorado
Dallas & Fort Worth
Disney World & the Orlando Area
The Far West
Florida
Greater Miami, Fort Lauderdale, Palm Beach
Hawaii
Hawaii *(Great Travel Values)*
Houston & Galveston
I-10: California to Florida
I-55: Chicago to New Orleans
I-75: Michigan to Florida
I-80: San Francisco to New York
I-95: Maine to Miami
Las Vegas
Los Angeles, Orange County, Palm Springs
Maui
New England
New Mexico
New Orleans
New Orleans *(Pocket Guide)*
New York City
New York City *(Pocket Guide)*
New York State
Pacific North Coast
Philadelphia
Puerto Rico *(Fun in)*
Rockies
San Diego
San Francisco
San Francisco *(Pocket Guide)*
Texas
United States of America
Virgin Islands *(U.S. & British)*
Virginia
Waikiki
Washington, DC
Williamsburg, Jamestown & Yorktown

Foreign Guides

Acapulco
Amsterdam
Australia, New Zealand & the South Pacific
Austria
The Bahamas
The Bahamas *(Pocket Guide)*
Barbados *(Fun in)*
Beijing, Guangzhou & Shanghai
Belgium & Luxembourg
Bermuda
Brazil
Britain *(Great Travel Values)*
Canada
Canada *(Great Travel Values)*
Canada's Maritime Provinces
Cancún, Cozumel, Mérida, The Yucatán
Caribbean
Caribbean *(Great Travel Values)*
Central America
Copenhagen, Stockholm, Oslo, Helsinki, Reykjavik
Eastern Europe
Egypt
Europe
Europe *(Budget)*
Florence & Venice
France
France *(Great Travel Values)*
Germany
Germany *(Great Travel Values)*
Great Britain
Greece
Holland
Hong Kong & Macau
Hungary
India
Ireland
Israel
Italy
Italy *(Great Travel Values)*
Jamaica *(Fun in)*
Japan
Japan *(Great Travel Values)*
Jordan & the Holy Land
Kenya
Korea
Lisbon
Loire Valley
London
London *(Pocket Guide)*
London *(Great Travel Values)*
Madrid
Mexico
Mexico *(Great Travel Values)*
Mexico City & Acapulco
Mexico's Baja & Puerto Vallarta, Mazatlán, Manzanillo, Copper Canyon
Montreal
Munich
New Zealand
North Africa
Paris
Paris *(Pocket Guide)*
People's Republic of China
Portugal
Province of Quebec
Rio de Janeiro
The Riviera *(Fun on)*
Rome
St. Martin/St. Maarten
Scandinavia
Scotland
Singapore
South America
South Pacific
Southeast Asia
Soviet Union
Spain
Spain *(Great Travel Values)*
Sweden
Switzerland
Sydney
Tokyo
Toronto
Turkey
Vienna
Yugoslavia

Special-Interest Guides

Bed & Breakfast Guide: North America
1936...On the Continent
Royalty Watching
Selected Hotels of Europe
Selected Resorts and Hotels of the U.S.
Ski Resorts of North America
Views to Dine by around the World